ETHNICITY AND THE STATE

Political and Legal Anthropology Series
Myron Aronoff, Series Editor

1. *Ideology and Interest, The Dialectics of Politics*
2. *Culture and Political Change*
3. *Religion and Politics*
4. *Cross-Currents in Israeli Culture and Politics*
5. *Frailty of Authority*
6. *State Formation and Political Legitimacy*
7. *Outwitting the State*
8. *Early State Economics*
9. *Ethnicity and the State*

Political and Legal Anthropology
Volume 9

ETHNICITY AND THE STATE

Edited by

Judith D. Toland

Transaction Publishers

New Brunswick (U.S.A.) and London (U.K.)

ISSN: 1060-2720
ISBN: 1-56000-058-9 (cloth); 1-56000-617-X (paper)
Printed in the United States of America

Contents

Figures and Tables   vii

Introduction: Dialogue of Self and Other:
Ethnicity and the Statehood Building Process   1
    Judith D. Toland

1. Nationalism and Ethnicity: Images of Ecuadorian   21
    Indians and the Imagemakers at the Turn of the
    Nineteenth Century
        Blanca Muratorio

2. Ethnicity and the State: The Hua Miao of Southwest   55
    China
        Norma Diamond

3. Ethnicity and the Security Forces of the State: 79
    The South Asian Experience
        Angela S. Burger

4. Ethnicity, Nationalism, and the Role of the   103
    Intellectual
        Anya Peterson Royce

5. Ethnicity and the State in Northern Ireland   123
        Joan Vincent

6. Batak Heritage and the Indonesian State: Print   147
    Literacy and the Construction of Ethnic Cultures in
    Indonesia
        Susan Rodgers

7. Ethnicity and State-Building: The Case of the   177
    Palestinians in the Middle East
        Emile Sahliyeh

8. Jewish Ethnicity in Israel: Ideologies, Policies, and   201
    Outcomes
        Herbert S. Lewis

9. Conclusion: Ethnicity, the State, and Moral Order   231
      Ronald Cohen

About the Contributors   259

Index   263

Figures and Tables

Figures

1.1	The Inca and His Queen	29
1.2	Indian from Otavalo	31
1.3	Indians in Obraje	32
1.4	Indigenas del Oriente	33
1.5	Cotos Indians at the Napo River	35
1.6	Inhabitants of Quito	38
1.7	Potter	39
1.8	Delousing	42
1.9	Indian from the Capital	44
1.10	Streetsweeper	45
5.1	Cultural Areas in Modern Ulster	131

Tables

3.1	Comparison of Central Reserve Police Recruitment Patterns by State, 1973 and 1980–1982	97
3.2	Comparison of CRPF and BSF Recruitment by State, 1980–1982	98
5.1	British and Irish in Ulster	130

Introduction:

Dialogue of Self and Other: Ethnicity and the Statehood Building Process

Judith D. Toland

The Problem

The state has always been at risk of promoting and maintaining social environmental degradation because of the propensity of federal policymaking to focus on self-maintenance at the expense of those individuals and groups that are deemed peripheral to the system. In the world of physics, Prigogine and Stengers (1984) might define this system of ordering as "far from equilibrium" because of its propensity for being extremely sensitive to the external influences of its marginalized people.

In the language of physics, small inputs from the periphery of open systems are apt to produce startling effects that continuously cause the system to reorganize in strangely different ways. These seemingly "small" inputs create the ongoing possibility of the system's fluctuating subsystems reaching a point of division and disintegrating into chaos and/or leaping to new, higher levels of organization.

The disintegration of large monolithic states such as the USSR and the aftermath of the federation of small ethnic statelets into regional communities may be one possible form of that higher level of organization. The unrealistic expectations of ethnic purity present in the Yugoslavian struggle may constitute the chaos of the process. The idea of a "pure" nation state with one monolithic voice has never been and probably never will be a reality.

Another higher form would certainly be the achievement of pluralism with equal respect for, and equal representation of, all ethnic groups within one state. However, the backlash of ethnic hatred experienced in those states with expanding plural populations signifies the disequilibrium that can occur when the mature state resource base is stretched.

Many years ago Hugo of St. Victor said "perfectus vero cui mundue totus exilium est", (. . . he is perfect to whom the entire world is as a foreign land). He suggests that the dynamics between individuals and between culturally distinct groups should be equipollent, equal in weight and validity. Studies of statehood throughout time and space, however, have shown us that although the nature of state society has always been plural, the presence of pluralism, that exists as a form of rule only when there are policies and expectations that serve the interests of all ethnic groups, irrespective of their differences, has not yet been fully realized. In other words, the state as a plural entity has yet to successfully practice pluralism and realize St. Victor's vision. This phenomena bears witness to what Prigogine and Stengers are proposing; that we view disequilibrium, not equilibrium, as the natural state of all open systems.

Throughout the past 5000 years, states have evolved into complex political structures of cultural diversity because of a number of factors, the most important being the imposition of a conquering culture on another, colonial expansion, boundary redefinition, and/or voluntary or involuntary migration of outside cultures to a host territory or a territory that has been redefined. It can be said then, that the nature of a state society has always been plural. But because the state is a politically autonomous unit ruled by a culturally distinct and politically privileged group, to survive this group has had to maintain its system of authority in accordance with a charter of moral rights. This charter has traditionally legitimated the group's cultural right to place authority, and thereby power over a diverse many, in the hands of a privileged few.

In addition, this group has had to operationalize its alleged right to defend state territorial boundaries and to control the movement of people across these boundaries. It has had to be capable of distinguishing between those who are subject to its authority and those who are not through an institutionalized criteria for membership. It has also had to have a pool and division of labor sufficient to generate enough revenues to support the state machinery and its system of works. And when the charter of moral rights falls short of the expectations of the populace, a more tangible source of order has had to be defined through institutionalized bodies of domestic and foreign order keeping.

Although ethnic diversity is a characteristic of all state populations, the nature of that diversity is related to how each state has carried out its building process. The dynamics of interethnic relationships are characterized by each state's needs for territorial jurisdiction, control of population movement, access to resources and adequate supplies and distribution of labor.

The concept of ethnicity, seen as the sense of peoplehood held by members of a group sharing a common culture and history within a society, is the key to understanding why St. Victor's vision of pluralism on local, national, and international levels has not been, and very likely may never be, achieved. In looking at the structuring of states from prehistory to the present we find that images of peoplehood have been deliberately manipulated by decision makers within the dominant culture as they carry out social, economic, and political state building needs that reflect their priorities, and by decision makers within subordinate cultures as they try to better position the social, economic, and political needs of their group vis-à-vis others. Therefore, the maintenance of the state over time depends on the ongoing legitimation of the moral authority of the dominant group through an ongoing reification of their values and beliefs and expectations for behavior over those of other groups (see Cohen and Toland 1988).

The papers in this volume illustrate the historical process of ethnic manipulation by dominant/subordinate groups and the ensuing dialogue of self and other that invariably occurs at local, national and international levels in the state building process. It is proposed that this dialogue constitutes an ongoing state of disequilibrium that culminates in division and disintegration into chaos and/or structuring of a higher order. What is important to understand in this collection is that the power of a sense of peoplehood cannot be underestimated as a coalescing force. Whatever its origin or its context, whether it be recent and artificially constructed in response to immediate need or ancient and organic, growing overtime, it has the potential to crosscut race, class, and gender. It can be sanctified and resanctified by mythical, spiritual origins and relatedness to territory; legitimated and relegitimated by written and unwritten charters of shared joys and sorrows; and maintained by the human need to belong to, and be apart from, a larger group. It is reinterpreted, recreated, enlarged upon, or modified if the odds against it are too great. Very rarely, however, is it ever totally disregarded. Human need and the flexibility of belief is what makes it so vulnerable to manipulation.

The history of state building has shown us that those in power have tried, with little success, to eradicate ethnicity through genocide, bury it under accusations of "tribalism," discredit it with the mindframe of "modernization," relegate it to local rather than national political arenas, and until recently, generally wish it away through the silence of such organizations as the United Nations.

But both Barth (1969) and De Vos (1975) confirm that ethnicity can never be eradicated because it constitutes the psychological boundaries that are necessary to structure cultural interaction. And Pandian (1985) reminds us that these boundaries are maintained according to the historically generated symbols that give meaning to each group's heritage. Historically, the state has been a system of ordering that has depended on the symbols of its dominant culture to represent what is desirable, good, and true against the backdrop of subordinate cultures whose symbols have often come to stand for the very opposite of what has been deemed acceptable.

Cultural Hegemony and Ethnic Manipulation

Culture, defined as that system of values and beliefs that gives meaning to behavior, can, as Said (1983) points out, be seen as essentially "combative," as the assertively achieved and won hegemony of an identifiable set of ideas over all others within a society. Insofar as culture has been seen by many as representing that which is best in humankind, and in the state as the realization of that best in a material reality, the power of culture is linked with the power of the state.

The conclusion of Matthew Arnold's *Culture and Anarchy* (1969) illustrates this point: "because a State [is an entity] in which law is authoritative and sovereign, a firm and settled course of public order is requisite if man is to bring to maturity anything precious and lasting now, or to found anything precious and lasting for the future. Thus in our eyes, the very framework and exterior order of the State, whoever may administer the State, is sacred; and culture is the most resolute enemy of anarchy, because of the great hopes and designs for the State which culture teaches us to nourish" (1969).

Here Arnold makes the clear distinction between the culture of the State and that which stands outside that culture as anarchy. In other words, as Foucault (1972) reminded us, culture is an institutionalized process that makes appropriate a whole set of meanings through the articulation of language and defines what is inappropriate through silence.

Said (1983) ties the notion of cultural "combativeness" to the construction of the "other." With the assimilation of culture to the authority and exterior framework of the state go as well such things as "assurance, confidence, and the majority sense," that is, the entire matrix of meanings we usually associate with "home, belonging, and community." Outside this range of meanings stand anarchy, the culturally disenfranchised, and all those elements opposed to the link of a dominant culture with the state; what he calls the "others" or the "homeless."

Muratorio's chapter illustrates how the construction of a state culture selectively creates images of self and other in nineteenth-century Ecuador. In trying to convince Europe that Ecuador was a viable economic player in the international market, the coastal bourgeoisie, buoyed by their successful production of cacao, construct their own cultural hegemony in an era when commercial success and cultural progress are perceived to be closely intertwined. "Mestizaje," the concept of Ecuador as a nation of mixed bloods, European and Indian, becomes one of the most important "master fictions" of the new order. It hides, and yet still maintains, the asymmetrical relations of power between Colonials and Indians. As Muratorio states, "it creates the illusion that the Other, as forged by the dominator, can be brought into the 'imagined community' . . . through the doorway of 'natural' ties." In other words, according to Wilentz (1985) they appear to make their hierarchy appear "natural" and "just" to both rulers and ruled. To do this they incorporate, ignore, suppress, and reinterpret the symbol systems of the indigenous Indians.

For example, Muratorio cites a report documenting the suitability of exhibits for Ecuador's participation in the 1891 Historic American Exposition in Madrid that is based on the creation of two sets of images for the Indian, "savage" and "cultured." The Jivaro, as the savages, are considered outside the new national image and unsuitable for exposure because they are "dull" and "stubborn," "they are good for nothing," lack "civility," "morality" and "decency," and are "too fond of alcohol." On the other hand, the Otavalo Indians, supposedly descended from the Caras and the Incas, have "royal blood," "correct features," "vigorous forms," and are "intelligent, hard working, sober, of good manners and accustomed to neatness, order and cleanliness." In short, they are the Indian in the "mestizaje" image, not the Jivaro.

Diamond's chapter on the conflict between Chinese state culture and the cultures of minorities further illustrates the institutionalization of self/other relationships by the dominant power. She tells us that the concept of "wenhua" does not translate into the neutral terminology of culture as understood by Western thought. Rather than meaning that system of values and beliefs that gives meaning to the economic strategies, social organization, and political ideology of all integral groups, it refers to a more judgmental concept of culture as being either present or absent, high or low. Those groups that practice the state-approved system of thought are said to have culture. Furthermore, this culture is measured as being "wenming" or civilized. A group's degree of culture and degree of civilization rests upon how closely that group emulates the state guidelines. Minorities are recognized in China and given autonomous status but generally considered to be "backwards," "primitive," and "uncivilized." Civilized culture parallels the belief system of the Han

Chinese as it relates to advanced technologies, social organization, and attendant ideology.

Diamond looks at the minority status of the Hua Miao and determines that because of their cultural "primitiveness" with regard to subsistence technologies, social organization, and religious beliefs, they have been considered "not ready to enter the industrial age" in China. "Before they can become workers, they must first become peasants." In trying to turn the Hua Miao into peasants, the state, through its policymaking and reforms, has made it increasingly difficult for them to practice their traditional slash-and-burn agriculture and pastoralism, keep their unranked social order with its emphasis on large extended families, and adhere to their choice of religious beliefs, either animism or Christianity. In addition, Hua Miao dress and ritual festivals have been coopted by the state through the "manufacture" of traditional costumes as designated by the tourist board and the "performance" of traditional songs and dances with proper political messages as interpreted by the state.

The social, economic, and political structural boundaries of the state, then, can be said to be formed by the dominant group defining the inclusiveness/exclusiveness nature of its membership through the institutionalization of the self/other, we/they dynamics basic to individual human interactions. As Young (1976) suggests, ethnic identity must be looked at as both a subjective and objective phenomenon, one that is shaped through the constantly reoccurring subjective questions of ego as to "who am I" and within the collectivity as to "who are we" and the inevitable corollary, the objective questioning of the significant others as to who is he, she, or they?

The concept that one cannot understand the meaning of what something is, unless the meaning of what something is not is articulated, summarizes the nature of this kind of dualistic thinking. While this is the most basic form of conceptual ordering, and a far cry from the complexity of multivariate analysis that underlies a more holistic approach to problem solving, it is still the dynamic at work in the maintenance of cultural hegemony within statebuilding. The values and beliefs that uphold the structure of most early states equally define the lack of rights of those subordinate "others" who maintain the foundation of state order as well as the rights of the dominant group who creates and carries out this order.

In tributary states, Gailey (1985) points out that the placing of liens that selected out labor from subsistence productive kinship groupings according to gender, age, class, and race facilitated a kind of biological reductionism that served to maintain subordination through differences. It could also be argued that values and beliefs in industrial societies have influenced policymaking to enforce similar inequities for women, the elderly, the poor, and those of color considered ethnic minorities.

The desired end result of the legitimation of the dominant group's culture is the achievement of consent on the part of the subordinate group(s) to the existing system of order. However, as I have argued elsewhere (Toland 1987, 1988), consent is primarily based on the maintenance of "a perception of mutuality" that members of a state share with the dominant group. Perception of mutuality can be initially achieved through the reification of a system of values and/beliefs on the part of the dominant group, but to be maintained over time the perception must be validated by continued evidence that the trade-off, occurring when the loss of a certain amount of freedom on the part of the subordinate group(s), balanced by the gain of security and attention to well-being from the dominant group, is worthwhile.

A dominant group's credibility depends on keeping that perception of mutuality realized. Those regimes that loose credibility have to extend their authority through the increased use of sanctions and systems of coercion. In general, the degree of complexity and use of these sanctions and systems of coercion appear to be directly related to the degree of credibility held by the dominant group.

Burger's chapter illustrates how the systems of coercion used to maintain order among diverse populations in Pakistan, Sri Lanka, and India manipulate the very dynamic that they are mandated to control, ethnicity. Pakistan and Sri Lanka are examples of the state using disproportionate numbers of "core" or "heartland" ethnic groupings in their security forces to quell internal ethnic conflicts. In the case of Sri Lanka, this proved not to be successful and the government had to turn to outside forces from India to make sure that its policies of Sinhalization did not promote confrontations from the opposing ethnic group, the Tamils.

The Indian case study, however, indicates what appears to be the establishment of a paramilitary with integrated forces and north Indian leadership counterbalanced by an army with class-based units whose top leadership tends to come from linguistic and ethnic groups from southern and eastern states. This ethnic "balancing" policy appears to be successful in allowing the state to control large numbers of violent incidences while still keeping its own power base intact. Time will tell how long manipulation of ethnicity at the security level is acceptable in trying to deal with obvious ethnic inequities at economic and sociopolitical levels.

Gramsci (1971) argues that consent and coercion will always coexist to form the main contradiction of the state. He characterizes the cultural hegemony of the dominate group as "the spontaneous consent" given by the great masses of the population to the general direction imposed on social life by the dominant fundamental group. He suggests that this consent is historically caused by the prestige (and consequent "assurance, confidence, and majority sense") that the dominant group enjoys because of its position and function in the world of production. Although this world of production is the base from which the dominant group is able to, in actuality, carry out its part of the mutuality bargain, Gramsci implies, that it is the values and beliefs regarding redistribution or access to this production that determines whether consent will be achieved. In other words, even if the redistribution of production by the dominant group does not meet the subordinate group's needs, there is room for credibility if the values and beliefs surrounding the area of production are promising. With this notion it appears that the prestige of the group and its belief system does more to shape reality for the subordinate groups than the ability to deliver goods and services. A case in point is the cultural charter of the dominant Eurocentric power structure of the United States that "promises" equality in the pursuit of health, wealth, and happiness without deliverance.

This perspective, which at first appears to justify the classic Marxist "dominance maintained by ideology" approach, opens up a new area for thought with Gramsci's subsequent claim that the ordinary individual has two contradictory consciousnesses. The first is implicit in his activity and unites him with all his fellow workers in the "practical transformation" of the real world. The second is "superficially explicit or verbal," and one which he has inherited from the past and uncritically absorbed. It is this verbal conception that molds the culture of a specific social group and thereby, influences moral conduct and the direction of will, with varying efficacy but often powerfully enough to produce a situation in which the contradictory states of consciousness "[do] not permit of any action, any decision or any choice, and produces a condition of moral and political passivity" (1971).

In other words, the achievement of cultural hegemony has further levels of complexity, being related to more than just prestige within the world of production or fascist duplicity within a traditional ideologue. It relates, first, to the historicity of values and beliefs, the in-place, taken for granted canons and standards that, as Said (1983) points out, have become, over time, "natural," "objective," and "real"; and second, to the propensity of human thought to selectively ignore that which it cannot effectively grapple with at the moment. History tells us, however, that the life of the moment is directly related to the degree of discrepancies inherent in a credible/incredible hegemonic interaction.

The emphasis of the individual in theoretical considerations of the state is important. It recognizes what Gramsci calls "spontaneous philosophy" on the part of subordinate state members, the development of a way of thinking that is "unofficial." He points out a number of ingredients in this unofficial language that indicate individual response: the selective use of language; the conventional wisdom underlying "common sense"; the empirical knowledge underlying "good sense"; and the indigenous cultural values and beliefs of the subordinate group that are all pervasive inspite of the fact that attempts are often made by the dominant group to marginalize this type of communication as "folklore."

Adamson (1980) notes that cultural hegemony can also be characterized as "a process of continuous creation" because given its massive scale, it is bound to be uneven in the degree of legitimacy it commands and thereby leaves some room for "antagonistic" cultural expressions to develop. It is useful, here, to understand antagonistic as also meaning "alternative," "spontaneous," or "folkloric" cultural systems of values and beliefs developed by subordinate groups that seek to distinguish their perspective from that of the dominant group. These systems of thought constitute what can be seen as the external voices in an internal/external, dominant/subordinate, self/other cultural dialogue that constitute the disequilibrium present in all state building.

Royce, in her chapter on the manipulation of ethnicity as an "alternative" voice at a regional level by the Isthmus Zapotec of southwestern Mexico, concentrates on the role that Zapotec intellectuals play in defining the Indianness of their people in a non-Indian state. Through the creation of a "Zapotec style" during the last half of the nineteenth century that would distinguish the "indiginesmo" of the region in relation to newly arrived foreigners, Isthmus Zapotec elite have managed to maintain a strong presence for their people at the local, regional, and national levels of Mexican politics. Those who adhere to maintaining the Zapotec Style are considered to have "guendabianni," or culture/intelligence, for they are the "makers of light." They are *hombres bien preparados.*

The observable components of this style include elements of dress, language, music, visual art, dance, food, and fiestas. These are complemented by fundamental Zapotec values, the most important being *"guendalisaa,"* meaning the "sense of kinship, relatedness, and cooperation" that maintains the Zapotec notion of peoplehood. Royce points out that there are two important facets of Zapotec style: that it is eclectic and flexible; and that it was developed and is maintained by the Zapotec cultural and economic elite.

An active literary movement began in the 1930s with the publication of the journal, *Neza,* [the Road] and reappeared in 1968 as *Neza Cubi,* [the New Road]. It reaffirms that the strength of Zapotec culture lies in its ability to remember the achievements of previous generations. It sends a message endorsing the notion of progress but not at the expense of abandoning the brilliance of the Zapotec past. As long as Mexico follows "the Road," defined by the Zapotec style, the Zapotec will make the journey with the state. This has been seen most recently with the successful rise of the political party, COCEI *(Coalicion de Campesinos, Obreros y Estudiantes del Istmo)* strongly endorsed by Zapotec intellectuals. The Zapotec, by maintaining a strong ethnic identity and linking that identity to populist movements supporting rural peoples have managed to create a political dialogue with the predominant ruling culture; and one in which their "alternative" voice may be heard and understood at the national level.

In trying to understand ethnic manipulation in the state building process it is also important to consider, as Keyes (1981) suggests, that because all social interaction bears the seeds of potential disproportion, ethnicity creates a form of social action that orients people in their pursuit of self-maintenance. And as Rabushka and Shepsle (1972) point out, because the need for group security in a plural society generates a mobilizing imperative for its members, the logic of coalition formation within this risk-laden environment reduces this need. Ethnicity can be seen, then, as a defense mechanism against inequality or as Vincent, in her chapter on Northern Ireland, shows us a "masking" of inequality with the eradication of the culture history of the Irish Catholic "others."

The fact that British sovereignty rests on "controlled neglect of its peripheral domains," namely, Northern Ireland, is no news to political theorists. Vincent points out, however, that this brand of territorial politics may be directly responsible for the resurgence of an Ulster Scot ethnic identity for Northern Ireland's non-Irish population. Since 1968, several attempts to establish a separate sense of Northern Irish cultural identity have not come to fruition. However, Vincent documents that as of 1989 the newest attempt is underway. She cites Rory Fitzpatrick's volume *God's Frontiermen: The Scots-Irish Epic* as the spearhead of a "strategically constructed" campaign to reidentify Ulster Scots ethnicity.

Vincent shows how, Fitzpatrick, adopting the tone of a "civilizing colonist," points out how the transformation of "preexisting Catholic medieval values and an indolent pastoral economy" within Northern Ireland was accomplished by the Ulster Scots. He goes on to claim that "the Scots so predominated in numbers, in the toughness of their culture and in the determination with which they acquired land, that the *whole Plantation enterprise took on Scottish characteristics and the name Ulster Scots came in time to be applied to the entire non-Irish population of the Province"* (emphasis added). According to Vincent, this "hegemonic utterance" is not realistic. Neither is Fitzpatrick's message that the identicality of Ulster Scots, Presbyterianism, Orangeism and Ulster Unionism comprises an implicit claim for Northern Irish ethnic identity. To be effective, she maintains, historiographers will "have to reconstruct the old linguistic argument pitting Celts (the Irish and Scots) against Anglo-Saxons (the hated English) . . . they will have to reconstruct the ancient population flows of Gaelic-speaking peoples to and fro across the narrow waters between Ulster and Scotland from time immemorial . . . they will certainly have to rethink Fitzpatrick's perceptions of pastoralism and Catholicism." All appear to be unlikely. Thus we have another example of a dominant political force reconstructing a cultural identity that will more successfully keep it in place in times of risk.

As Cohen (1978) reminds us, ethnicity is first and foremost "situational." It is a dynamic process in which the interactive situation determines the level of inclusiveness used in setting up the self/other relationship. In other words, how the identity is subjectively or objectively perceived relates to what is important at the time to include in the identification criteria. What is important is going to relate to who the individuals or groups are within the interaction, what biological and cultural heritages are at stake, why the interaction is taking place, what the self interests or group interests are that have to be satisfied and if it is a situation where both parties are equal.

Identities, therefore, are not static, they are fluid, forever in process to include all the social roles individuals may assume and all the functions groups may perform in differing situations within the social arena. Ethnic affinity may or may not be a choice at a particular time within a particular situation for either individual or group. Self identity, at a particular moment may be contingent upon a more complex set of variables than peoplehood. So, those who attempt to develop a rigorous set of criteria for ethnic inclusiveness or identity build their arguments upon sand (Young 1976). There are as many criteria for ethnic inclusiveness or identity as there are situational interactions for individuals and groups.

Rodgers, in her case study of the Angkola Batak of Northern

Sumatra, points this out with reference to ethnic fluidity taking place throughout Southeast Asia. For the Batak, the concept of "adat," implies conformity to supposedly "ancient, prototypically correct patterns of behavior and speech" bestowed on them by their ancestors. These ancient village heritages, however, are constantly being "reconfigured" and at times, "invented" at both the local and the state level to depict Angkolaness.

At the local level, the Angkola Batak have tried to do two things at once: be faithful to ancient Angkola traditions by maintaining "adat," and be "maju," or progress minded in conjunction with the state goals of Indonesia. Rodgers tells us that they take great pains to glorify their "ancient village heritage" as a "morally excellent and specifically Angkola tradition whose distinctive character and content should be maintained within the larger nation." In other words, they try to identify Angkolaness with the matrix of all things important to the state. She illustrates this point with examples from a series of Angkola "culture guides" that have been written to extoll the correctness of Angkola village customs and indicate to modern readers that they should pay attention to this exemplary behavior if they are to understand the true nature of the Indonesian character. On the other hand, at the state level, Angkola customs and traditions are trivialized in comparison to the importance of all citizens living by the principle of "Indonesian Unity." Government publications present the Angkola as a small subsociety of a larger, vaguely defined ethnic unit, the Bataks, who are, in turn, presented as a small part of a large, multiethnic nation. Angkola culture emerges as nothing more than a collection of ceremonies, family rules, and old sayings without political significance. The core of "adat" sayings or social practices are translated as part of a larger Indonesian context thus minimalizing the uniqueness of Angkola identity in favor of the principle of "Indonesian Unity."

When we speak of inclusiveness, we by unspoken definition, imply exclusiveness. And as Southhall (1970) notes, the two are not always so well defined. It is imperative, therefore, that we recognize the importance of "interlocking, overlapping, and multiple collective identities" that may be present in the interaction of self and other, and we with they. As Cohen (1978) and Aronson (1976) tell us, it is important to note that the qualities of inclusiveness and exclusiveness create a social distance scale, or a forum for consensus/dissensus, engagement/disengagement that is appropriate at the time.

Sahliyeh's chapter on the Palestinians illustrates how the boundaries of inclusiveness/exclusiveness are manipulated in the preservation of self in the state-building process. In his case study of the Palestinian statehood movement, Sahliyeh defines ethnic inclusiveness/exclusiveness in terms of the Palestinian's "deep sense of deprivation and grievances" based on their physical dispersal and their attachment to the land. The collective agony produced by their "crisis environment" has forged a strong ethnic and nationalistic identity for the Palestinians. Despite their "physical dispersal, [and] the oneness of language, race, religion, and common political aspirations" that they share with other Arabs, the Palestinians recognize themselves as a new, distinct, ethnic and national group. As with the Israelis, group solidarity is maintained and has been intensified over time relative to perceived threats to their physical presence on commonly claimed/occupied land.

Various mobilizing agents, such as, the Palestinian traditional elite, the militant counterelite, mass organizations, and the PLO with its various functions, have shaped the Palestinian's desire for statehood through the creation of many different forums for dissensus, as have the 1967 war, Israel's occupation of the West Bank and the Intifada. Throughout this process the Palestinians have created and recreated different social distances within their own ranks and between themselves and varying Arabs states, Israel, and nations exterior to the Middle East arena. The recent Persian Gulf crisis has been a cause for further realignment and rethinking of these social distances. Throughout this process, however, the collective agony has not diminished, nor will it until the formation of a state becomes the "requisite framework for the fulfillment of . . . [the Palestinian] political, social, cultural and economic identity and existence."

Lewis's case study of the ethnic diversity of Jews within Israel further illustrates how what is/is not to be included in the concept of a state-mandated sense of peoplehood is manipulated in the statebuilding process. The formation of the Jewish state after 1948 was based on the idea that "the Jewish people is one people," and the reality that the Jewish people were a "far more complex melange of peoples" than had ever been imagined. After the Law of Return was promulgated in 1950, a mass immigration of Jews included an almost equal division of groups coming from post-World War II Europe and groups coming from Morocco, Tunisia, Libya, Egypt, Yemen, Iraq, Iran, Turkey, and India. In the 1950s the pioneering Israeli elite envisioned full integration and unity, politically, culturally, and socially, among all Jews with differences being obliterated over time and a "new type of Jew" with the "favorable qualities and characteristics" of all the tribes of Israel emerging. They referred to this "fusion of the exiles" as *"mizug galuyot."* Apparently, this has yet to happen.

Lewis tell us that the early goal of fusion, in reality, ended up as fission. Although there are substantial differences within the groupings of European and Oriental Jews there are even wider differences between them in terms of material culture, education, hygiene, and domestic practices. The Israeli elite of the 1950s saw themselves as modern secular socialists and they were not about to sanction the traditional patriarchal structure of the "backward" countries in which the father was the unchallenged potentate with all the rights and privileges. They tried to create a type of social climate that centered around the education of the child, in which an individual's status is measured in terms of "ability, character and achievements," not family connections. In other words, "they had a clear mandate: to make the immigrants over into the kinds of modern Jews and Israelis that their ideology had envisioned."

By the 1970s they had a real problem, an ethnic divide or "two Israels," made up of modern Western European-thinking Jews vs. traditional Eastern European/Oriental-thinking Jews. It was claimed that the policy of *"mizug galuyot"* had been responsible for the "deculturation, marginalization, educational and cultural deprivation" of all those outside the dominant elite or Western European thinking group. A general "rethinking" resulted with policies formated to "enrich" school curricula, celebrate diverse "traditions," and subsidize intercultural "gatherings." In general, the policies became more sensitive and thus more inclusive of cultural differences among all Jews rather than continuing to adhere to the former exclusivity of the Western European mandate.

Contemporary thinking regarding the forum of consensus in Israel still favors "the Jewish people is one" concept but that "Jewish people" is now seen as encompassing a larger ethnic base.

The final point to be considered with regard to ethnicity and state building is that ethnicity has a peculiar handicap in states that have built their charter on democratic principles. Values and beliefs generated to maintain systems extolling individual rights have little use for the collective rights of groups. It is much easier and safer to propose and maintain a "myth of rights" for faceless individuals than to meet the demands of a more defined collectivity (Scheingold 1974).

Enloe (1981) suggests that ethnic intensity varies in democratic societies in relation to how strong the state's impact is on the potential group member's self-perception of their identity, the ethnic group's resources for communal organization, and the group's acceptance by other ethnic groups in such political processes as elections and petitioning. Within the United States, for instance, she states that antimachine campaigns, civil service reforms, regularization of welfare services, the institution of professional city managers and nonpartisan city elections can be seen as unsuccessful efforts to demobilize ethnicity at the local and state levels. Marginalizing attempts at the federal level can be seen in the establishment of specialized groups such as the BIA and INS to deal specifically with Native American and Hispanic groups and defuse their political presence through selectivism, and the legitimization of broad-based ethnic categories such as black, Hispanic, Asian and Native American that obscure specific problem solving.

Within such national institutional systems as higher education, the concept of ethnicity, itself, is manipulated to marginalize the voices of ethnic minority groups. So called "ethnic studies" courses have been created to fulfill cultural diversity requirements within the monocultural halls of academe. The generally held assumption that those who are "ethnic" are those who are not easily assimilable into the ranks of white society is further enforced with this thinking.

National campaigns for elected office in the United States in the last decade, based on the creation of images of the white Anglo-Saxon knight fighting wars against poverty, drugs, and illiteracy, have depended on the negativization of ethnic minority images.

Beginning with Bush's identification of societal "evil" as personified by the Willie Horton image, national campaigns have continued to characterize the black male as "criminal," "addictive," and "illiterate" and the black female as "the witch of reproduction" or "the mother of poverty" (Samuels 1991). These negative associations create a false reality that obviates the statistics that tell us the majority of rapists and drug users are white males and that illiteracy is not color blind.

Ethnic intensity for the pursuit of group interests in the United States, however, appears to take place in spite of national, state, and local efforts to disperse, deny, discredit, and/or make dependent, collective relationships. We have only to look at the revitalization movements of African Americans rediscovering and reinterpreting their culture heros and heroines to promote the cohesiveness needed to continue their fight for civil rights; Native Americans restructuring the rituals of the Grandfathers to help regain lost treaty rights and the Grandmothers to help regain gender equality within the tribe; Mexican Americans redefining the concepts of Chicano, La Raza, and the journey from Aztlan to validate their fight for labor equity; and such newly arrived peoples as the Hmong from Southeast Asia who are reinventing their ceremonial traditions to combine different tribal customs into a pan-Hmong sense of peoplehood.

Conclusion

The intensification of ethnic activism and conflict was once thought to be shortlived with consequences that "probably will not be widespread" (Despres 1984). We see, now, how misguided this viewpoint was. The state, through its nature of incorporation of many into a united one, articulated with an official origin myth, charter, and dominant system of values and beliefs, has always constituted a more-or-less believable, stable/unstable entity at the ethnic level.

Gramsci (1971) tells us that the prestige of the values and beliefs of the dominant ruling group of the state system will cover for economic inequalities. But history has made clear that prestige in the world of production, in a capitalistic or socialistic state, cannot suffice to silence the "others" excluded from that world. The internal/external, inclusive/exclusive, self/other dialogue is ongoing. And those "alternative" voices in the dialogue are breaking the silence for "others" denoted not only by ethnicity, but by race, gender, age, sexual choice, varying mental/physical abilities, and differing world views. The fight continues but the contestants and the rules are changing along with the possibilities for the outcome. Disintegration and reordering appear to be an ongoing cycle with ethnic manipulation a given ingredient of social, economic and political change within the process of statehood.

References

Adamson, Walter L. 1980. *Hegemony and Revolution: A Study of Antonio Gramsci's Political and Cultural Theory.* Berkeley and Los Angeles: University of California Press.

Arnold, Matthew. 1969. *Culture and Anarchy,* ed. by J. Dover Wilson, (1869 reprint). Cambridge: Cambridge University Press.

Aronson, Dan R. 1976. "Ethnicity as a Cultural System: An Introductory Essay." In Frances Henry (ed.), *Ethnicity in the Americas.* The Hague: Mouton Publishers.

Barth, Fredrick. 1969. *Ethnic Groups and Boundaries: The Social Organization of Cultural Differences.* Boston: Little, Brown and Co.

Cohen, Ronald. 1978. "Ethnicity: Problem and Focus in Anthropology." *Annual Review of Anthropology* 7:379–403.

Cohen, Ronald and Judith Toland. 1988. *State Formation and Political Legitimacy,* Political Anthropology Series, 6. New Brunswick, N.J.: Transaction Publishers.

Despres, Leo A. 1984. "Ethnicity: What Data and Theory Portend for Plural Societies." In David Mayberry-Lewis (ed.), *The Prospects for Plural Societies.* Proceedings of the 1982 American Ethnological Society.

DeVos, George. 1975. "Ethnic Pluralism: Conflict and Accomodation." In George DeVos and L. Romanucci-Ross, (eds.), *Ethnic Identity.* Palo Alto, Cal.: Mayfield Publishing Co.

Enloe, Cynthia. 1981. "The Growth of the State and Ethnic Mobilization: The American Experience." *Ethnic and Racial Studies* 4, 2, April:123–36.

Fitzpatrick, Rory. 1989. *God's Frontiersmen: The Scots-Irish Epic.* London: Weindenfeld & Nicolson.

Foucault, Michel. 1976. *The Archaeology of Knowledge,* trans. by A. M. Sheridan Smith, New York: Harper & Row.

Gailey, Christine. 1985. "The State of the State in Anthropology." *Dialectical Anthropology* 9, 1–2:64–89.

Gramsci, Antonio. 1971. *Selections from the Prison Notebooks,* ed. and trans. by Quentin Hoare and Geoffrey Nowell Smith. New York: International Publishers.

Hugo of St. Victor. 1961. *Didascalicon,* trans. by Jerome Taylor. New York: Columbia University Press.

Keyes, Charles F. 1981. "The Dialectics of Ethnic Change." In Charles F. Keyes (ed.), *Ethnic Change.* Seattle: University of Washington Press.

Prigogine, Ilya and Isobelle Stengers. 1984. *Order Out of Chaos.* New York: Bantam Press.

Rabushka, Alvin and Kenneth Shepsle. 1972. *Politics in Plural Societies: A Theory of Democratic Instability.* New York: Charles E. Merrill Publishing Co.

Said, Edward W. 1983. *The World, the Text, and the Critic.* Cambridge, Mass.: Harvard University Press.

Samuels, Deborah D'Amico. 1992. "A Not-So-Hidden Disgrace: What Talk About Literacy Says About Race." For publication in *Transforming Anthropology,* 1992.

Scheingold, Stuart. 1974. *The Politics of Rights,* New Haven, Conn.: Yale University Press.

Southhall, Aidan. 1970. "The Illusion of Tribe." *Journal of Asian and African Studies* 5, 1–2.

Toland, Judith. 1987. "Discrepancies and Dissolution: Breakdown of the Early Inca State." In Henri J. M. Claessen (ed.), *Early State Dynamics.* Leiden: E. J. Brill.

————. 1988. "Inca Legitimation as a Communication Process." In Ronald Cohen and Judith Toland (eds.), *State Formation and Political Legitimation.* New Brunswick, N.J.: Transaction Publishers.

Wilentz, Sean. 1985. "Introduction: Teufelsdrockh's Dilemma: On Symbolism, Politics, and History." In Sean Wilentz (ed.), *Rites of Power.* Philadelphia: University of Pennsylvania Press.

Young, Crawford. 1976. *The Politics of Cultural Pluralism.* Madison: University of Wisconsin Press.

1

Nationalism and Ethnicity: Images of Ecuadorian Indians and the Imagemakers at the Turn of the Nineteenth Century

Blanca Muratorio

> *No matter how democratically the members of the elite are chosen (usually not very) or how deeply divided among themselves they may be (usually more than outsiders imagine), they justify their existence and order their actions in terms of a collection of stories, ceremonies, insignia, formalities, and appurtenances that they have inherited or, in more revolutionary situations, invented.*
> —Geertz, "Centers, Kings, and Charisma"

By royal decree, in 1891 Spain invited American and European countries to Madrid to commemorate the fourth centenary of the discovery of America. The center of the celebration was occupied by two joint historical exhibitions that opened in *El Palacio de la Biblioteca y Museos Nacionales* in October 1892. One was the Historic American Exposition, intended to illustrate the state of civilization of the New World in the pre-Columbian, Columbian, and post-Columbian periods. The other, the Historic European Exposition, was to exhibit "the evidences of the civilization of

Europe at the time when the New World was discovered and colonized" (Report 1895).[1] In addition, at the request of the Royal Commission in charge of the celebrations, the American countries were encouraged to "reproduce" in the Parque de Madrid some "primitive dwellings or monuments" and to send (live) "Indians to inhabit them" (Informe 1892).[2] In preparation for the Historic American Exposition, the Ecuadorian Organizing Committee *(Junta Directiva)* had to request funds from Congress and consequently to justify the characteristics and merits as well as the cost of the objects and Indians that were to be sent to represent the country. One such request is made in a document presented to the Ecuadoran Congress in 1892 by the minister of the interior and foreign affairs, Leonidas Pallares Arteta, who was also chief delegate of the Ecuadoran committee in charge of the exhibit (Informe 1892). Further information on the Ecuadoran participation on the Exposition was obtained from the General Catalogue (Catálogo 1893).

This essay will examine the explicit and the unspoken yet unhidden images of Ecuadoran Indians represented in those documents and at the Madrid exhibition. The dominant visual images of Ecuadoran Indians (mostly in engravings, drawings, and water colors) circulating among intellectuals, artists, and other powerful producers of public images at the turn of the century, undoubtedly contributed to the construction of the images apparent in the documents. They also seem to have influenced the selection and hierarchization of the artifacts actually presented at the exhibition. I will argue that those narrative and visual images of the Indians became incorporated as important elements in the political rhetoric of an emerging nationalist ideology. It was articulated by those class groups who, at the turn of the century, were in a position to use the power of the state to write the text and to shape cultural traditions. I will then attempt to contextualize those images by providing the socioeconomic and political characterization of the period in Ecuadoran history when those representations were made and "used." That is, how and why they were incorporated or excluded from a more comprehensive image the Ecuadoran elite was forging of the country as a whole, both as an emerging nation state (since 1830) before the mother country and the rest of Europe, and as a viable economic player in the international market. Blessed by an increasingly profitable cacao boom at the turn of the century, the new coastal bourgeoisie in control of the state was looking to the outside world to gain legitimacy as a "civilized" society. It was trying to construct its own cultural hegemony in an era when commercial success and cultural progress were perceived to be closely intertwined. The tradition that the Ecuadoran elite "invented" for the country at that particular time was intended to convey this message, and was manufactured primarily for external, not internal consumption. Two world's fairs (Paris 1889 and Chicago 1893) as well as the Madrid Exposition — which is our particular concern here — provided an irresistible ritual stage to display and test this developing feeling of a new national self. However, in analyzing this particular historical instance in the social construction of national identity it becomes evident that *"mestizaje"* — the concept of Ecuador as a nation of mixed bloods — Indians and Europeans — begins to emerge as one of the important "master fictions" (Geertz 1985) of the new political order. Since then, *mestizaje* became the "ethnic component" in the larger discourse of nationalism, significant for both external and *internal* consumption. Although it served to legitimize their domination, subordinate groups participated in maintaining this master fiction, until its own contradictions provided the basis for their own autonomous ethnic consciousness and resistance.[3]

As Sider has noted, "[t]he *process* of domination imposes a dialogue between dominators and dominated. Each must speak to the other for the economic and political transactions to occur" (1987, 22, emphasis added). As part of an *ideology* of domination, however, *mestizaje* hides this dialogue by turning it into a monologue — the monologue of the Self who has incorporated the Other or is in the process of doing so. It creates the illusion that the Other, as forged by the dominator, can be brought into the "imagined community" — the useful term by which Benedict Anderson (1983) refers to national social identities — through the doorway of "natural" ties. As such, the ideology of *mestizaje* is riddled by the same contradiction that Sider sees as the fundamental one in the colonial encounter between Europeans and Indians: a contradiction between the [European] "impossibility and the necessity of creating the other as the other—the different, the alien—and incorporating the other within a single social and cultural system of domination" (1987, 7).

While master fictions remain the unchallenged first principles of a political order, they have the power to make "any given hierarchy appear natural and just to rulers and ruled" (Wilentz 1985, 4). Like other master fictions, *mestizaje* was invented by the dominant turn-of-the-century elites for the subordinate peoples in order to hide and maintain the asymmetrical relations of power between whites and Indians that they had inherited from the colonial administration. As the "ethnic master fiction" in the official ideology of nationalism, *mestizaje* remained unchallenged until the 1970s. It is in this decade when indigenous organizations started to publicly contest it by advocating a new imagined community that conceives of Ecuador as a country embodying a plurality of autonomous nationalities.

The Narrative Images and Their Display

In his capacity as chief delegate of the Organizing Committee, Mr. Pallares Arteta was in charge of collecting, buying, and organizing all the exhibits to be sent to the Historic American Exposition. The participation of Ecuador is regarded in his report to Congress as "a very special testimony of love, deference and gratitude to Columbus" and to the "heroic Spanish nation" that "gave him her unquestioned support" and "brought [us] civilization and Christianity."[4] It is also considered a matter of national honor, since Ecuador has to show the Mother Country that "the conquered nations are now powerful and *flourishing*," and "have finally deserved the seed of civilization [she] planted in the New World." The report is rich in such rhetorical imagery about the country and its distinguished citizens as well as its generous foreign friends, all of whom have contributed to the exhibition with their intellectual productions and private collections.[5]

It is precisely the rhetoric of historical texts like this that provides clues to the process by which the dominant groups produce and reproduce their hegemonic cultural meanings by incorporating, ignoring, or suppressing the symbol systems of the dominated groups. The document also describes in detail several "important Inca and Caras" artifacts, the collection of medals and coins, and other "minor and ornamental" objects all of which will be included in the Ecuadoran Hall at the exposition. Finally, the author supplies us with two vivid and contrasting images of contemporary Ecuadoran Indians: the "savages," of whom the "Jíbaro" and the "Záparo" are given as examples, and the "Indians from Otavalo." These two images emerge in the narrative text through the "compelling" reasons given by Pallares Arteta point by point to explain to the congressmen why the first group of Indians should not be sent to the *Parque de Madrid* to be housed in the "primitive dwellings," and why the second constitutes "the most suitable group" for that exhibit.

To start with, the "savages" will never be convinced of the need and advantages of the trip. Even if they were, they would most certainly cause "serious inconveniences" for the person in charge, given the fact that their "dullness" and "stubbornness" prevent them from following any instructions. Besides, they don't speak Spanish and not even Quichua, "they are good for nothing," "lack the most elementary notions of civility, morality or decency," are "too fond of alcohol" (an obvious embarrassment to the government if caught by the police). Moreover, they would not even be able to perform their job of "keeping the dwellings neat and tidy." By contrast, despite the fact that the Otavalo Indians are not "pure," according to Mr. Pallares, they remain "outstanding" for their "correct features," their "above-average height" and "their vigorous forms," characteristics that they allegedly have "preserved" from their "Caras" ancestors. In addition, they are "intelligent, hard working, sober, of good manners and accustomed to neatness, order and cleanliness." Most important, however, the Otavaleños have "special abilities" such as their "San Juan dances," their "ball game" (similar to the "most popular Spanish Jai-Alai"), and their *totora* boats with which they could sail the lakes of the Madrid Park. All these exotic talents would not only attract and entertain the public, but the small fee that would be charged for this entertainment, may "even help to pay for all the expenses incurred in transporting and housing the Indians themselves" (Informe 1892).

The section of the General Catalogue (Catálogo 1893) of the exhibit devoted to Ecuador[6] contains a long introduction presenting the "official" history of the country from its pre-Columbian past to the present, and an itemized list of the 1,327 artifacts included in the different collections exhibited. The great majority of those items are pre-Columbian artifacts designated under the all-inclusive category of "Incásicos." Among them one should note a facsimile of Inga Pirca "Palace" in wood, commissioned especially for the occasion, by Mr. Pallares in Cuenca, five figures excavated from San Pablo, which were very "similar to the Egyptian mummies," and a large stone found in the province of Manabí "with resonant qualities" reported to have been used by the "Caras" Indians to sound warnings. Dr. Antonio Flores, who had finished his term as president of Ecuador in 1892, was president of the exposition commission. He personally presented a collection of twenty ethnographic artifacts "belonging to the Jíbaro tribe" that included mostly necklaces, feather crowns, and feather earrings, and that had been "presented to him while President of the Republic by the Cacique Charupe, Chief of the Macas tribe." Another private collection included a "life size figure of a Jíbaro Indian with two sets of dresses" and a specimen of a "desiccated and shrunken head of a Jíbaro Indian called Tamaguari, chief of an Oriente tribe, Canelos, year 1590." To complete the "ethnographic" exhibit there were a series of "curiosities" of contemporary Indians exhibited all together in one large panoply, and four "paintings of Indian customs."

In the text of the introduction, which contains the official history of the country, the author (anonymous) incorporates an already existing "mythic history" (see Murra 1963, 792) most probably invented in the eighteenth century by the Jesuit Juan de Velasco "for reasons of regional chauvinism" (see Salomon 1981, 433). This invented history refers to the "Caras" (Cara or Caranqui tribe or nation) as the first civilizers of Ecuador, who, after entering through the coast proceeded to build an empire. According to the author, the "Caras" conquered the inhabitants of the kingdom of Quito who allegedly were living in "a state of barbarism." Soon after the Inca conquest of Ecuador, the "Caras" princess Paccha was married to Huayna Capac and Atahuallpa the last Inca emperor was her son. The Incas themselves are presented in this conjectural history as possessing "great noble character," and their religion "although erroneous," is not considered "bloodthirsty," since the sacrifices performed by them "corresponded to the gentleness of their beliefs." In sum, the image of the Incas is that of "a very advanced civilization."

The only other powerful image of Ecuador present in this introduction takes the reader into the contemporary scene, not in the Highlands but on the Coast, and specifically in the city of Guayaquil. There one can find "several banks enjoying solid credit," "a vertiginous commercial life," and a place where "all the people are well off due to the abundance of well remunerated work." Finally, this "main port of the Republic" is reported to export "more than half a million quintals of cacao annually," in addition to the increasingly important exports of rubber and coffee (Catálogo 1893).

The Imagemakers' Kaleidoscope

In the narrative texts just mentioned, it is evident that the organizers of the exhibit (mainly Antonio Flores and Pallares Arteta), carefully orchestrated an economic representation of the country to promote the already dominant interests of a specific class: the coastal merchant bourgeoisie. In this picture, the image of the Indian is conveniently left out, since in the immediate experience of the imagemakers, Indians were the dispossessed peasants from the Highlands who were forced to work in the cacao plantations. However, their wretched reality is artfully inverted and hidden under the general image of an alleged prosperous and well-remunerated coastal population.

When dealing with "cultural progress," the other term in the nineteenth-century equation of economic success linked to advanced civilization, the imagemakers engage in a very selective use of the images of Indians current at the time, emphasizing the *past* and the *future* rather than the present. The past is brought to life in the images of the "Incas" and the mythical "Caras." Their history cannot be denied (since their artifacts are actively being excavated), but it can be adequately touched up and reinvented or fictionalized to demonstrate historical continuity and to legitimize the origins of all Ecuadorians. They are not to be considered second-class Europeans, but the descendants of a "noble" and "aristocratic" race. Neither liberal democracy nor the Enlightenment but "aristocratic racism" (Muratorio 1980), which traced the ancestry of Ecuadorans to the historic Indian aristocracy—real or mythical—constituted an important pillar in the social construction of national identity. It selectively ignored the contemporary Indians.[7] Thus Juan Montalvo, the nineteenth-century Ecuadorian essayist refers to his country as "the land of Atahuallpa" (1923). As Hobsbawm has pointed out, invented traditions "might foster the corporate sense of *superiority* of élites—particularly when those had to be recruited from those who did not already possess it by birth or ascription" (1983, 10, emphasis in the original).

Furthermore, this image of the "Incas" also catered to a European public who, already by the mid-nineteenth century, had demonstrated great interest in their history. Honour notes that Prescott's history of the Incas was widely read in England and in the United States (1975, 180). Europeans had also seen representations of the Incas in images that compared them to the great civilizations of the Egyptians and the Romans, or to the great Sun King, Louis XIV (see image from the Encyclopedia Londinensis, figure 1.1, found in a shop in Quito).[8] It is in the context of this universe of discourse that Pallares Arteta compares the five figures excavated from the San Pablo site with Egyptian mummies. Honour also points out that while at the great international exhibitions of the mid-nineteenth century, the Latin American states were "represented almost exclusively by natural products," an exception was made regarding the Incas and the Aztecs. Even the Royal Academy of London had exhibited a painting by John Everett Millais entitled *Pizarro seizing the Inca of Peru* (1975, 183).

In contrast to the historic Incas, the image of the Otavaleños is designed to represent the future. Within the nineteenth century scheme of progress, the Otavaleños symbolize for the authors, what all the Indians might and should become if the process of civilizing them is allowed to take its "natural" course. That positive perception of the Otavaleños, which makes of them the "mould image" of highland Indians to this day, was fashioned very early on. It was certainly already current by the turn of the century; as Hassaurek

FIGURE 1.1

The Inca and His Queen. Engraved for the *Encyclopaedia Londinensis*, 1823
(page bought by the author in a Quito shop).

remarks, "There is a general belief at Quito that the Indians of Otavalo, and especially the women, are handsomer and cleaner than those of Pichincha, Latacunga, etc., but I have been unable to discover the slightest foundation for such an opinion" (1967, 157–58). The Otavaleños are also singled out because they are considered to have started the process towards civilization with one advantage: that of having "inherited" and "preserved" some of the best physical traits, cultural characteristics, and skills of their "Caras" ancestors (see also Stutzman 1981). After all, even in mythical history, the "Caras" had ended up establishing their empire in the Otavalo area (see Salomon 1981). Besides, their reported behavior and general "clean" attitude as hard workers and as respectful of order, may be regarded as a good example of the effectiveness of liberal ideology and laissez-faire economics. In the image that emerges from the text, this belief is reinforced by the fact that all of the Otavaleño skills in sports and the arts are considered marketable (see figure 1.2). This asset is particularly important before a European audience living in an era when—as Breckenbridge points out—"the modern entertainment industry began to take shape in European urban centers" (1989, 200). The harsh and oppressive realities discarded from this idealized image of the Otavaleños have been thoroughly examined by Salomon (1981), and can also be seen in some of the images until recently kept hidden in the privacy of hacienda homes, like the photograph of the hacienda *obraje* from the Otavalo area shown in figure 1.3 (discovered in 1989).

When the narrative text in the documents is examined in conjunction with the ethnographic artifacts exhibited, the image that emerges of "the savages" appears at first sight to be the most transparent, but actually it turns out to be riddled with ambiguities. It can be seen as composed of at least three different images: the savage as "nature," as "infidel," and as "Jíbaro." First, in the Informe (1892), the Jívaro and Záparo Indians are just presented as examples of all savages. Their image is constructed in the semiotic field that considers the savages as part of nature. They are regarded as equal to the animals in the sense that they lack any "sensible language," they seemed to be compelled by their nature to be "stubborn" and "dirty," and are deprived of any notion of social,

FIGURE 1.2

Indian from Otavalo. Painting from the Castro y Velázques collection. *From Ecuador Visto por los Extrànjeros* (Quito: Salvat Editores Ecuatoriana, 1983).

FIGURE 1.3
Indians in Obraje. Photograph courtesy of Fernando Espinosa de los Monteros
(Ibarra, Ecuador).

civilized life: "their essence is privation" (Ryan 1981, 537). This
image of the savage conforms to the ideology that Berkhofer refers
to as "scientific racism," in which social progress, racial hierar-
chies, and Darwinian biology converge. According to Berkhofer,
the result of this convergence is a savage that not only has "darker
skin" and "bad manners," but an "inferior organic equipment as
well" (1978, 59) (see figure 1.4). For Pallares Arteta the imagemaker, the savages are contained within the cage of their psychological nature. Because of their "dullness," they cannot help themselves. Taussig, for instance, has pointed out how an experienced
traveler like Simpson, who visited the Ecuadoran Oriente in the

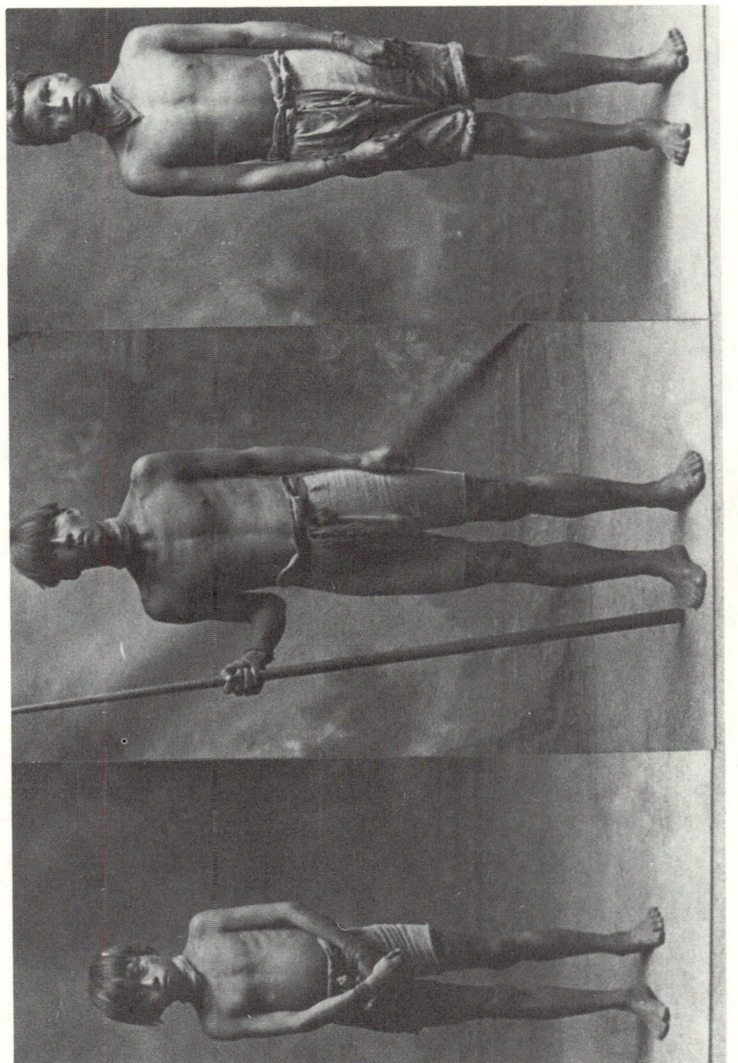

FIGURE 1.4
Indígenas del Oriente. Photograph, series 20, nos. 83 and 87. Fondo Jijón.
Banco Central del Ecuador.

1870s, powerfully describes the Záparo with all the characteristics that make them just one more animal group in the jungle (1987, 97). In fact, in many of the European travelers' illustrations, the savages graphically become one with nature, as literally part of a tree, or hanging from it like monkeys (see figure 1.5). The Other is considered merely a part of the savage landscape, observed by the gaze of the civilized Self. As Gordie points out, "the sense of belonging to nature associated with the indigene creates an immediate organicist metaphor which is often then used, in a somewhat circular form of logic, to justify the emphatically natural indigene" (1989, 21).

In a brief paragraph in the introduction to the exhibit catalogue, the author presents a second image of the savage. In the context of describing the general resources of the country, the following statement is made:

> The Republic counts with 1,200,000 inhabitants, without including the population of the Oriente region, which is inhabited by several tribes of Indians that are gradually being incorporated into the life of Christian civilization, thanks to the efforts of the government and the missions. (Catálogo 1893)

Here, the savage as "infidel" is given the possibility of incorporation into the scheme of evolutionary progress. In his analysis of how the seventeenth and eighteenth centuries assimilated new worlds, Ryan argues that "paganism was the most inclusive, unambiguous category of Otherness" (1981, 525). Because paganism was considered a transhistorical category like Christianity, it served to guarantee the Indians' humanity and, eventually their conversion, finally proving "the unity and identity of all mankind" (ibid.). Contrary to the first image of the savages "as nature," the representation of them as "pagans" and "infidels" brings them back into history, but a history whose pace is only in the power of the Self to advance.

Finally, the third image of the savage as "Jíbaro" emerges primarily out of the ethnographic exhibit, which is dominated by a great number of artifacts of their material culture, by a full-size figure of a Jívaro Indian, and by a *tsantsa,* the shrunken head for which they became so famous in Europe. I will argue that by selecting the Jívaro to represent physically (but not personally) the image of the savage, the imagemakers were responding on the one hand to

FIGURE 1.5

Cotos Indians at the Napo River. Drawing by Vignal based on a sketch by
Wiener. From *Grabados sobre el Ecuador en el Siglo XIX.* Le Tour du Monde
(Quito: Banco Central del Ecuador, 1981).

their own ambiguous love-hate relationship with this Amazonian group, and second, to the demands of their European audience who in the nineteenth century had developed a morbid fascination with the "scientific mysteries" of the Jívaro *tsantsas* (Taylor 1985, 259–60). In her article, "The Invention of the Jívaro," Anne Christine Taylor has made a perceptive analysis of the complexities of that image in the Ecuadoran mind from colonial times to the present. She argues it oscillated between two polar opposites: at the negative extreme, the Jívaro were considered the quintessential savages defying all the canons of European civilization, at the positive extreme they were regarded as the "indomitable nation" and as a model for the new Ecuadoran nation to emulate. Taylor describes this second side of the image as follows:

> Thus, those subversive Indians (Jívaro) come to symbolize the Republican virtues with which Creole society likes to endow itself: the warrior passion, a strong attachment to freedom, the machismo of the individual fighting against an indomitable Nature, in opposition to the pompous nobility of the European urbanites, decadent, effeminate and lovers of oppression. (1985, 258)

This multifaceted and contradictory image of the "Jíbaro"—the invented Jívaro—fitted perfectly the intentions that the image-makers wanted visually displayed at the Madrid exhibit: to impress a cultivated European public, and to heighten their newly acquired sense of national identity and pride.

The Visual Landscape at the Turn of the Century

In an article on the historical analysis of photographs at the Carlisle Indian School, Malmsheimer underscores the mutual research advantages of looking at photographs in close interrelationship with verbal historical documents:

> Not only, then, do words provide the necessary context for the interpretation of photographs, but photographs provide an essential and hitherto neglected visual context for the complete historical understanding of words. From this point of view, photographs are not so much reflections of a past material actuality as they are, like words, examples of a past symbolic reality. (1985, 54)

If we add other forms of art to photographs, this research strategy is equally productive when used in the analysis of images of Ecuadoran Indians at the turn of the century, as I hope to demonstrate in the discussion that follows. On the one hand, many of those images were produced by artists specifically to illustrate foreign travelers' narratives or lyrics of popular songs, and often they were mirror images of those already available in the travelers' publications. On the other, the powerful image manipulators, who shared the social world and the appropriate semiotic codes of painters and writers, took those images for granted as part of the then current hegemonic visual landscape.

Two types of representations of Indians dominated that visual landscape: the foreign travelers' drawings and engravings, and the "Costumbrista" watercolors by Rafael Salas, Agustín Guerrero, and Joaquín Pinto.[9] Two, that is, until one looks more closely and several of the images start to blur and become one (see figures 1.6 and 1.7). Here the written texts — primarily the travelers' accounts — provide the communication context and the framework of power relations within which the images were constructed and actually used, allowing us to decipher their meaning.

The list of European travelers who visited Ecuador during the nineteenth century is long and distinguished. It includes foreign diplomats, scientists of all kinds, ethnologists, adventurers, artists, and commercial and government envoys. Most of them had social connections at high levels of government; they stayed in the haciendas and private residences of important landowners and were in contact with the Ecuadoran intellectual and artistic community. It was then fashionable for travelers to write and illustrate detailed accounts of their experiences in books or journal articles published in Europe, all of which became extremely popular with a nineteenth-century public obsessed with precise and tangible realism (see Munsterberg 1982). When they were not traveling accompanied by their own artists, the travelers often searched for illustrators among the local pool. They also commissioned paintings to take back with them to Europe, especially to France and Italy where "ethnographic and *costumbrista* publications were much in fashion" (Vargas 1984, 428). Most foreigners wanted to take back

FIGURE 1.6

Inhabitants of Quito. Drawing by Fuchs based on a sketch by Ernesto Charton. From *Grabados sobre el Ecuador en el Siglo XIX. Le Tour du Monde* (Quito: Banco Central del Ecuador, 1981).

FIGURE 1.7
Potter. Watercolor by Joaquín Pinto. From *Ecuador Pintoresco* (Quito: Salvat Editores Ecuatoriana, 1977).

images of the "exotic" and "typical" indigenous populations, and the *costumbrista* painters seem to have obliged. The scientists, like the vulcanologists Stübel and Reiss, were more interested in landscapes, and the Indians then became attached to nature as an appendage (Vargas 1984, 376, 428; Castro Velázquez 1980, 471). According to Vargas, *costumbrismo* as a pictoric genre was born inspired by the detailed narrations and meticulous drawings of two famous foreign travelers; one French, E. Charton who published in "Le Tour du Monde," and the other an Italian, Gaetano Osculati, who arrived in Quito in 1847 (1984, 376). Friedrich Hassaurek, a North American diplomat, in his book *Four Years Among the Ecuadorians* (1967 [1867]) had this to say about the painter Rafael Salas:

> It was only at my suggestion that Rafael Salas, one of the best painters in Quito, left the beaten track, and undertook to paint Ecuadorian scenery and costumbres [customs] . . . Mr. Salas often told me that his principal supporters were the foreigners who came to Quito from time to time. The natives seldom pay more than $16 or $20 for a large-sized portrait. (1967, 113–14)

According to Castro y Velázquez, the first mention of *costumbrista* paintings is found in the work of Miguel María Lisboa, "Relacao de uma Viagem a Venezuela, Nova Granada e Equador," written in 1866, in which we learn that Lisboa asked Salas (a relative of Rafael Salas) for a series of paintings of "indigenous costumes" (1980, 471).

Towards the end of the nineteenth century, Joaquín Pinto became the undisputed fashionable artist. He could count among his clients the minister of France, who bought twenty-three of his watercolors; other important diplomats; and the Frenchman F. Cousin, who commissioned a collection of a hundred of Pinto's watercolors of *costumbrismo indígena* (Vargas 1984, 405).

Costumbrismo in painting has been characterized as a reaction against the academicism and sombre religious iconography of colonial art, influenced by Spanish literary romanticism (Castro y Velázquez 1980, 470), and as a development out of the liberal individualism born in the new Republican period and reflected in the innumerable portraits of the independence heroes (Samaniego

1980, 456–65). Seen in conjunction with other contemporary artistic developments in music and literature, *Costumbrismo* also reflects the newly acquired feelings of "deep nationalism" that made the artists "turn their eyes" towards the "indigenous heritage" and towards the "discovery of their own landscape" (Gallegos Donoso n.d., 11–15). For instance, Juan León Mera, a writer now famous for his novel *Cumandá,* set among Jívaro Indians, also wrote the lyrics for the Ecuadoran national anthem personifying the *Patria* (nation) and a collection of "indigenous and popular songs,"[10] some of which were illustrated by Joaquín Pinto. Augustín Guerrero the painter, was also a musician and wrote a history of Ecuadoran music. He was commissioned by Marcos Jiménez de la Espada to compile a collection of "indigenous and popular melodies" for the Museum of Natural Sciences in Madrid, that was presented at the 1881 Congress of Americanists (Hallo 1981, 21). He was also the founder of an art school by the name of "Democratic School Miguel de Santiago," whose motto was "Liberty, Equality, and Fraternity" and its emblem "the Phrygian cap on the painter's pallet." Hallo quotes Guerrero's motives for founding the school as follows: "Culture has been maintained up to now as servile imitation; we must be inspired by nature, and throw ourselves into original production with a deep national sense. Only then will we be able to achieve our own complete independence and nationality" (quoted in Hallo 1981, 23). Both intellectuals and politicians were creating the cohesive symbol systems and meaningful ritual practices of the national community.

The realism of dress and adornments in the *Costumbrista* paintings of Indians, as well as the specificity of occupations and events in which they are depicted, often mirrors the descriptive realism of the travelers' narratives as shown in the picture by Guerrero of a woman delousing a child, or Pinto's rendition of the same event (figure 1.8). This image matches Hassaurek's following description:

There is nothing more loathsome, however, than to see the common people crush lice between their teeth. In the entrances of houses, on the marketplaces, in the groceries and greenshops, and in a variety of other places open to the

FIGURE 1.8

Delousing. Watercolor by Joaquín Pinto. From *Ecuador Pintoresco* (Quito: Salvat Editores Ecuatoriana, 1977).

public eye, men, women, and children may be seen picking lice off each other's heads, and crushing them between their teeth. (1967, 55–56)

The Indians behind the costumes are represented as types, as Vargas says, "for the functions they perform for society" (1984, 403). The power of the image is conveyed by the frame in which the Indians are constrained, not by the human identity of those occupying the roles. If we look at the two extremes of what is really a continuum, (figures 1.9 and 1.10), the watercolors reveal a highly stratified and rigid social world where the Indians play a role strictly demarcated by the hegemonic signmakers. The lonely figures are totally decontextualized; they are even deprived of their own natural surroundings because they have now become part of an urban landscape. They are presented as a milestone on the unilineal road towards acculturation and miscegenation. They are also frozen in time. Exercising what Fabian (1983) calls "chronopolitics," the imagemakers have deprived them of their own cultural time.

The Imagemakers and Their Times

I have argued that the three world's fairs of the nineteenth century in which Ecuador participated provided the dominant elite with a stage to " invent a new tradition" about the past, the present and the future of the country. In this imagined community, the images of the Indians were suitably accommodated to fit the main ideological currents of the period and to serve the interests of the imagemakers. Here I intend to provide the social and political context that would allow us to situate the authors and manipulators of those images and to better understand their assumptions. Hobsbawm argues that there are certain periods in the history of nations that seem to be more prone to produce the "invention" of traditions. He says,

We should expect [the invention of tradition] to occur more frequently when a rapid transformation of society weakens or destroys the social patterns for which "old" traditions have been designed, producing new ones to which they were not applicable, or when such old traditions and their institutional carriers and promulgators no longer prove sufficiently adaptable and flexible, or are otherwise eliminated: in short, when there are sufficiently large and rapid changes on the demand or supply side. (1983, 4–5)

FIGURE 1.9

Indian from the Capital. Watercolor by Agustín Querrero. Hallo Foundation Collection. From Wilson Hallo, ed., *Imágenes del Ecuador del Siglo XIX* (Quito: Ediciones del Sol, Quito y Espasa-Calpe, 1981).

FIGURE 1.10
Streetsweeper. Watercolor by Agustín Querrero. Hallo Foundation Collection.
From Wilson Hallo, ed., *Imágenes del Ecuador del Siglo XIX* (Quito:
Ediciones del Sol, Quito y Espasa-Calpe, 1981).

In many different ways, this statement accurately characterizes the situation of Ecuador at the turn of the nineteenth century. The society was going through a process of social, economic, and political transformation that would finally bring about the consolidation of liberalism and the demise of conservative hegemony. It is a period of transition that came to be known as *"Progresismo"*—a period when the old traditions of conservative authoritarianism, blessed and staunchly defended by the all encompassing power of the Church, were becoming obsolete and a new hegemony was being fashioned by increasingly assertive sectors of the bourgeoisie and the landowning class, both from the Coast and the Highlands. They were sustained by cacao, which brought unprecedented wealth to Ecuador, then the world's leading exporter (Chiriboga 1980, 116). This period also marks a political beginning for Ecuador. For the first time in its history, political conflict was contained within a representative legal framework and in structured political parties that channeled the dominant economic and ideological interests (Ayala 1982, 189). These are some of the economic and political dimensions of domination that provided the paradoxes and contradictions implicit in the attempt to build a republican nation state, seeking simultaneously to create the Indians as alien Others and as fellow nationals (see Sider 1987).

Progresismo was a brief attempt to constitute a third political movement on the basis of constitutional government, respect for civic rights and religious tolerance. It also espoused a new economic role for the state as a vehicle for the emerging economic power of the coastal bourgeoisie (Ortiz Crespo 1981, 273). Two of the three presidents who dominated this progressive period interest us here: José María Plácido Caamaño (1884–1888), and especially Antonio Flores (1888–1892), who was officially involved in the Madrid exposition both during his presidency, and in 1892, as the highest representative from Ecuador. Plácido Caamaño belonged to a family who, since colonial times, had owned Tenguel, the largest cacao plantation in the world. During his visit in 1885, the geographer Teodor Wolf described Tenguel as "the most valuable in the Republic" (Chiriboga 1980, 165). During his tenure as president, Plácido Caamaño enthusiastically promoted foreign investment and the incorporation of Ecuador into foreign markets

(Ayala 1982, 191). He was also known for his "ability to tame the fierce day laborers of Tenguel" (quoted in Ortiz Crespo 1981, 273). A large number of these workers were part of the mass of indigenous small peasant producers who, dispossessed by the landgrabbing efforts of the highland landowners, were migrating to the Coast to join the labor pool demanded by the cacao boom (Chiriboga 1980, 62–63). Charles Wiener, another of the famous foreign travelers, after a visit to one of the largest cacao plantations, described the life of those workers as "patriarchal." By contrast, a few years later, the Liberal leader Eloy Alfaro denounced their condition as "disguised slavery" (Chiriboga 1980, 117). According to the bourgeoisie and their foreign friends, that indigenous population could not be incorporated into the public images being produced for international consumption. However, their reality was being expressed more violently in the *montoneras* or armed bands led by Alfaro, whose struggle finally brought about the triumph of liberalism and the first effective legislation to ameliorate the situation of the Indians.

Antonio Flores succeeded Caamaño to the presidency in 1888, and was even more concerned than his predecessor to put Ecuador economically and culturally into the international arena. He was born to the job (literally, as son of the nation's first president he was born in the National Palace). He was educated in Paris and at the University of San Marcos in Lima, where he occupied the chair of universal history. From 1860 onwards, his life was spent mostly in the major European capitals and in Washington where he held several important diplomatic posts (see Larrea 1974). Flores was a modern intellectual of his time, a cosmopolitan and an internationalist. In addition he had strong economic and social connections with *"La Argolla"* (The Ring), an important group within the Guayaquil commercial and financial bourgeoisie. Most of the members of *La Argolla* were related by blood or marriage to the Caamaño and Flores families. While in office, Flores designed policies in accordance with the current ideas of progress and laissez-faire economics, and was a strong supporter of foreign immigration.

One particular incident at the very beginning of Flores' administration is quite relevant to our topic and will serve to illustrate the symbolic conflict between old and new traditions, between obsolete and emerging hegemonies at that time. In his first message to Congress, Flores requested funds in the amount of 10,000 sucres for Ecuador's participation in the 1889 Universal Exposition in Paris. "It should be obvious to you"—he said to the legislators—"the benefits that these expositions bring to the countries involved; they become known as producers and the exchanges are instituted. From this rendezvous of industry emerges a fertile movement towards economic well being" (quoted in Ayala 1982, 192). This event, which most modern countries would consider routine, provoked a state crisis in Ecuador at that time. The Conservative-controlled Congress, which included members of the clergy, was outraged. They regarded the Paris Exposition as an "impious event," in celebration of the centenary of that "horrendous monster" that was the French Revolution (Ortiz Crespo 1981, 275; Ayala 1982, 193). New newspapers were created to defend one or the other side in the controversy. In Cuenca, one such newspaper conceived of the whole nation as dedicated to the Sacred Heart and set against the Centenary of '89 (Ayala 1982, 193). Flores personally asked for the Pope's intervention to try to stop the clergy from participating in the debate. Having his request for funds denied by Congress, Flores went as far as resigning from the presidency, a resignation which of course was not accepted by a then panic-stricken Congress. Finally, Flores got his funds from the Guayaquil merchants and financiers, who were more than willing to participate in a world's fair where most of the Hispano-American nations would primarily be exhibiting their raw materials (with the side exhibits of archaeological and botanical collections). As Ayala notes, in the Paris Exposition the merchant bourgeoisie gave a visible sign of its power in the international scene: "against the vote of Congress, the national flag was displayed for the first time thanks to private financing" (1982, 204–5)—a powerful symbolism of the new hegemony.

Concluding Remarks

There is a long tradition in the anthropological literature on Ecuador dealing with the complex interrelationship between national and ethnic identity.[11] As one of the main contributors to that scholarship, Norman Whitten, in a recent article, calls for the interpretation of nationalist and ethnic culture "as complementary and mutually reinforcing systems of symbols sustained by dialogic discourse" (1988, 303–4). This essay is intended as a contribution to that tradition. Adopting a historical perspective, it has focused attention on the Self as the main speaker in that dialogue. The occasion of the four-hundredth anniversary of the Discovery of America and the Madrid Exposition, provided the Ecuadoran elites with an enticing scenario in which to enact what Hobsbawm would characterize as its "rite of passage" as a new nation (1983, 10). In the formative stages of defining this corporate Self, the emergent coastal bourgeoisie invented a historic continuity with a refashioned Indian past. It looked to images and the rhetoric of "race" and "aristocracy" to validate state formation and nation building. Thus, the ideology of *mestizaje* emerged as a dialectical process of selective exclusion and inclusion of the subordinate Other. As the dominant imagemaker, the bourgeoisie used the Indians as "semiotic pawns" (Gordie 1989, 10) for its own semiotic interests, and to legitimize its own very real economic achievements. The drive behind these achievements was the nineteenth-century ideology of liberal democracy — known in this particular period of Ecuadoran history as *Progresismo*. Through this discourse, the bourgeoisie was hoping that Ecuador would become a player in the international market, and occupy its proper place within the community of civilized nations.

Historically, the same tensions and contradictions between these two "essentialist" and "epochalist" principles (see Geertz 1973, 240–41, passim and also Whitten 1988, 303–6), allowed for a dialectics of accommodation and resistance among indigenous peoples. They accepted the impositions of the state and the lures of social *mestizaje,* occasionally challenging both by participating in different forms of resistance movements and everyday defiance. Furthermore, despite the fact that the material and social basis of their cultures continued to be undermined, indigenous peoples were able to retain an autonomous sense of their cultural history. Their symbolic universe even had its own distinctive ways of incorporating the history of the white Other (see Hill 1988).

As Lears argues, "even the most successful hegemonic culture creates a situation where the dominant mode of discourse — and each visual or verbal text within it—becomes a field of contention where many-sided struggles are constantly fought out" (1985, 591). In the last two decades, the Ecuadoran indigenous peoples are increasingly becoming their own imagemakers both in the national and the international arena. Their present contest with the national society is as much a contest over power, as it is a contest over symbols and definitions of self and ethnic-group identities. This conjuncture should make the analysis of the dialogic discourse even more interesting.

The research upon which this article is based is part of an ongoing project on Images of Ecuadorian Indians from 1892 to 1992, currently supported by a University of British Columbia HSS Grant (S89-1565). Research assistance was provided by Alexandra Martinez in Quito and by Jill Fitzell in Vancouver. I also want to acknowledge the assistance of Ronald J. Mahoney, Head of the Department of Special Collections at California State University, Fresno, who promptly provided me with copies of the U.S. Report (1895) and Catálogo General (1893) for this otherwise "obscure" Columbian Historical Exposition at Madrid. An earlier version of this essay was presented as part of the session "Images of ethnicity in Andean South America" at the 88th Annual meeting of the American Anthropological Association, Washington, D.C., November 1989. My thanks to Marigay Graña for her friendly editorial comments.

Notes

1. This article will only deal with the Historic American Exhibit. It is relevant, however, to quote here the reasons given by the Spanish authorities for the European exposition: "to teach the people of today what were the elements of civilization with which, on the side of the arts, Europe was then equipped for the tasks of educating a daughter, courageous and untamed, but vigorous and beautiful, who had risen from the bosom of the seas, and who, in the course of a few centuries, was to be transformed from a daughter into a sister—a sister proud in aspiration and power" (Report 1895).
2. It is difficult to say at this stage of the research if this part of the exhibit ever took place. Documents gathered so far make us believe it never happened. It is not mentioned in the comprehensive United States report on the exhibit, although other "less striking" events are noted, such as the meeting of the Congress of Americanists at La Rabida (Huelva), and the unveiling of a monument to commemorate the Discovery (Report 1895).
3. This same idea is developed by Silverblatt (1988) for the Andean peoples fighting against the cultural hegemony of the Incas, and by Sider (1987) for the period of the early confrontation between Europeans and native Americans.
4. Unless otherwise stated, all translations from the Spanish are my own.

5. Federico Gonzalez Suarez contributed to the exhibit with his monumental work *Historia del Ecuador* (the first three volumes), an Archaeological Atlas, and a plan carved in wood of the old city of Chordeleg. D.A. Cousin exhibited a collection of 1,000 pieces of "Inca" artifacts, which had already received an award at the 1889 Paris Exposition.
6. My analysis of the Ecuadoran exhibits at the exposition is based on this catalogue. I have not yet been able to find a photograph or any other visual documentation of the Ecuadorian Hall. The United States Report (1895) contains a picture of the U.S. Hall. It represents quite closely the ideological style of nineteenth-century exhibit displays.
7. In more general terms for Spanish America, my interpretation here differs from that of Benedict Anderson. He argues that there was little "reverse racism" in the anticolonial movements (1983, 139) and that Mexican mestizos traced their ancestry to the Aztecs or the Mayas out of a democratic feeling (idib., 140). However, one must remember that, like the Inca, the Aztec and Maya were highly stratified societies with identifiable aristocracies.
8. The Incas, who also invented a holy ancestry for themselves as part of the process of state formation and consolidation (see Silverblatt 1988), probably would not have objected to this image.
9. Searching for pictorial images of Indians in antiquarian shops and private collections in Quito, I found this phenomenon repeated with monotonous regularity. A large number of anonymous and undated watercolors and oil paintings of Indians can be found in private collections in Ecuador. In all probability, they were produced and circulated at around the same time.
10. Mera wrote two poems, "Melodías indígenas" ("Indigenous melodies") and "La Virgen del Sol" ("The Virgin of the Sun") in which he pretends to rescue the pre-Columbian past. In his collection of popular songs, the lyrics were "expurgated" of bad grammar and of verses "offensive to morals and persons" (Gallegos Donoso n.d., 11,14).
11. It is difficult to do justice here to all the contributors to that tradition. Among the most salient works see Whitten (1981, 1985, 1988), Stutzman (1981), Salomon (1981), Muratorio (1984), Reeve (1985), Fine (1986). Recently, Mary Crain (1990) has published an article entitled "The Social Construction of National Identity in Highland Ecuador." Our interpretations of this phenomenon coincide in several important points. My analysis differs from hers, primarily in reference to the cultural and ideological elements that enter into the construction of that national identity at the turn of the nineteenth century, and the first decades of the twentieth century.

References

Documents

Informe Junta Central del 4° Centenario del Descubrimiento de América. Informe del Ministro del Interior y Relaciones Exteriores al Congreso ordinario 1892. Archivo-Biblioteca de la Función Legislativa, Quito. (Informe 1892).
Catálogo General de la Exposición Histórica, Americana de Madrid 1892, Tomo

I 1893. Department of Special Collections. Henry Madden Library (Catálogo 1893).
Report of the United States Commission to the Columbian Historical Exposition at Madrid 1892–93. Washington 1895. Department of Special Collections. Henry Madden Library (Report 1895).

Other References

Anderson, Benedict. 1983. *Imagined Communities. Reflections on the Origin and Spread of Nationalism.* London: Verso Editions and NLB.
Ayala, Enrique. 1982. *Lucha Política y Orígen de los Partidos en Ecuador.* Quito: Corporación Editora Nacional (Segunda Edición).
Berkhofer, Robert F. Jr. 1978. *The White Man's Indian. Images of the American Indian from Columbus to the Present.* New York: Alfred A. Knopf.
Breckenridge, Carol A. 1989. "The Aesthetic and Politics of Colonial Collecting: India at World Fairs," *Comparative Studies in Society and History* 31:3, 195–216.
Castro y Velázquez, Juan. 1980. Un Importante Momento en la Pintura Ecuatoriana: El Costumbrismo. In *Libro del Sesquicentenario. II Arte y Cultura. Ecuador: 1830–1980.* Quito: Corporación Editora Nacional.
Chiriboga, Manuel. 1980. *Jornaleros y Gran Propietarios en 135 años de Exportación Cacaotera (1790–1925).* Quito: Consejo Provincial de Pichincha.
Crain, Mary. 1990. "The Social Construction of National Identity in Highland Ecuador." *Anthropological Quarterly* 63:1, 43–59.
Fine, Kathleen. 1986. "Ideology, History, and Action in Cotocollao: A Barrio of Quito, Ecuador." Ph.D. dissertation, University of Illinois at Urbana-Champaign.
Gallegos de Donoso, Magdalena. n.d. Juan León Mera y Joaquín Pinto, Testigos de su Tiempo. In Juan León Mera, *Cantares del Pueblo Ecuatoriano.* Quito: Museo del Banco Central del Ecuador.
Geertz, Clifford. 1973. *The Interpretation of Cultures.* New York: Basic Books.
———. 1985. "Centers, Kings, and Charisma: Reflections on the Symbolics of Power." In Sean Wilentz (ed.), *Rites of Power. Symbolism, Ritual and Politics Since the Middle Ages.* Philadelphia: University of Pennsylvania Press.
Goldie, Terry. 1989. *Fear and Temptation. The Image of the Indigene in Canadian, Australian, and New Zealand Literatures.* Kingston: McGill-Queen's University Press.
Fabian, Johannes. 1983. *Time and the Other: How Anthropology Makes Its Object.* New York: Columbia University Press.
Hallo, Wilson. 1981. *Introducción.* In Wilson Hallo (ed.), *Imágenes del Ecuador del Siglo XIX Juan Agustín Guerrero 1818–1880.* Quito-Madrid: Ediciones del Sol y Espasa-Calpe.
Hassaurek, Friedrich. 1967[1867]. *Four Years Among the Ecuadorians.* Carbondale and Edwardsville: Southern Illinois University Press.
Hill, Jonathan D. 1988. *Rethinking History and Myth. Indigenous South American Perspectives on the Past.* Urbana: University of Illinois Press.
Hobsbawm, Eric. 1983. "Introduction: Inventing Traditions." In Eric Hobs-

bawm and Terence Ranger (eds.), *The Invention of Tradition.* Cambridge: Cambridge University Press.

Honour, Hugh. 1975. *The New Golden Land: European Images of America from the Discovery to the Present Time.* New York: Pantheon Books.

Larrea, Carlos Manuel. 1974. *Antonio Flores Jijón, su vida y sus obras.* Quito: Corporación de Estudios y Publicaciones.

Lears, T. S. Jackson. 1985. "The Concept of Cultural Hegemony: Problems and Possibilities." *American Historical Review* 90, 567–93.

Malmsheimer, Lonna M. 1985. "Imitation White Man: Images of Transformation at the Carlisle Indian School." *Studies in Visual Communication* 2:4, 54–75.

Montalvo, Juan. 1923. *Siete Tratados, por Juan Montalvo,* 2 vols. Paris: Casa Editorial Garnier Hermanos.

Munsterberg, Marjorie. 1982. The World Viewed: Works of Nineteenth-Century Realism. *Studies in Visual Anthropology* 8:3, 55–69.

Muratorio, Blanca. 1980. "Protestantism and Capitalism Revisited in the Rural Highlands of Ecuador." *The Journal of Peasant Studies* 8:1, 37–60.

———. 1984. "Dominant and Subordinate Ideologies in South America: Old Traditions and New Faiths." *Culture* 4:1, 3–17.

Murra, John. 1963. "The Historic Tribes of Ecuador." In Julian H. Steward (ed.), *Handbook of South American Indians,* vol. 2: *The Andean Civilizations.* New York: Cooper Square Publishers, Inc.

Ortíz Crespo, Gonzalo. 1981. *La Incorporación del Ecuador al Mercado Mundial: La Coyuntura Socio-Económica 1875–1895.* Quito: Banco Central del Ecuador.

Reeve, Mary-Elizabeth. 1985. "Identity as Process: The Meaning of Runapura for Quichua Speakers of the Curaray River, Eastern Ecuador." Ph.D. dissertation, University of Illinois at Urbana-Champaign.

Ryan, Michael T. 1981. "Assimilating New Worlds in the Sixteenth and Seventeenth Centuries." *Comparative Studies in Society and History* 23:4, 519–38.

Salomon, Frank. 1981. "Weavers of Otavalo." In Norman E. Whitten, Jr. (ed.), *Cultural Transformations and Ethnicity in Modern Ecuador.* Urbana: University of Illinois Press.

Samaniego Salazar, Filoteo. 1980. El Retrato en el Ecuador. In *Libro del Sesquicentenario II Arte y Cultura: Ecuador: 1830–1980.* Quito: Corporación Editora Nacional.

Sider, Gerald. 1987. "When Parrots Learn to Talk, and Why They Can't: Domination, Deception, and Self-Deception in Indian-White Relations." *Comparative Studies in Society and History* 29:1, 3–23.

Silverblatt, Irene. 1988. "Imperial Dilemmas, the Politics of Kinship, and Inca Reconstructions of History." *Comparative Studies in Society and History* 30:1, 83–102.

Stutzman, Ronald. 1981. "El Mestizaje: An All-Inclusive Ideology of Exclusion." In Norman E. Whitten, Jr. (ed.), *Cultural Transformations and Ethnicity in Modern Ecuador.* Urbana: University of Illinois Press.

Taussig, Michael. 1987. *Shamanism, Colonialism, and the Wild Man. A Study in Terror and Healing.* Chicago: The University of Chicago Press.

Taylor, Anne Christine. 1985. "La Invención del Jívaro. Notas etnográficas sobre un fantasma occidental." In Segundo E. Moreno Yánez (ed.), *Memorias del*

Primer Simposio Europeo sobre Antropología del Ecuador. Quito: Ediciones Abya-Yala.

Vargas, José María. 1984. "El Arte Ecuatoriano en el Siglo XIX." *Cultura* 7:19, 349–420.

Whitten, Norman E., Jr. (ed.) 1981. *Cultural Transformations and Ethnicity in Modern Ecuador.* Urbana: University of Illinois Press.

———. 1985. *Sicuanga Runa: The Other Side of Development in Amazonian Ecuador.* Urbana: University of Illinois Press.

———. 1988. Historical and Mythic Evocations of Chthnoic Power in South America. In Jonathan D. Hill (ed.), *Rethinking History and Myth. Indigenous South American Perspectives on the Past.* Urbana: University of Illinois Press.

Wilentz, Sean, ed. 1985. *Rites of Power. Symbolism, Ritual and Politics Since the Middle Ages.* Philadelphia: University of Pennsylvania Press.

2

Ethnicity and the State: The Hua Miao of Southwest China

Norma Diamond

The People's Republic of China is both a developing country and a strongly nationalistic major civilization, a combination that raises a particular set of problems for the minority peoples within her political borders. On the eve of the 1949 revolution, China could still be described as an agrarian society. Over 85 percent of her population was engaged in agriculture and rural subsidiary industries with the family (household) as the unit of production. Though peasants were engaged in the market economy, the bulk of what they produced was for their own immediate subsistance. Even areas along major trade routes or near central markets and treaty ports that were engaged in cash cropping of tea, silk, cotton, soybeans, and the like, strove for self-subsistance as a buffer against the market. Commercial and manufacturing enterprises in the towns and cities were often small scale and utilized family labor, while modern industrial and business enterprises were not highly developed, or were owned and managed by foreign entrepreneurs. Indeed, the new rulers of the State themselves described the country as semi-feudal, as a semi-colony, and as in the early stages of capitalist development. Some of this backwardness could be attributed to the inroads of Western imperialism and Japanese aggression and the rest to tradition. In the "Great Leap" of the 1950s, Mao promised that China would soon catch up with Europe through her own determined efforts.

Comparing herself today to the industrialized West, the Soviet Union, or neighbors like Japan, Taiwan, Singapore, and Hong Kong, China sees herself lagging behind. Still, her belief in her own cultural superiority, the sense of being the Middle Kingdom, the center of the civilized world has persisted through the decades of socialist experiment, perhaps reaching its height in the puritanical excesses of the Cultural Revolution (1966–1976). To some extent, it has been reinforced by the presence within her borders of a large population of varied ethnic groups whose social organization, cultural practices, and economic strategies differ markedly from those of the Han Chinese, or Chinese proper. These other societies are regarded as representing earlier levels of social evolution, following the schema laid out by Lewis Henry Morgan and Friedrich Engels. They are viewed as living examples of primitive communal society, patriarchal slave society, and in a few cases feudal society (with cultural survivals of traits from the two earlier ones). In this framework, the Han Chinese represent the highest level of development, based on their position at the start of socialist construction, their achievements over the past four decades, and their role in guiding social change among the minority peoples. Unfortunately, the costs of developing China proper have left few resources to spare for the border regions where most of the minorities live. The gap has grown wider rather than narrower over the years.

The Han account for 93.3% of the population, according to the 1982 census figures (*Minzu Yanjiu* 1983, 80). The remainder of the population is distributed among some fifty-five recognized national minorities *(shaoshuminzu)* as defined by the state. These range in population size from a few thousand to several millions. The actual number of groups and total population may be larger. In the 1950s they were the majority population over some 60 percent of China's land area. Some are pastoralists, or mixed oasis farmers and stock raisers, some are mountain-dwelling, slash-and-burn agriculturalists, a few gain a sizeable part of their livelihood from hunting, trapping and fishing, and a few seem not all that different from the Han in terms of their economic base. With these few exceptions, they live in the areas less suited to Han modes of livelihood, areas that until relatively recently were remote from direct political control by the state, or areas that came under Chinese control only in the past few hundred years.

The Han Chinese majority themselves are only now becoming a culturally and linguistically unified nationality. Differences in ecological setting and degree of access to transport routes and urban centers have led to a number of regional variations that are recognized at the level of popular discourse. Some of the differences are quite marked. The North China loess plateau and Yellow River plains areas are dependant on wheat and millet and similar crops that rely on rainfall rather than irrigation and that can survive climatic extremes. South of the Yangtze River there is a world of navigable streams and rivers, of irrigated rice paddy, mountain rice terraces and upland forest. Double-cropping and even triple-cropping are possible in the warm south, and living standards were generally higher there than in the north. The south is more linguistically and culturally diverse than the northern plains and hilllands. Indeed, the sense of Han unity stops along the banks of the Yangtze. The southern coastal regions are also more densely populated, more commercialized and urbanized. It is a world seen by the northerners as soft, indulgent, luxurious and morally weak. Conversely, southerners see the northerners as rough, uncultured bumpkins.

The linguistic uniformity of the north, the cradle of Chinese civilization is due in part to a long history of migrations within the area in response to droughts, famines, floodings of the Yellow River, invasion, and internal warfare. The current inhabitants of the northeast fringe are for the most part the descendants of nineteenth- and early twentieth-century migrants from Shandong and Hebei. The populations of the Sichuan basin descend from settlers of the early Qing dynasty (mid-seventeenth century and following) in the aftermath of a bloody rebellion that caused severe depopulation. The Qing government proclaimed the area open to soldiers and civilians who would be assisted with draft animals, seed, and a five-year tax exemption, and newcomers poured in from the northern provinces of Gansu, Honan, Shensi, Anhui, as well as from the southern regions of Guangdong, Fujian, and Zhejiang (Ho,

139–41). The linguistic accomodation seems to have been to Mandarin, so that a speaker from Beijing can be understood through most of the area, from Sichuan in the west out to the easternmost part of the Shandong peninsula.

In the southern regions, linguistic unity vanishes. Settlement by Han Chinese began in the Tang dynasty (ca.600 A.D.) and the population balance of the country did not shift toward the south until the twelfth or thirteenth century in the wake of the Mongol invasions. Successive waves of migration engulfed the indigenous peoples of the southeast, assimilating them to Han Chinese cultural patterns yet at the same time creating regional subcultures marked by language and local custom. Rivers and mountains hampered free travel between localities, and local isolation led to increasing differences.

In identifying China's minority peoples, the government has taken language as a key feature. At the same time, the language differences between those classified as "Han" are smoothed over by refering to them officially as "dialects." However, the languages of the south are not simply dialects of Mandarin. They are at least as different as French is from German, and in some cases the distance seems far greater than that. Linguists recognize at least five Chinese languages, further subdivided into dialects of greater or lesser distance from each other (Ramsey, 87–115). Our Beijing speaker could manage with only small modifications to make himself understood across north China, but would be incomprehensible among the Yue language speakers of Guangdong and Guangxi, the Min language speakers of Fujian, the Xiang speakers of Hunan, the Wu languages of the coastal areas of Shanghai and the Yangtze Delta, the various Gan dialects of Jiangxi and Hunan, or the pockets of speakers of Hakka throughout the south. There is clear difference in tonal systems, vocabulary, and grammatical features. Indeed, only in schoolrooms and government offices where a standard Mandarin *(putonghua)* is now enforced as the language of the educated and the language of officialdom would he feel at home.

In the past, as now, an ideographic writing system linked the upper classes and officialdom across the various Han-settled areas. An educated person might speak Yue at home and on the streets, but he could easily read something written by a Gan speaker. Indeed, most Chinese admit that Tang poetry rhymes better when read by a Yue speaker than by someone from the north. Modern writing, which is based on the word order and idiom of a standardized Mandarin rather than the formal grammar of classical writing *(wenyen)*, presents some problems to speakers of the other languages, and learning to speak a correct *putonghua* involves more than refining ones pronunciation.

Since 1949, the state has done much to erase differences in local custom among the Han by defining much of peasant tradition and local traditions as "feudal." Weddings, funerals, festivals, styles of dress, choices of recreation all come under state control, while Mandarin is spread not only by the schools but also on television, radio, movies and public events. The minorities are the sole outpost of cultural diversity.

A few of the recognized minorities also speak Chinese. The Manchus (now estimated at 4.3 million) adopted Han written and spoken language after their conquest of China in 1644, though they retained some cultural features of their own. The 7.3 or more million Hui speak the Chinese language of the areas in which they are settled and there are Hui communities all over China. Many are indistinguishable from the Han except that they are followers of Islam. The Chinese insist they are the descendants of foreigners from the Middle East or Central Asia, and therefore an ethnic group. The languages in common use among the 14 million Zhuang of Guangxi and Guangdong are the local Chinese dialects, but in recent years the government has pushed to revive the Zhuang language. Aside from these few exceptions, the languages of the minority peoples are something other than Mandarin or one of the other Chinese languages, although state expansion and colonization of the borderlands and interior regions has been going on for many centuries. This is particularly true in the southwest, where a strong drive for pacification and settlement did not take place until the seventeenth century. Indeed, the process of political incorporation was not effectively completed until the nineteenth century for the provinces of Yunnan and Guizhou, the early twentieth century for the mountain areas of Sichuan, and remains somewhat problematic for Tibet, for areas along the Burma border, and in the northwest Xinjiang Autonomous region. And the recognized minorities speak Turkic, Mon-Khmer, and Altaic languages totally unrelated to Sino-Tibetan, or speak languages of the Tibeto-Burman or Miao-Yao branch which are very distant from any of the Chinese languages.

As suggested earlier in this paper, the criteria for minority status does not rest solely on language. If it did, a good case could probably be made for the Hakka or for speakers of Cantonese. The other oft-cited criteria are that the group shares a common territory, a common economy and a common psychology, by which most writers mean customs, beliefs, and life-styles (Ma Yin 1985). Yet even these official criteria do not explain the present classification of the various minority peoples. Even before 1949, few still held a clearly marked territory: some populations had expanded into areas already settled by other ethnic groups, while others had retreated higher into the mountains to avoid further conflict with an expanding Chinese state. Most of the frontier/borderland microregions of the southwest and northwest became home to a mix of ethnic groups who usually lived in separate villages and married amongst themselves but who were interdependant through trade and exchange of services, or landlord/tenant relations, or temporary military alliances, or (less commonly) intermarriage during the years of the Qing dynasty (1644–1911) and the Republican period (1911–1949). Not only did they share territory and economy, but the local economies were often tied to the national market.

In the most simplistic terms, what defines a *shaoshuminzu* is that its members are not Han in significant features of ideology and practice, and the state is willing to recognize this. Many groups have asked for recognition as minorities, or to be reclassified as a different minority and have been refused. Unlike the imperial state of the Ming and Qing dynasties, current postrevolution policies toward these populations no longer favor dispersion, forced migration or extinction, nor do they openly support the goal of assimilation to a Han Chinese model that marked the policies of the Republican period. The various policy pronouncements since 1949 emphasize that the ways and customs of the minority nationalities are to be respected and protected by law, and specify that the minority people have the right to use their own languages, follow their own religious beliefs and continue their traditional culture. However, these freedoms do not include the right to continue their traditional economic and political organization if these are at variance with the requirements of a socialist state and the current majority definition of morality. It is also understood that customs and practices that are adjudged to be "backward" should be reformed, usually through persuasion but where necessary by reference to the legal system. From the various writings about the "nationality question," one senses that many of those working on nationality affairs believe and hope that with education and economic changes and the advance to a true communist society ethnic (cultural) differences will fade away and a new shared pan-national culture will emerge. This is seen as a desirable goal since the underlying assumption is that the minority areas are "backward" not only economically but also culturally. Respect for cultural diversity operates weakly in Chinese thinking, even in a socialist society, and the minority peoples defined as representatives of earlier stages of human history are seen as being in need of guidance and tutelage so that they can catch up with the Han Chinese majority.

With this background, let me turn to a focus on one particular minority group, the Hua Miao (Flowery Miao) of the Yunnan-Guizhou plateau. The term "Hua Miao" was used to distinguish them in the gazetteers of the eighteenth and nineteenth century, and continues in the literature of the Republican period. This earlier literature refered to White Miao, Black Miao, Green Miao, and a number of others to distinguish the various peoples speaking one of the dialects within the four or more Miao languages. Miao language speakers are also present in Thailand and Vietnam and usually refered to as Hmong. Current Chinese terminology groups all of these as Miao. Officially, there are over five million Miao in China, and the government makes no distinction between the subgroups. The Hua Miao call themselves *Ad hmaob,* though when speaking Chinese they will refer to themselves as Hua Miao. They number some 250,000 and are speakers of the Dian Dongbei branch of the Miao language. Government writing about them glosses over linguistic and cultural differences within this larger "Miao" catagory, a position that parallels the use of the term

"Han" for grouping all speakers of Chinese languages (except of course Hui, Manchu, and Zhuang) into a single category, regardless of local variations.

According to government policy, where one or more of the national minorities form a sizeable percentage of the population in an administrative area at the level of county or above, the administrative posts should be held by representatives of the minority groups. In these "autonomous areas" the minorities should share proportionately in political posts and the local organs of administration are granted control over economic development, education, cultural activities, public health, and the like in order to protect the cultural heritage of the peoples involved. In such areas some of the rulings in effect elsewhere in China can be modified. For example, the one-child policy urged in the Han areas does not have to be followed, or the legal age of marriage can be reduced (Ma 1985, 25–31). In theory, the minority cultures are allowed to follow their own culture and to change at their own pace.

The Hua Miao, unlike some of the other Miao peoples, are sufficiently scattered or intermixed with other populations so that they do not have their own separate autonomous region as do the more numerous and concentrated Black Miao of the Qiandongnan Autonomous Prefecture of eastern Guizhou. A sizeable segment are located in western Guizhou, just across the border from Yunnan, in the Weining Autonomous County, where they are the minority of the minorities in a mixed area dominated by Yi people and the Moslem Hui and a growing Han population. This area was not open to resettlement by Hua Miao who were residing outside of Weining County at the time of the establishment of the Autonomous County in 1954. Nor can their descendants settle there except for those women who can transfer residence at the time of marriage to a Weining resident. The reverse cannot be done easily, since the Han Chinese expect that a woman joins her husband's household at marriage.

As for the Hua Miao areas of settlement in Yunnan, they are not incorporated into autonomous counties or prefectures. At best, and this is a recent development, they form part of special townships *(minzu xiang)* and are represented in township administration along with other minority representatives and often a Han

Chinese majority. Since 1949, Han Chinese populations have been resettled in Yunnan's northeast and along the borders with Guizhou, brought in to develop mining, forestry, industry, or to fill cadre positions and thereby improve the economy of the area and provide tutelage to the indigenous minority peoples. The towns themselves are unmistakeably Chinese settlements. The minorities live in their smaller villages, located for the most part on the less desireable mountain lands. Schools, clinics, government offices are located within the town, easily accessible to the town residents, and several hours walk over rough mountain trails from the outlying villages. That, at least, is the case for the Hua Miao located in the Yunnan-Guizhou border area, in Zhaotong, Yiliang, and Xuanwei prefectures and even for the smaller communities of Hua Miao in Anning county, some of whom were moved there by government decree from the Weining autonomous county.

With few exceptions, the Hua Miao continue as an uplands population, living at altitudes of 1200 meters or more in areas of less interest to the incoming streams of Chinese settlement. On these mountain slopes, Chinese patterns of agriculture are impossible. Only in the valleys is irrigation sometimes feasible, and the winters are cold, with frequent frosts and snowfalls. Crops are dependant on rainfall, rice cropping is out of the question save in the more protected valleys, and even wheat does not grow well under the climate conditions of the highlands. Traditionally, the Hua Miao practiced slash-and-burn agriculture relying on hardy crops such as oats, barley, millet, and buckwheat. Access to the highlands was eased and expanded by the introduction of New World crops such as potatoes and corn in the sixteenth century. Both of these were quickly accepted by the Hua Miao and by the nineteenth century if not earlier had become valued staples. Additionally, some land was used for growing hemp (to be spun and woven into cloth), for rape (a source of cooking oil) and for tobacco. Hua Miao agriculture was combined with pastoralism: sheep and goats are found throughout the Hua Miao areas of settlement, and in the lower altitudes of the Weining region horses and cattle were also important in the past. In the mountain forests the Hua Miao hunted game for the table (pheasant and deer were highly prized) and for sale at the periodic local markets, and also gained some income through the sale of furs. The forests were also a source of honey, nuts, mushrooms, edible wild fruits and vegetable plants, and herbals and roots for medicine.

However, it would be misleading to present this as a self-sufficient egalitarian system. The Hua Miao were tied to the regional economy in a variety of ways. For one, they participated in the local markets, which met once every five or ten days, exchanging goods for money to buy items they could not produce for themselves. Livestock, wool, and hides were sold to Hui and Chinese traders. The market demand for medicinal herbs brought buyers from all over China and Tibet. In exchange, the Hua Miao purchased farming tools, metalware, pottery, soy sauce and sugar, and even the occasional luxuries of silk, cotton, and silver jewelry.

Opium was also an important feature of the economy until the 1920s: the Hua Miao grew it, but they had no control over its sale, and very few were attracted to its use. Most Hua Miao villages were tenant communities on lands held by Han or Hui, or more commonly in this area, by members of the elite strata of the Yi (also called Nosu or Black Yi). In the pacification of the region, large tracts of land were awarded to the Yi nobility by the expanding Chinese state. In return for the right to claim rentals and labor service, the Yi "native officials" *(tu si)* collected taxes for the state and generally maintained law and order within the boundaries of their estate holdings. This feudal system lasted until the 1920s. The Hua Miao met their obligations to these overlords by the forced growing of the opium poppy, payments in kind or in cash or a specified number of days of labor service (agricultural work, collecting of firewood, household service, transport work). However, as tenants they were free to move residence, to change landlords and to make their own marriage arrangements, rights that were not granted to the slave class within Yi society. Within the ethnic stratification of the area, the Hua Miao ranked below the Yi nobility and freeborn classes, and below the Hui and the Han, but their status was better than that of the Yi slaves — some of whom were Han who had been forced into slavery. Relations between the Hua Miao and their Yi overlords were tense but in general the Yi made no attempt to force the Hua Miao to assimilate to Yi cultural practices, and at times the Miao fled from the Han to the protection of the Yi.

Internally, the Hua Miao were not stratified, though there were differences in wealth and general standard of living between communities and between individuals within communities. But there were no marked social classes and no ranking of lineages, a point that leads the present government to regard the Hua Miao as very primitive and close to the "primitive communal society" as described by Morgan and Engels. Moreover, it was not until well into the twentieth century that the Hua Miao were allowed to purchase land. Few could afford to and even fewer were interested in doing so. Land purchase was a package that involved a transition from slash-and-burn shifting agriculture to intensive settled farming (not feasible except in the valleys and lowlands, far from Miao areas of settlement) and the giving up of pastoralism and forest hunting and gathering. The result was that few Hua Miao became landowners and those who did owned only a couple of acres. In the government surveys of land ownership and exploitation of labor done in connection with the Land Reform movement of the early 1950s, it was impossible to target any of the Hua Miao as members of the landlord class or even as rich peasants (Li Zhaolun 1982). Only a few qualified as middle peasants (owning sufficient lands for their own use without engaging in the exploitation of others) while the majority was classified as poor peasants and landless tenants.

During the Land Reform period, national policy was for the lands of the landlords and even of the rich peasants to be distributed to those in the poor peasant category, along with household goods, sections of housing, draft animals, and farm tools. However, the Hua Miao did not benefit greatly from land reform. It was repeatedly stated that the Hua Miao prefered to live on the higher mountain slopes, their situation treated as a matter of choice rather than adaptation. The more fertile valley lands were distributed to the Han, the Hui, and Yi. Draft oxen and ploughs were almost useless in the mountain areas, and were similarly distributed to the residents of the valleys and lower slopes. Land reform demarcated the mountain agricultural and pasture land holdings for the Hua Miao villages and their componant households. This, together with household registration and restrictions on any future shifting of residence or opening up of new lands effectively put an end to slash-and-burn techniques of mountain-land exploitation, and a ceiling on the size of herds. Individuals and entire communities were locked into place, unable to move to unworked areas. Under later land use policies they could not allow lands to remain fallow for a time. While the land distributions would have seemed generous for lowlands irrigation farming, they were insufficient for shifting drylands agriculture or pastoralism. Soon after, unopened forest lands came under state ownership. This restricted or even ended the earlier utilization of forest resources for timber, charcoal, firewood, the collecting of various forest products, and hunting activities.

During the subsequent collectivization campaigns (mid-1950s till 1979), the Hua Miao were pressured by state directives that placed an emphasis on the production of wheat and corn and that urged the abandonment of "coarse grains" (millet, buckwheat, oats) that did not qualify for filling the quota of taxes and grain sales to the state. Corn had always done well in the highlands, but the wheat yields were disappointing. In many years, the Hua Miao were unable to meet their grain quotas for the state, and were so badly off that they were eligible for relief grain. As for potatoes, those fell outside of the approved crops set by the state, despite their role as a staple and an appropriate offering to guests. By Han definition, potatoes are a vegetable, a side dish to be grown on collective land only after grain quotas are met. Han areas across the northern China plain suffered similarly from substituting wheat and corn for the millet and kaoliang previously raised, and areas that had adopted the sweet potato as a staple found the state unwilling to accept it as a part of the grain quota or to purchase it except at a very low price. In eastern China, four pounds of sweet potato were state-valued as the equivalent of one pound of wheat or corn (Diamond 1985).

Han food preferences also affected pastoral activity. Neither lamb nor goat are widely eaten by the Han. The state urged the raising of pigs and poultry, and set quotas for delivery of pork to the state. These were also hard to meet, given the problems of grain shortage for animal fodder. However, even without that policy, the pastoral segement of the economy was in decline. Herding was collectivized, which proved less efficient than management by a few related households. It had also become difficult with the restrictions on pasture lands. Nor could pastoral produce easily reach the market since the entrepreneurial Hui merchants who had once traveled the area buying hides, wool, lambs, and kids were no longer allowed to do so. The shutdown of the local markets between 1966 and 1979 was the final blow. One might note here that the neighboring Hui villages were also under pressure to raise pigs, despite state rhetoric about respecting the customs and religious beliefs of the minorities, while Hui in the cities and towns suffered from decline in availability of lamb and goatmeat.

On the positive side, Land Reform and collectivization had ended the payment of rentals and labor service to landlords and put more land into food crops, but even so, the standard of living began to decline through the 1960s and 1970s. By the 1980s, despite the easing of collectivization and the return to more liberal economic policies, the Hua Miao were clearly lagging behind other groups within their areas. Han cadres assigned to local minority work, and even some of the acculturated Miao cadres in the region, attribute the poverty of the Miao communities to "backwardness," conservatism, or survivals of their primitive state. In 1985, the time of my fieldwork there, Hua Miao yearly per capita incomes were about 1/5 of the national average for all rural communities in China. There was only subsistance farming and pastoralism on a small scale. There were no industrial ventures or profitable agricultural sidelines. Illiteracy was high, a result in part of the absence of schools in the small Hua Miao villages and the reluctance of parents to send small children to the far-off township schools dominated by Han Chinese. Medical facilities were nonexistant.

Accusations of backwardness, conservatism, and primitive survivals cut cruelly in this case since one of the internal markers of their ethnicity is their widespread conversion at the turn of the century to the evangelical Protestantism brought by the China Inland Mission and the English Methodist Church. They were one of the most dramatic success stories of the missionary effort in southwest China, or China generally, with tens of thousands of converts and adherants. This was more than token Christianity.

Along with the conversions and baptisms came literacy, on a fairly wide scale and a strong sense of unity and local pride.

The first missionaries among the Hua Miao belonged to the Bible Christian Church, a dissenting Methodist sect, that placed great importance on the ability to read the Bible for oneself. With missionary assistance and encouragement, a simple phonetic script was developed in 1905 and in the following years the New Testament was translated in full into Dian Dongbei. Hymnals and study guides were also produced, and a series of school primers. In the 1930s and 1940s a small newspaper was published. Village chapels, built with communal effort, functioned also as one-room primary schools and centers for adult education. The mountain community of Shimenkan (Stone Gateway) in northwestern Guizhou served as the headquarters of church activity. In addition to its own large primary school, it offered secondary schooling and teacher training. At least thirty Hua Miao continued on and graduated from university in the decades before 1949. Some of these became ordained Methodist ministers or doctors and one became a well-regarded anthropologist (Yang Hanxian). Generally the local chapels were served by lay preachers who were trained at Shimenkan. Other young people received training as nurses and agricultural extension workers. At various points in time, agricultural and industrial extension programs were held at Shimenkan. New strains of potatoes were introduced, fruit orchards were planted on the hillsides of many villages, vegetable gardens were encouraged, and a number of Miao learned the techniques of carpentry, brickmaking, and masonry. More efficient looms were designed for home production of cloth. During the prerevolutionary decades, some villages benefited from collective endeavors to build bridges and roads, and pipe systems that brought water into the community. Teams of medical workers, from Shimenkan or from the church-affiliated hospitals in nearby Zhaotong City, traveled around the area periodically. Even those who were not interested in becoming church members participated in the economic innovations, accepted treatment from the medical workers, and sent their children to the schools.

The Hua Miao thus had a headstart on modernization. In 1949, they possibly had the highest literacy rate of any ethnic group within the Yunnan-Guizhou border area. Girls as well as boys had been trained in the seventy-five or more village schools, there were thousands of middle-school (secondary school) graduates who had remained in the area, and most of the college graduates had returned to serve as doctors, teachers, technicians, and church leaders. Although the state drew on that pool for cadres during the 1950s, it assigned many of the chosen to other areas. For those who remained, ties to the Christian church were a handicap and used in subsequent political campaigns as evidence of their political backwardness (as opposed to cultural backwardness) and possible disloyalty. The village schools were closed and the teachers transfered to other work, including ordinary agricultural labor. During the Anti-Rightist campaign of the late 1950s, and particularly during the Cultural Revolution, the surviving teachers, lay preachers and ministers, and former middle-school students were repeatedly brought out for "struggle meetings" where they were accused of having ties with foreigners, of being members of the former ruling party, the Guomindang, and of being secret counterrevolutionaries.

The village schools remained closed until the 1980s when some of them were allowed to reopen. Education lagged, and in the thirty-five years following Liberation, only one Hua Miao graduated from university. In the available schools, instruction and the texts were in Mandarin. Some of the older Miao speak and read Mandarin; in the church schools the early years of instruction were in Dian Dongbei, with a gradual transition to spoken and written Chinese. By middle-school they were using the same textbooks that were standard all over China. Most children, however, learned little Mandarin at home and the only reading materials in many households were in Dian Dongbei script. The state refused to recognize this as a valid writing system since it was connected to the Church and devised with the help of foreign missionaries. The Hua Miao were declared preliterate. Yet there was no alternative writing system for them until 1983, when the first school primers appeared in a new romanization of Dian Dongbei. The primers and romanization devised earlier for Miao in eastern Guizhou were useless to them. Oddly enough, the new primers *(Ad Hmaob Ndeud)* use the older writing system as a guide to the reading of the new romanization, which in turn is based on the Latin (foreign) alphabet.

Despite state promises that minority languages would be used in the schools, these primers were not in wide use in 1985 – 86. They remained a token gesture. The township schools continue to serve a mix of ethnic groups, with Han Chinese predominating, and Mandarin of a Yunnan variety continued as the classroom language. Teachers in the area schools are not given any special training in the minority languages.

State policy on religion held that minority religions could continue in practice, save for those aspects that were physically harmful or in some way wasteful of economic resources. Christianity was recognized as one of the indigenous religions of the Miao, as well as some other ethnic groups. Even so, the churches in the Hua Miao area were closed and the practice of Christianity forbidden at some point in the late 1950s. The Hua Miao continued to hold Christian worship services, meeting in private houses or in forest clearings and caves in the hills, under lay leadership. Reportedly, these were not much different from village chapel meetings, except that they were now illegal and participants could be punished. But there were other differences, of course. Prior to 1949, intervillage services were common, and at Shimenkan there were several days of religious activity around major church festival days. Some 10,000 or more people might travel in from the surrounding area to attend. These large meetings could no longer take place. Indeed, given the restrictions on travel outside of ones own commune, the local churches groups operated in isolation. A few moved toward a more millenarian stand than what had been taught by the Methodist Church and the China Inland Mission. Picking up on doctrines brought by the Seventh Day Adventists, who had sought converts in the late 1930 and 1940s, they began actively preaching and preparing for the Second Coming and the end of the world. Yet others developed services that centered on long hours of singing and dancing.

Elsewhere in China, the churches operated openly until the start of the Cultural Revolution in 1966. Then they too were closed, not reopening until the late 1970s and early 1980s. The reopenings occured at the same time in the Hua Miao areas, under the guidance of the Three-Self Church (the state-approved religious body). However, there were very few surviving ordained ministers in the Hua Miao communities by then, and few youth educated sufficiently to be accepted to seminary. House churches continued, the local Miao village cadres tending to look the other way on such activities. Where there were reopened churches, congregants were willing to walk five or six hours to attend, often starting off at dawn, sleeping over and returning the following day. But this could not be done too often; the township cadres I talked with pointed out that such activities interfered with production and should not be encouraged.

The situation was not any better for the non-Christianized Hua Miao who wished to follow traditional religious activities. Worship of nature spirits, shamanistic rituals, exorcism of evil forces, and rites to secure the safety of the household and the village were all attacked as "superstition" and strongly discouraged. They have not been openly revived though some undoubtedly continue in secret. The only aspects of traditional religious activity that have survived are the social-recreational segments of religious festivals, particularly the "Flower Mountain Festival." This was an intervillage festival that included song contests between groups of young unmarried men and women, musical performances on the lu-sheng pipes and dances. It served the function of bringing marriageable young people together in a large assembly so that they could establish relationships and eventually select their own spouses. The current Flower Mountain Festivals have been coopted by the state as a purely cultural interethnic event under government sponsorship. The songs and dances have been revised to carry politically correct messages, the flirtations and pairings off that used to occur are discouraged, and so too is the followup of the festival in which small groups of young men would journey around to visit the villages of the girls that each was interested in courting. The audience for the performances is no longer limited to Hua Miao — it has become a cultural diversion for Han Chinese and others — and parents express concern about allowing their unmarried sons and daughters to attend.

Under state regulations and state-inspired changes, marriage and residence patterns have been forced to change. They are becoming more and more like the model Chinese pattern for marriage where, despite the changes in law and lip service to marriage on the basis of choice, marriages are still thought of as obtaining a daughter-in-law for the family. In the past, parental consent was certainly desirable in any marriage arrangement, and parents sometimes used their influence in bringing prospective spouses to the attention of their unmarried offspring. But "arranged marriages" were not the norm as they were among the Han Chinese population, and the young people involved knew the prospective partner prior to marriage and had a say in the final decision. Love and mutual attraction were important. The usual interpretation of this by Han scholars and cadres is that among the Miao (all Miao, and many other ethnic minorities as well) marriage was based on "free love" and involved sexual promiscuity prior to marriage and perhaps even afterward. The love songs at festivals, the open association of young men and women, and courtship practices continue to be seen as evidence of a primitive mentality, inappropriate in a socialist society, though in China's cities courtship and choice in marriage is regarded as the progressive way to proceed.

Hua Miao villages are small, on average between twenty and thirty households, which means in effect that the real marriage pool involves a number of villages. During the 1960s and 1970s travel became increasingly restricted. Local officials in charge of the collective brigades or communes had no sympathy when five or six able-bodied young men picked up their lu-sheng pipes and disappeared on a courtship journey for four or five weeks. Parents were urged to play a larger role in making good marriage arrangements for their children.

In all fairness, it should be mentioned that the foreign missionaries and the religious leaders that they trained were also unenthusiastic about some of the aspects of Hua Miao courtship, particularly premarital sex and a fairly young age at marriage. They substituted intervillage sports meets, weekend hymn sings and prayer meetings interspersed with picnics and games, in hopes that these would provide an adequate means for young people from small hamlets to meet others their own age and make their own marriage choices. Attendance at the schools or special training programs at Shimenkan also brought young people together in natural circumstances. They also pushed for later marriages, with the young people urged not to marry until they had finished their schooling or until they were eighteen. The only clear restriction was that church members should marry other church members. But they never suggested parental control over marriage and it is ironic to find Han cadres taking that as a model when it is on the wane in Han areas. One could argue that the traditional Hua Miao marriages are more in keeping with a modernizing society.

The Hua Miao also take a more egalitarian view of gender. The Han still regard sons as more valuable than daughters; daughters are "water spilled on the ground," raised for the benefit of another family. Among the Hua Miao both sons and daughters were valued and received a portion of family property at the time of marriage (livestock and household goods) in order to set up their own household. The new household could be in the boy's village or in the girl's village, or even in a third community where one or the other had relatives and economic opportunities. Only the youngest son was expected to remain in the parental household, and he inherited the house and remaining property at their death. However, by the mid-1950s, the state looked with disapproval at these flexible residence patterns. Except in unusual circumstances, it expected women to join their husband's village and household at marriage. State control over building materials, and the collectivization of livestock made it difficult to do otherwise.

Other cultural features of Miao life have been under attack as well. As mentioned earlier, the Hua Miao women spin and weave their own wool and hemp in order to make clothing for the family. Men, more than women, have switched to ready-made standard "Chinese" dress for work, but continue to wear traditional clothes when attending church, or market, or social functions of any sort. The patterns of the women's batik skirts vary by locality but are a distinctively Hua Miao dress and valued as such. Though China's television and magazines get a lot of mileage out of the colorful and varied clothing of the minorities, one finds that in the minority areas themselves these marks of ethnicity are discouraged. The cadres say that they are wasteful of work time and of local resources, or that they are inappropriately immodest or both. The Hua Miao are repeatedly pressured to "modernize" by adopting the same dress as the rural Han Chinese. Attempts at this visible assimilation were at their height during the years of the Cultural Revolution. Bands of revolutionary activists belonging to one or another faction of youthful Red Guards or more adult elements descended on the villages, insisting that the women replace their batik skirts with baggy blue trousers, and cut off their long hair. In the 1980s, the use of force was replaced by persuasion. In the town of Yiliang, a factory misleadingly named "Nationalities Clothing" turns out the drab unisex clothing favored during the Cultural Revolution. Elsewhere, factories produce approximations of "minority dress" for cultural festivals or theatrical performances. But in most areas, the Hua Miao cling to home production of their traditional dress, save for the acceptance of inexpensive sneakers in place of straw sandals or bare feet.

Despite the reopening of free markets and the more relaxed economic policies of the 1980s, the Hua Miao seem to have benefited little. State-assisted development is directed toward the Han populations, who in these mountain areas are much poorer than those on the plains or in the urban centers. For example, there are now development projects for scientific livestock breeding and expansion of pasture acreage. But the Australian technicians brought in to facilitate this project in Yunnan found themselves working not with Hua Miao or Yizu who have been engaged in pastoralism but with rural Han Chinese who were encouraged to branch out into this activity as a way of expanding their incomes. Mining and forestry work in Xuanwei prefecture has created new towns and generated income, but the workforce is Han Chinese, brought from elsewhere if necessary. The given reason for these policies is that minorities (like the Hua Miao) are not ready to enter the industrial age. Before they can become workers, they must first become peasants.

China's minority policies, whether at the level of ideology or of local practice, needs to be seen in the larger framework of the way that the State thinks about "culture." The term *wenhua* does not translate well as "culture" in the way that it is used in Western social science. It is not a neutral term referring to economic strategies, social organization, ideology, values, and behaviors learned by people as members of a society. Rather, it is judgmental: one can speak in Chinese of peoples having a "low" or a "high" level of culture, and most of the national minorities are said to have a very low or backward level of culture, or in a few cases to have no culture at all. What is meant is advanced technology, a system of social organization and attendant ideology that parallels that of the Han Chinese, and Culture (with a capital C) in the sense of a written literary tradition, artistic productions and professional artists.

Another term in use is *wenming,* which roughly translates as "civilized," a feature where once again the minorities are seen to fall short. During the 1980s a campaign has been under way in China's rural areas to create "civilized villages" and "civilized households" under Party leadership. What this means is unclear, but it appears to mean living up to a model of prosperity, morality, and modernity as defined in current political thinking. If the minorities fail to live up to the ideal standards, so too does much of the population. Posters everywhere in the cities urge people not to litter, not to spit, not to use rough language and not to shout or quarrel in public, and there are repeated campaigns to locate and reward "civilized households" and "civilized villages" nationwide.

Yet despite the desire to transform all of China into a cultured and civilized country, the State has at various times come down heavily on those very features that made China admired as a major center of world civilization. Buddhism and Taoism have suffered the same fate as Christianity in terms of state controls, restrictions on the size and recruitment of clergy, and the forced closure for long periods of temples and monasteries. Local temples and lineage halls were converted into Party headquarters or storage buildings. The literature and arts of Imperial times were scorned, and even forbidden, replaced by didactic plays and stories extolling the Party and the socialist road, and paintings of sturdy and smiling workers, peasants, and soldiers. Folksongs, folktales, traditional opera all came under criticism, and if revived emerged with revised texts and new themes. The distrust of Culture extended to the arts and literature produced in the 1920s, 1930s and 1940s, though much of that had been socially critical and even radical in its critiques. Finally, in the lunacy of the Cultural Revolution, even the revolutionary productions of the 1950s came under attack. The cadres in charge seemed to have a deep distrust of Culture.

One needs to keep in mind that China's socialism was built on the base of a semifeudal society, a vast bureaucratic agrarian state in which an indigenous bourgeoisie did not have time to develop and in which Western colonialism had only a tenuous hold in a few coastal urban centers. Modern schooling was limited to the big cities and larger towns, and the emergent modern intelligentsia/ white collar workers/technicians strata was small at the time of Liberation in 1949, and politically suspect for having more than a primary school education. In some rural areas, even a primary school education was suspect. Much of the working class was first-generation, and a disproportionate segment of that relatively small class was composed of young women and children. China was a nation of peasants, and the recruits to the Party were drawn primarily from the peasantry, particularly among those who had participated in the war against the Japanese, in the Civil War or the Korean conflict. Army experience had given them some minimal formal education and a sense of what lay beyond the boundaries of their villages and local marketing areas, and the experience of participation in revolutionary struggle or armed combat. It is not unfair to say that the vast majority of the new cadres appointed to various levels of the State bureaucracy and local bureaucracies were semiliterate, distrustful of the heritage of Chinese culture that they associated with the former ruling classes, and equally distrustful of "foreign learning" that smacked of imperialism and the elites of the treaty ports.

Even today, the majority of Party members have not gone beyond primary school levels of formal education. The 1980s campaigns against "spiritual pollution" and "bourgeoise liberalization" are of a piece with the closedmindedness of the Cultural Revolution. There is fear of the new, of the old, and of the "foreign" whatever its source, and deep suspicion of China's own traditions and mixed cultural heritage. Nobody really seems able to define what is meant by the Party's calls for building a "Socialist Spiritual Civilization," and the cadres protect their careers by finding political grounds for rejecting most things that are offered up toward that goal.

Cultural diversity is suspect, even though revised minority songs and dances are performed on prime-time television. In the name of socialist culture, the State exercises control over social organization, social practice, and intellectual production, but the minorities remain distinctively different. Every year there is a spate of articles in the government-controlled press stressing the need to educate and train minority cadres so that reform can effectively take place from within. The established Minorities Institutes, which train such cadres, teach standard Chinese and basic Marxism-Leninism-Mao Zedong thought to short-term students, and more academic courses to others. There is no practical training that would further economic development. Few minority youth make it to regular universities and technical colleges, and when they graduate they can be assigned anywhere in the country by the States, not necessarily to their home areas.

The shortage of trained indigenous personnel for the minority areas is not the only factor holding back economic development. As suggested earlier, government planning for modernization plays a significant part. The new factories in Tibet provide employment mainly for Han Chinese recruited elsewhere. Vast numbers of Han have been brought into the Xinjiang Uighur Autonomous Region to staff primary and secondary industries so that by now the Uighur are truly a minority in their own region. In northern Yunnan the driveable roads stop at the valley towns that are Han settlements. The extension of electric power lines also stops there.

In addition, groups like the Hua Miao have been set back by past government policies, and by failure to distinguish more clearly between local populations and to understand their cultures. Policies that may work well with one are not necessarily suited for another. Even the recent policy that dissolved the collectives in favor of household contracting for agricultural lands and other productive resources is not universally welcomed among minorities where lands were held in common by the village or by lineage segments. Speaking specifically to the Hua Miao case, the return of herd ownership to the households is welcomed, but individual assignment of pasture land is not. Han cadres administering the program cannot grasp the idea that a flock of sheep do not, indeed cannot, graze the same small plot of mountain land every day year round.

Like some other minority groups, the Hua Miao are nervous

about government policies on any issue. They have seen them switch back and forth over four decades. Despite the promise of autonomy and tolerance they feel that they are looked down on, and that they are under pressure to give up all but a few token of their traditional heritage. They are troubled by the increasing number of Han in their areas, and incursions on what were once common lands and free resources. The socialist years have widened the economic gap between the minorities and the Han Chinese, and they have increased the feeling of separateness and ethnic identity.

Research for this paper was carried out with the cooperation of the Yunnan Academy of Social Sciences, the Central Minorities Institute (Beijing), the Methodist Missionary Society (London) and the University of London School of Oriental and African Studies. Funding was made possible by the Luce Foundation History of Christianity in China Project and the Wang Institute Fellowship for Chinese Studies program.

References

Diamond, Norma. 1985. "Taitou Revisited: State Policies and Social Change." In William L. Parish (ed.) *Chinese Rural Development: The Great Transformation.* Armonk, N.Y. and London: M.E. Sharpe.

Ho Ping-ti. 1959. *Studies on the Population of China, 1368–1953.* Harvard East Asian Series. Cambridge, Mass.: Harvard University Press.

Li Zhaolun (editor). 1982. *Yunnan Miaozu Yaozu Shehui Lishi Diaocha* Source Materials for Research on the Social History of China's National Minorities Series. Kunming: Minzu Chubanshe.

Ma Yin. 1985. *Questions and Answers about China's Minority Nationalities.* Beijing: New World Press.

Minorities Commission of Zhaotong (Yunnan) and Weining (Guizhou). 1983. *Ad Hmaob Ndeud.* Zhaotong: Zhaotong Printing House.

Ramsey, S. Robert. 1987. *The Languages of China.* Princeton: Princeton University Press.

3

Ethnicity and the Security Forces of the State: The South Asian Experience

Angela S. Burger

The most dangerous violence that governments and states encounter is likely to be ethnic and/or religious. Class conflict may be troublesome, but without significant elite participation or overlap with other societal cleavages, can usually be spatially and temporally limited with low or moderate uses of force. In most societies the vertical linkages between and among classes in villages, towns, districts, and so on, are sufficiently strong to sunder horizontal class ties. Furthermore, scholars as diverse as Edelman (1964) and Hrebenar (1982), using different approaches, both conclude that the lower classes can be defused by offering symbolic reassurances that the leaders will try to ameliorate their grievances.

Ethnic and religious conflict, by contrast, is far more serious for a regime. If the groups in question are not regionally concentrated, the conflict can spread rapidly through the state, due to the "complementary habits" and facilities of communication which define "that people" at that time (Deutsch 1966, 96–99). If concentrated geographically, the conflict may not necessarily be separatist, but it is likely to be difficult to control. On the one hand, if the security forces are perceived as an alien "them" by at least one of the major parties in the conflict, the most basic efforts to restore order are

79

likely to raise questions of whose law, and whose order. On the other hand, use of sizeable numbers of the dissident ethnic group(s) may bring division or desertion within the forces.

Governments are always and everywhere concerned with protecting themselves as well as their states from attack and defeat. For many governments the sure knowledge of their legitimacy, their moral authority to rule, in the populace and especially among elites, markedly lowers the internal threat.

New governments cannot assume their legitimacy will be so acknowledged, and are therefore likely to pay particular attention to the security forces upon which they must rely to protect both themselves and the state. A critical concept in analyzing policies followed towards those forces is the government's perception of threat. Direction of threat, along with its classification or definition, can change over time, either with the same or different directive personnel. Governments will endeavor to counter threat with appropriate policies towards the police and the military, in composition of both rank and file as well as officers, and in pattern of usage.

If the prime fear is attack by another state, differing in ethnic, racial or religious composition from one's own, a government may recruit heavily among threatened border populations even though they be minorities within the state, because they would be defending their homes as well as the state. If, however, the neighboring state or its military, shares similar characteristics with one's border populations, a government might well leaven the fighting forces with a judicious mix of "heartland" troops.

If the concern is not interstate war, but internal strife, the calculus changes dramatically, and varies depending on the definition of the threat. If the threat is seen to emanate from a particular person, that person can be jailed, exiled, or eliminated. If the threat is defined demographically, efforts can be made to divide that construct (i.e., divide the poor on social or racial lines). If the threat is perceived as ethnic or religious, the choices are broader, ranging from accommodation to assimilation, to repression. If the threat is perceived in terms of one or more issues, then policies to handle that issue can be adopted. Much depends on whether the cleavages are singular or multiple, cross-cutting or congruent.

No matter how the threat is defined, and what policies are adopted to diminish the problem, governmental leaders in the third world are likely to presume the paramount importance of the military forces, especially the army, for maintenance of state and governmental security. Governments rely on the military to protect themselves but must be concerned simultaneously with preventing the military from overthrowing them. The juxtaposition of both concerns can lead to adoption of policies regarding ethnicity that may not seem immediately obvious. For example, overrepresentation in the officer corps by a minority ethnic group may be a safeguard against a coup. If ethnic tensions run high, the populace would not accept such rule for long (Enloe 1980a). As Talleyrand once said, one can do almost anything with swords except sit on them.

A case can be made, however, that the most important security forces for governmental maintenance are those of the police; the police are in daily contact with the citizen body, often being the nexus of interaction between "government" and "individuals," whereas the military are likely to be semi-isolated on military bases. The greater the level of brutality and discrimination by the police, the more likely their actions will create antagonism. In an ethnically skewed force, there is a greater likelihood of police brutality and/or discrimination towards members of ethnic groups not their own. Resentment over incidents among the adversely affected then tend to become multiplicative rather than additive. Relatively minor incidents can trigger major civil disturbances. Inability of the police to maintain peace and good order requires intervention by the military (Bowden 1978).

One theory associated with causation of military coups is the recurrence of military interventions to restore order in society. The perception of disorder as a consequence of civilian government policies or actions—including police behavior—is critical. Frequent or large-scale civil disturbances demonstrate the existence of a political vacuum. Eventually, military leaders, concerned about the "failure of politicians," take over (Horowitz 1980, 3–20; Johnson 1962, 69–89, 7–67; von der Mehden 1964, 97–99).

A second theory asserts that coups occur because the military is a part of society, not separate from it. Ethnic, religious, and class cleavages are found in the military as well. The skew may differ from that in society, but no matter what the skew, the military intervenes to settle the conflict on its own terms, by its own preferences (Huntington 1968, 192–98; Lofchie 1972, 19–35; Veliz 1967, 66–118).

A third theory stresses the corporate interests of the military, which overthrows a government to further its own, rather selfish, interests. Such interests might include its share of the budget, its perks, its preferences in weapons, strategy, and tactics. A coup might occur after an end to a long period of ethnic conflict that had seen large increases in the military as well as behavioral excesses. Contemplated reductions as well as disciplinary actions might well trigger a corporate military response (First 1971, 20; Thompson 1973, 1–147; Dowse in Leys 1969, 213–16).

A fourth theory stresses the ambitions and private motives of key individuals in the military. While the ability to bring about a settlement of disputes or obtain civil control may lead individuals in the military to be aware of their powers, abilities, and support, this particular theory makes it impossible to predict conditions likely to lead to coups (Decalo 1976, 14–21).

Police forces rarely initiate coups, but their behavior vis-à-vis citizens can create problems which affect both civilian government and the military in terms of their perceptions and actions (Enloe 1980b).

Governments have limited options available regarding ethnicity policy within the police and military, and between them. A structural option is to establish one or more paramilitary forces to augment the police, so that the military will rarely be called upon to restore civil order. That structural option makes it possible for a government to adopt different ethnic policies between multiple forces. Basically the government can

1. Ignore ethnicity (although this does not make the problem disappear).
2. Counter-balance ethnic groups within the forces.
3. Deliberately provide for dominance by a preferred ethnic group in one or all of the institutions.

The purpose of this paper is to explore which of these options have been chosen and why with reference to the security forces of India, Pakistan, and Sri Lanka, in South Asia. All were British colonies with similar though not identical political experiences from the British period. All three have plural, multiethnic societies. But while India has remained under civilian rule throughout, and save for a short period of Emergency, politically competitive, Pakistan has experienced long and frequent periods of military rule alternating with civilian, and has lost a significant part of the original state because of inability to handle ethnic questions. Sri Lanka has had uninterrupted civilian rule, has put down two attempted coups, and has had a change of party at the national level at every election save that of 1988. However, since the early 1970s, and escalating after 1983, it has experienced civil war on ethnic lines, which brought Indian military intervention in 1985. The friction took on a new dimension with the onset of violence between groups within the majority as well as within the largest of the minority communities. Analysis of these three cases provides us with an opportunity to study the relationship between sociopolitical conditions and ethnicity policies towards the security forces.

Initial Policy Choices in India and Pakistan

To ignore ethnicity seems, on the surface, to be the most unlikely policy for any of the three states to follow, because the British deliberately utilized ethnicity in staffing the military for so many decades. The British used terms such as "class" or "martial race" in a markedly narrow definition that, according to Ellinwood, reflected sociocultural realities of that time (1981, 94). In 1904, for example a rather broad category of "Punjabi Muslims" was identified as particularly suitable for recruitment. So were Gaur Brahmins, a much narrower subcaste. But Bhuinhar Brahmins, another subcaste, were not to be recruited because they "are generally too quarrelsome and fond of intrigue to render their enlistment desirable" (Ellinwood 1981, 95 quoting Bingley; Nicholas 1918, 18).

The British did not allow all-Muslim units to exist after the Mutiny of 1857, and decided the men of Oudh were no longer a "martial race." Instead, the Gurkhas and Punjabis were. The irony is that it was the soldiers of Oudh who had defeated the Gurkhas and Punjabis. Why did the British change their view? In the Mutiny, civilians in Oudh had sided with the mutineering soldiers, while Punjabis and Gurkhas had been perfectly willing to suppress them (Enloe 1980, 36). The change in policy illustrates the effect of a change in perception of threat.

After independence it was inconceivable that the British policies could be maintained. Oudh is part of Uttar Pradesh in the Hindu and nationalist heartland, the state from which all but one prime minister of India has come. It would be inconceivable for a nationalist independent government to accept the British reasoning on recruitment. When Pakistan was created, it had to have Muslim units. The Royal Indian Army was divided, but although during World Wars I and II, Punjabi Muslims comprised the largest single group in the army, there were no units to transfer en toto.

Independence and partition into two states came simultaneously, and were accompanied by extensive Hindu-Muslim rioting. The army had to be used to restore order. Neither India nor Pakistan could afford to ignore ethnicity from the very beginning of independent states. War between the two countries, as well as between India and the People's Republic of China, plus civil unrest on communal lines within each country have made it impossible to disregard ethnicity.

Changing Policy Choices in Sri Lanka

In Sri Lanka, unlike India and Pakistan, ignoring ethnicity was policy from independence until around 1962. Under the British the officer corp in the military and the police greatly overrepresented the ethnic and religious minorities of the state; Horowitz estimates that about a fifth of the military officers were Ceylon Tamils (either Hindu or Christian) who comprise about 11 percent of the population, and another fifth, the Burghers who were only about 4 percent of the population. Sinhalese, with over 70 percent in the population had only about 50 percent of the officers. Buddhists were outnumbered by Christians, in sharp contrast to societal representation (1980, 66–67). As late as 1957, 29 percent of the gazetted police officers were Burghers, and another 19 percent Ceylon Tamil. Sinhalese were less than 50 percent, and Buddhists only 25 percent.

How is this acceptance of a minority-skewed ethnic composition to be explained? Absence of a foreign threat may be one factor. The pattern of internal disorder over a century might be another. Civil disturbances historically had pitted Sinhalese against Catholics in 1883 and 1903, Sinhalese against Muslims in 1903 and 1915, Sinhalese against Tamils in 1915. De Silva points out that the majority Sinhalese usually started the riots (1986). A government might find greater security in a military that overrepresented the minorities, it was more likely to be interested in containing the conflict than extending it, while less likely to challenge the civilians for control of government. Labor strife, which occurred among discreet sets of workers, was also containable.

Against this background, a key factor appears to have been the domination of government and politics by a small, highly westernized and educated elite, who acquired power without having to organize and mobilize the people in a nationalist movement. The "moderate reformers" were able to win significant changes early; for example, legislators were chosen in elections under universal adult suffrage in 1931, two decades earlier than in India. Independence was gained as a consequence of events in India, but without the mass mobilization associated with Gandhi. In a uniquely British cultural pattern, the Sri Lankan elites expected and obtained deference from the masses. This narrow elite communicated using English, usually wore Western dress, and shared social habits. They valued "professionalism" in the military and police, as did the westernized officer corps of both institutions. Ethnicity was not relevant in the early years of independence.

Under the pressures of competitive party politics, it was only a matter of time before an opposition party would appeal to the majority, the nonwesternized, Sinhalese-speaking Buddhists, to win control of government. The Sri Lankan Freedom Party (SLFP) charged the country was dominated by an English-speaking elite, that Tamils were overrepresented in the government, in the most prestigious positions — economic, professional, governmental — and in the universities.

Sinhalese Buddhist militants in the SLPF, who won in 1956, took immediate steps to adopt Sinhalese as the official language, and require its proficiency to continue in public-sector jobs or enter the university. Their policies led to protests by Tamils, followed by civil disturbances. The focal point was language, not religion (Kearney 1978; Roberts 1979). The direction of threat to Sinhalese politicians was obvious, and policies were adopted to balance Tamil and Sinhalese officers by "sandwiching" them in the police, and choosing top officials for political reliability rather than professional abilities. Tamil commanders in the military were replaced with militant Sinhalese before being sent into Tamil areas.

Sinhalese dominance in both military and police was adopted after a coup attempt was put down in 1962. The plot ("Operation Holdfast") was uncovered literally hours before it was to commence. It was led by both army and police officers, who were of that small English elite, heavily Christian, and while Sinhalese were in the majority, Tamils and Burghers were overrepresented (just as they were in the officer corps itself). Of those from the army, there were considerably more from the artillery (which served only English food — no rice or curries) than the infantry (Horowitz 1984, 78–83). The group was opposed to the strident communalism of the Sinhalese Buddhist politicians. The second coup theory seems most appropriate, that which claims the security forces are part of society and intervene to see that "their group" wins. Here, however, the identification was shifting with religion (non-Buddhist) being added to language.

The coup attempt cemented the direction of threat for the Sinhalese Buddhist politicians in power, who then moved to establish Sinhalese dominance. Discriminatory public policies particularly in university admissions led to further protests. As time went on, even when Sinhalese instigated civil disturbances against the Tamils, the government blamed the Tamils.

What were the consequences for choosing Sinhalization? One, Tamils who suffered the brunt of discrimination began to wage terrorist attacks and to demand a separate state.

Two, in 1983, for several days neither police nor army moved to quell the massive riots between Sinhalese and Tamils. Indeed Sinhalese policemen actively incited citizens to attack Tamils in several locations. The riot was triggered by funerals of Sinhalese soldiers killed by Tamil rebels (Dissanayake, n.d.).

A third consequence is more speculative. Observers noted that the President of Sri Lanka did not call on the police and military to act for several days, nor did he try to establish a curfew. Could it be that incidents of known insubordination were accompanied by other intelligence indicating the possibility that the security forces might fracture if used? That possibility would help explain why, immediately following the riots, the president established a paramilitary force, headed by a family member, and heavily Sinhalese, to use in counterterrorist activities. (Ironically, the first paramilitary unit trained was virtually eliminated by a terrorist attack on its way to its first posting. By that time, the rebel activity had reached the status of civil war. A small paramilitary force could not have coped with the level of activity.)

Fourth and less speculative, Sinhalization meant the police and military had great difficulty in obtaining intelligence about rebel demands, organization, strategy and tactics, and personnel, and concomitantly greater problems in controlling brutality and wanton killing of Tamils by the Sinhalese security forces. Emergency Acts were passed that made it easy for the security forces to torture, kill, harass, and cover up their actions (Burger 1985).

Fifth, Sinhalese fears about Tamils led to posting policies that aggravated ethnic tensions. Sinhalese were posted in heavily Tamil areas in ratios of up to 70 percent. The Sinhalese did not speak Tamil and few spoke English. Tamils speak Tamil, English, but halting Sinhalese at best. In Sri Lanka a three-year probationary period follows six months of training, during which time the probationary appointees are not allowed to marry. These greenest of police trainees were sent to the Tamil areas; the more senior used their marital status to beg off such dangerous duty. Short-term six-month assignments were made, meaning a steady succession of young, green, police, whose fears could feed on each others in the barracks where they were housed, apart from their officers who were given houses or allowances for living quarters more suitable to their social station. In 1984, the Deputy Inspector General who headed the police in the northern district of Jaffna, heavily Tamil, moved his headquarters to the capital of Colombo, in the south. Little wonder that the police became overly aggressive to cover their fear, and retaliated en masse when attacked by dissident Tamils. The police burned the magnificient public library in Jaffna, which was a repository of Tamil culture and history, and trashed colleges and libraries of the Tamils. Terrorist attacks against the military led to small groups leaving the base and wantonly attacking Tamil civilians. This breakdown of control within the security forces not only exacerbated ethnic relations, but made the Sinhalese governmental authorities reluctant to discipline the security forces for fear they might once again try to overthrow the government.

Sinhalization also prevented authorities from perceiving that they were recruiting extremist Sinhalese into police and army. Fear of the rising extremist Sinhalese Janatha Vimukhti Peramuna (People's Liberation Front) was a factor in accepting the Indian military presence on the island in 1985; the Army could not fight both threats to the regime at the same time. While the Tamil rebels, and Indian Government intervention, presented threats to the state, the extremist Sinhalese presented the most potent threat to the security of the Government.

The presence of Indian troops brought about an escalation of terrorist actions by the JVP, who attempted to assassinate the President and top cabinet officials in the Parliament building, killed over a hundred early voters in local elections in 1988, assassinated a number of public figures, set bombs in several public buildings, and were responsible for killing numerous civilians. One threat by the JVP, however, was sufficient to neutralize their presence in the security forces: the JVP threatened to kill not only security officers but also their families—and made good on that threat in a few cases. The police and military turned on the JVP, and by late 1989 had eliminated several top leaders as well as hundreds of rank-and-file members. Some but not all of the "death squads" are rumored to have come from the security personnel.

The Indian Government, with troops on the island, insisted on the establishment of local autonomy in the northern and eastern districts, along with elections on the structural change as well as on personnel. The largest and most potent fighting force, the Liberation Tigers of Tamil Elam (LTTE) apparently realized their electoral weakness, and, on the one hand, boycotted elections, and on the other, attacked Indian troops. For over three years the Indian army units fought the Tigers, experiencing the same difficulty as had the Sri Lankan military earlier. Damage to civilian life and property is reported to have been greater under the Indians than under the Sri Lankan troops, while the Indian troops were embarassed at their level of casualties. Elections put the ERPLF (Eelam Revolutionary People's Liberation Front) in control of local governmental bodies. In summer of 1989 the president of Sri Lanka, allied with the Tigers, demanded the withdrawal of the Indian Peace Keeping Forces, and after weeks of negotiations, phased withdrawal began. The Tamil areas are to have their own police forces, which have yet to be set up. The expectation is that, once the Indian troops have departed, the Tigers will attempt to eliminate the ERPLF leaders and any other obstacle to their acquisition of power (without elections). Those actions will pose extraordinary policy choices regarding police/military on the ERPLF and other non-Tiger Tamil organizations, as well as on the Sri Lankan government.

The Sri Lankan government has, over time, adopted every possible ethnic policy in and towards the security forces. The more communalized the police and military, the greater their difficulty in maintaining law and order in any part of the island. Their anti-Tamil policies have led to departure of all but one of the top Tamil police officers. Those Tamils in the middle and lower ranks of the police are viewed as "Uncle Toms" by the Tamils, but are distrusted by the Sinhalese. The subsequent adoption of extermination policies towards the JVP, whose members are difficult to distinguish from "ordinary" Sinhala, has resulted in forces accustomed to the use of brutality against civilians. Even if the Tamils within the police were "made available" to the Tamil-governed provinces for a nascent force, their position between the ERPLF and Tigers is likely to result in continued brutality. The Sri Lankan example, then, demonstrates the hazards of adopting both a policy of ethnicity as well as of brutality within the security forces, in terms of "peace and good order" within the state.

The Pakistani Experience

West Pakistan contains four provinces with differing ethnic groups in each: the Punjab, Sind, Northwest Frontier (with Pathans, etc.) and Baluchistan. East Pakistan was predominantly Bengali.

Ethnically, the original Pakistan Army (of both East and West) was overwhelmingly dominated by Punjabi Muslims, with about 60 percent of officers and sepoys coming from that one province, the next largest group coming from the Northwest Frontier Province, and very few from Sindh or Baluchistan. There were two Bengali battalions created (from East Pakistan). Troops from the four western provinces were integrated in all units, but the two Bengali units were kept separated (Cohen 1984, 42–43).

West Pakistanis viewed Bengalis much as Kipling portrayed the character Hurree Baba in *Kim:* short, fat, voluble, excitable, overeducated, cowardly, and lacking both the discipline and physical characteristics of a soldier. Their presence was "contaminating." The difficulty of creating a Pakistan Army in a short time, with insufficient officers and manpower, the need to create mythical ties to past glories (going back to Alexander the Great), perhaps made it easy to accept a prevailing ethnic stereotype. Having been accepted, it was not questioned.

After the military took over the government, Bengali representation in government as well as the military was nil. After the 1971 election, where the vote for Mujib Rehman's Bengali party assured it an absolute majority in the Pakistan Parliament, the West Pakistan Army moved into East Bengal and began systematically executing the educated and politically active. India sent in its army which quickly overcame the Pak forces which were interned in Prisoner of War camps for almost two years. The state of Bangladesh was formed, whose army and police are now both Bengali, in a dominantly Bengali state, and will not be further discussed. But for the military of West Pakistan, the combination of being termed the

"Butchers of Bengal" and then POWs makes this a shattering experience for a generational group.

What was the Pakistani governmental response to the defeat of its army? The civilian prime minister, Bhutto undertook no purge of the army in general, or of those in command specifically. He was critical, and made appointments to reform and "reprofessionalize" the army. He also established a paramilitary Federal Security Force for use in internal political control, which would mean he could avoid calling in the army to restore political peace. The military saw the paramilitary as a possible counter to their own power, and opposed it (Qureshi 1979; Cohen 1984, 53, 71, 119).

Within West Pakistan's military, efforts were made to open up recruitment to other ethnic groups. But Sindhis and Baluchs did not sign up. In 1979, Cohen reports the officer candidates to be 70 percent Punjabi, 14 percent from the North West Frontier, 9 percent from Sind, 3 percent from Baluchistan, and 1.3 percent from Azad Kashmir (1984, 52). Alternative recruitment or structure has been rejected, with overt reasons being most often economic. However, concern that changes would bring about "political trouble" indicates that officers in a politicized army have learned habits of political discretion. Cohen reports a prevailing undercurrent in discussion that downplays the military ability of Sindhis and Baluchs, similar to but not as intense as the attitudes towards the Bengalis. The Sindhis and Baluchis have begun to regard the Army as "colonial" in nature (1984, 44–47, 113–17).

The Pakistani police are provincial, with an "All-Pak" corp of top officers who are deputed to different areas. Punjabis dominate the All-Pak corp, while Punjabis who have moved into other districts have joined the respective provincial police forces. There is some resentment concerning the tentacles of Punjabis. In the late 1960s, rules of promotion were changed from more objective tests to give greater weight to an interview. This change is said to have led to more and quicker promotions of Punjabis by Punjabis, with consequent disaffection.

During the 1970s Baluch uprisings meant the Army had to support the police in that province. The experience politicized the military, who in 1977 overthrew the civilian government of Prime

Minister Bhutto. General Zia (a Punjabi), who was one of Bhutto's appointments to reprofessionalize the army, took control and had Bhutto (a Sindhi) executed.

In the 1980s dissidence in Sind has been considered most threatening. Zia's untimely death in an airplane explosion, was followed by elections which were won by Bhutto's daughter. Benazir, a Sindhi, played a delicate balancing act towards the Punjabi military officers who had led in the Islamization policies denigrating women. In late 1989, the announcement of her intention to retire immediately raised questions about the viability of any civilian successor and the possibility of military intervention again.

What of the frequent incursions of the military into civilian rule? The first occurred in 1958, and the usual analysis focused on the first coup theory, namely, the need to bring order out of chaos. Historically, the drive of Mohammed Ali Jinnah and other leaders to obtain a separate state had taken precedence over discussions about the form, direction, and nature of that state and its policies. The movement never became a well-organized party. Shortly after independence, Jinnah, the architect of the separate state, died. Then Liaquat Ali, the prime minister, was assassinated. When a constitution was finally drawn up and elections held in 1956, no party had a majority. Those who developed the first coup theory had cases such as that of Pakistan in mind, and Cohen reports the theory's popularity among the Pakistan military (1984, 105–10). However, Cohen also notes two competitive interpretations had surfaced: one was that ambitious generals who had concerns about the corporate army, its foreign policy and defense needs were responsible (i.e., the third coup theory), and the other was that the Punjabi military was intent on establishing Punjabi domination (1984, 110–17), which is the second coup theory.

The Pakistan military has been sufficiently politicized by past interventions and rule, for such long periods, that it might be considered, as in Brazil, "another political party." Richter (1978, 406–26) and Heeger (1977, 242–62) both suggest that Pakistan has become a praetorian state.

Pakistan, along with Sri Lanka, provides a case of ethnic dominance that is then associated with gross disaffection by minority ethnic groups. In this case, after the formation of Bangladesh, those in command accepted Punjabi domination. They would regard Punjabi domination not as a consciously chosen policy, but as an accident, "the way things are." Minorities do not perceive Punjabi domination in that light.

The Indian Case

For those wishing to study changes in ethnicity over time, there is no better test tube than India. Ethnicity is associated with religious groups (Muslims, Sikhs, Parsiis, Hindus), with linguistic groups (now largely organized in separate states), with groups of castes (such as the scheduled castes, formerly known as untouchables), with individual castes, or subcastes, and with tribes. To study the successful efforts of a caste over a large area to change both its name and classification in the *varna* system (i.e., four major divisions of caste in Hinduism: priest, warrior, merchant, peasant), between British censuses, raises the problem of considering such castes "ethnic groups" at that time. Weiner's study of the "sons of the soil" movement (1978) suggests that the linguistic determination has been increasing in importance, while Rajgopal's study of communal violence (1987) demonstrates the intensity of the religious-ethnic cleavage. The levels of violence between ethnic groups in India has always presented problems for the Government.

India inherited the bulk of the British Indian Army. The need for manpower to field six different expeditionary forces abroad during World War II, while still holding the fort in India, had led to the disappearance of the old theory of "martial races." Some Muslims opted to continue in the Indian Army, at all ranks, and the desire to show that the state was secular led to nondiscriminatory policies.

Analysis of recruitment and posting policies, as well as composition of the officer corps today are difficult. That information is not published, and scholars such as Stephen P. Cohen (1971) and Raju Thomas (1986) have not been able to ferret it out. After the Army's takeover of the Golden Temple in Amritsar, Punjab, from Sikh extremists, and the desertion of thousands of Sikh troops to defend the Temple, there was concern about the size of the Sikh contingent in the army. The official figure, cited by Thomas, was 10 percent

(1986, 83); Cohen suggested that the figure was chosen for political reasons, and that Sikhs were closer to 30 percent in the army. Even if they were close to 30 percent in 1984, the proportion might be considerably less in 1989. The desertions, plus the assassination of Prime Minister Indira Gandhi by Sikhs, probably led to a reclassification of the direction of threat, on the part of Rajiv Gandhi.

In organization, the service units, such as the Ordnance Corps and Army Service Corps are ethnically integrated. Fighting units have either of two structures. A few regiments recruit only one ethnic-linguistic class, such as the Maratha Light Infantry, or the two Sikh regiments. Other regiments have a different "class" (ethnic group) in each company or squadron. Major General Pravel states emphatically that commanders prefer single-class battalions under them, because of common mother tongue, common food habits, religion, customs, which help build esprit de corps. Class-company would be preferable to integrated (1986, 603).

Analysis of the police leaves some questions on ethnicity unanswered. India is a federal system, with linguistic states. The police as well as education are placed under state control. By and large, then, each state has an unarmed constabulary, and an armed police force, of its own ethnic-linguistic heritage, to maintain law and order and carry on other police functions.

India also has a small (by comparison) Indian Police Service. India follows the British pattern of recruiting on three levels, with differing education and training at each. Promotions between the levels are rather limited. The IPS is recruited for the top officer level, and postings are made on an All-India basis. Thus every state has some IPS officers from other states, and therefore, other ethnic groups. They are regarded as "outsiders," and will be moved on after a few years. Some states have asked that no more be sent (Bayley, 1983). The IPS, along with the Indian Administrative Service, is seen as a critical institution linking India's divergent states, languages, and ethnic groups. IPS is regarded as slightly lower in status than the IAS, but still prestigious, but it is difficult to determine the representation by state or ethnic groups.

The Centre (i.e., all India government and services) has experienced difficulties because police are under state control. On the one hand, when civil disturbances are widespread within one or several states, the state police sometimes need assistance. There have been occasions when the disturbances were linked to police action. On the other hand, when political partisan differences exist between states and the central government, or when there is a perceived political breakdown in the state, the center has felt the need to intervene with forces of its own. In addition, some border areas have been under armed insurgency, and in several areas terrorist activities have presented grave problems.

The Indian government has set up multiple paramilitary forces, each with a special mission, to cope with specific problems. The Railway Protection Force was set up in the 1880s. Another, the Central Industrial Security Force, provides protection and security in the government-operated industrial corporations. The Defense Security Guards protects ordnance factories, and military installations.

The Assam Rifles, with over 35,000 troops, battles insurgents in the northeastern frontier areas. The Indo-Tibetan Border Police tries to regulate the Indio-Tibetan border, and the Uttar Pradesh Special Police Force covers the border between Uttar Pradesh and Tibet. The Coast Guard, established only in 1976, regulates shipping and commerce in territorial waters.

More important politically are the Central Reserve Police (CRP) and Border Security Force (BSF). The CRP has its origins in British forces designed for use in the princely states. It is a mobile force, over 85,000 strong, in sixty-six battalions in 1982, used by the center in the states for internal law and order. The Border Security Force was initially set up to patrol the border, apprehend smugglers, serve as a trip wire if invaded, with the ability to defuse minor incidents, and relieve the military of functions it did not consider appropriate to its larger mission. However, the BSF, with over 85,000 troops in seventy battalions, is widely used for internal control. With the CRP and BSF available for civil disturbances, the military is brought in less frequently. After the 1984 Punjab crisis, the National Security Guards was established at a level of 5000, to be drawn from early retirees from the military, also to provide for internal order maintenance, but little is known yet of its activities.

In addition, a large Home Guards was established for use in disaster, promotion of health and welfare, protection of minorities, and for internal law and order. It is fundamentally a civil defense unit, though it has about half a million in personnel.

The existence of this many paramilitary forces is worth noting, as is the fact that the CRP and BSF each outnumber all the police forces of all the states combined. That all paramilitary together rival the army in size says something about balancing the forces.

Data on the recruitment to several of the paramilitary forces provides us with more precise knowledge of the composition of several of these paramilitary forces. Members of the Lok Sabha (Indian Parliament) and its committees were concerned in 1973 when they learned of the skew in recruitment, and made follow-up inquiries for 1980–82. The later data does show a slight increase in recruitment in states, such as Gujarat, which had had abysmally low representation. The CRPF remains, however, a northwestern force. Recruitment in the northeast is in the small border states, such as Tripura, rather than in the very large states of Bihar or West Bengal. The one southern state with more than the expected representation is Kerala. According to a former minister of state who supervised the paramilitary, the CRP has only 4 percent Muslims (India, Lok Sabha 1977).

The CRPF is a thoroughly integrated force, employing Hindi as the common language. Hindi is a north-Indian language. Yet the force is frequently employed to restore order in Telegu-speaking Andhra Pradesh, in Tamil-speaking Tamil Nadu, and in the Bombay-Ahmadabad areas in Maharashtra and Gujarat. Each unit has one CRPF commander and one local police commander to guide and direct it. The language problem, however, makes the CRPF a foreign occupying force. Even though Assam is overrepresented in the CRPF, in the 1983 ethnic riots, their small numbers may have been a factor in explaining why the Assamese turned on the CRPF when it appeared, necessitating bringing another security force.

Does the Border Security Force, which is more military in nature, have the same composition as the CRPF? Table 3.2 shows that while the BSF still resembles the CRP in its northern emphasis (plus Kerala), that recruitment from the Punjab, Jammu and

TABLE 3.1

**Comparison of Central Reserve Police Recruitment Patterns by State
1973 and 1980–1982**

Name of State	Percentage within CRPF		Over or Under Representation in Terms of State's Population 100% = Expected Recruitment	
	1973	1980–82	1973	1980–82
Southern states				
Andhra Pradesh	1.72%	2.71%	21.6%	34.13%
Tamil Nadu	1.54	3.26	20.48	43.35
Karnataka	1.62	1.90	30.28	35.51
Kerala	11.70	4.98	300.77	125.45
Middle states				
Orissa	1.34	3.56	33.50	89.00
Madhya Pradesh	2.85	2.89	38.02	38.03
Maharastra	4.47	3.46	48.58	37.61
Gujarat	.16	3.59	3.28	73.72
Northwestern states				
Uttar Pradesh	21.50	19.95	133.37	123.76
Haryana	12.31	13.58	672.68	742.08
Rajasthan	10.26	9.16	218.30	194.89
Punjab	7.41	3.55	300.00	143.72
Himachal Pradesh	4.89	2.12	776.19	336.51
Jammu & Kashmir	3.04	3.64	361.90	433.33
Delhi	.77	.81	104.05	109.46
Northeastern states				
Bihar	8.88	9.70	86.88	94.36
West Bengal	1.97	4.75	24.35	58.71
Assam	1.38	3.75	50.55	137.40
Tripura	.31	1.10	110.71	392.86
Manipur	.11	.88	57.89	463.16
Nagaland	.03	.03	33.33	33.33

Source: India, Lok Sabha. Public Accounts Committee, 133rd *Report of the Public Accounts Committee 1973–1974* (New Delhi: Lok Sabha Secretariat, April 1974), 56–57. India, Lok Sabha. Estimates Committee 1982–1983. 49th *Report on the Ministry of Home Affairs: Police (Including CBI)* (New Delhi: Lok Sabha Secretariat, 1983), 3–4.

TABLE 3.2

Comparison of CRPF and BSF Recruitment by State 1980-1982

Name of State	BSF	CRP	Over or Under Representation (100% = Expected Recruitment)	
			BSF	CRPF
Southern states				
Andhra Pradesh	.02%	2.71%	25%	34%
Tamil Nadu	2.74	3.26	36	43
Karnataka	2.19	1.90	41	36
Kerala	5.11	4.98	131	125
Middle states				
Orissa	1.12	3.56	28	89
Madhya Pradesh	7.21	2.89	95	38
Maharashtra	1.50	3.46	16	38
Gujarat	.60	3.59	12	74
Northwestern states				
Uttar Pradesh	19.30	19.95	120	123
Haryana	10.08	13.58	551	742
Rajasthan	6.62	9.16	141	195
Punjab	6.62	3.55	268	144
Himachal Pradesh	3.16	2.12	486	337
Jammu & Kashmir	6.17	3.64	735	433
Delhi	.64	.81	86	109
Northeastern states				
Bihar	9.80	9.70	95	94
West Bengal	1.47	4.75	18	59
Assam	8.65	3.75	316	137
Tripura	.95	1.10	339	393
Manipur	.38	.88	200	463
Nagaland	.17	603	189	33

Source: India, Lod Sabha. Estimates Committee. *49TH Report on the Ministry of Home Affairs: Police (Including CBI)*(New Delhi: Lok Sabha Secretariat, 1983), 3–4.

Kashmir, Madhya Pradesh and Assam are much heavier in the more military-oriented BSF than in the police-oriented CRP. Only 1 percent of the BSF are Muslims.

What about recruitment in the guerilla-fighting units, the Assam Rifles, and the Indo-Tibetan Border Police? The most striking feature of the Assam Rifles is that over half its recruitment in 1980–82 was from the one state of Uttar Pradesh. Assam contributed 8 percent, Nagaland and Himachal Pradesh 7 percent. Other states were minimally represented. The latter three states are border states; Uttar Pradesh is considered a "heartland" state even though its northern border is with Nepal and Tibet. The Indo-Tibetan Border Police has one third of its recruits from Uttar Pradesh and another 20 percent from Himachal Pradesh, and 16 percent from Haryana (all northwestern).

What the recruitment pattern suggests is the low regard for types of activities associated with military or police activities in the southern and middle states (except for Kerala). Since that pattern holds for four paramilitary forces, might we assume that the Army has difficulty recruiting in those states as well? Sikhs (Punjabis) with 10 to 30 percent in the army obviously prefer the "real" military to lesser forces, but it would seem reasonable to assume that the Army may overrepresent the same groups overrepresented in these tables.

If that assumption is correct then the data presented on the leadership of the army by Major K. C. Praval demonstrates a complex balancing policy among ethnic groups. Praval presented analysis of the Chiefs to show the "secular and non-regional character of the Army." Of the thirteen Indian chiefs, "three came from Karnataka, two each from Andhra Pradesh and Gujarat, and one each from Punjab, Bengal, Madhya Pradesh, Kashmir and Maharashtra" (1986, 609). Nine of the thirteen are from states that have very poor representation in the paramilitary forces. None are from Uttar Pradesh. Could a chief from a state with minor numbers in the army count on unquestioned support of class-based regiments, or class-company based regiments, and where the integrated regiments are nonfighting? Doubtful. Coup attempts tend to be led by lesser officers, but should one, or a few, class-based regiments, or class-company regiments, attempt a coup, other class-based regiments, et al., would have ethnic incentives to prevent their success, as would the chief.

Sanjay Gandhi's father-in-law was one of the top leaders of the BSF. Both the BSF and CRP were said to be politically loyal to Indira Gandhi, Sanjay, and perhaps still are to his widow, Maneka. When Janata came to power after the emergency ended, the topmost leader of the BSF was removed, but in promotions and transfers, the usual pattern was followed. There was no evidence that Janata tried to "repoliticize" the units in any other direction, either in the command structure or in lower echelons (Burger 1978). However, Bayley reported that when reelected, Indira Gandhi politicized the paramilitary forces in her favor (1983, 484–96). While the home states of top officials in these forces is not provided, their names are typical north Indian names.

These findings, nebulous though they may be, may indicate a paramilitary with integrated forces and north Indian leadership counterbalancing an army with class-based units whose top leadership tends to come from linguistic and ethnic groups from southern and middle, or eastern states, which provide few numbers to the Army. This is clearly unlike the pattern in Pakistan or Sri Lanka.

The Indian policy of "balance" may aid analysis and understanding of the maintenance of civilian governments, as well as the lesser levels of extralegal activities of the security forces. While the Indian police are from time to time and place to place charged with brutality, such actions are not endemic or "standard operating procedure." The security forces were said to have eliminated the Naxalite threat by extermination policies, but these actions were limited in time, and place.

Conclusion

Governments in plural states, concerned with their own survival as well as protection of the state itself, may think that adoption of policies to maximize representation of the "core" or "heartland" ethnic group from which the political leadership comes, will provide safety. The three cases here, however, indicate that such a policy opens the government to rebellion by minority groups and coups by the military. The Indian example indicates a clever and complex balancing policy, which has enabled the government to control extraordinarily high numbers of incidents involving violence of thousands while maintaining itself and protecting the state from outside enemies.

References

Bayley, David H. 1983. "Police and Political Order in India." *Asian Survey* 23 (April), 484–96.

Bingley, Capt. A. H. and Capt. A. Nicholas 1918. *Brahmans*. Calcutta: Superintendent, Government Printing, India.

Bowden, Tom. 1978. *Beyond the Limits of Law: A Comparative Study of the Police in Crisis Politics*. New York: Penguin.

Brown, John. 1982. *Policing by Multi-Racial Consent*. London: Bedford Square Press.

Burger, Angela S. 1978. "Janata, the Military and the Paramilitary." Unpublished paper presented at the Midwest Conference on Asian Affairs, Lincoln, Nebraska, October 20–21.

Burger, Angela S. 1985. "Police, Minorities and Terrorists in Sri Lanka." Unpublished paper presented at the Academy of Criminal Justice Education, Las Vegas, Nevada, April 1.

Burger, Angela S. 1987. "Policing a Communal Society: The Case of Sri Lanka." *Asian Survey* 27, n 7 (July), 822–31.

Cohen, Stephen P. 1971. *The Indian Army*. Berkeley: University of California Press.

Cohen, Stephen P. 1984. *The Pakistan Army*. Berkeley: University of California Press.

Decalo, Samuel. 1976. *Coups and Army Rule in Africa*. New Haven: Yale University Press.

De Silva, Kingsley M. 1986. *Managing Ethnic Tensions in Multi-Ethnic Societies: Sri Lanka 1880–1985*. New York: University Press.

Deutsch, Karl W. 1966. *Nationalism and Social Communication*, 2nd ed. Cambridge, Mass.: MIT Press.

Dissanayake, T. D. S. A. (n.d.). *The Agony of Sri Lanka*. Colombo: Swastika (Pvt.) Ltd.

Edelman, Murray J. 1964. *The Symbolic Uses of Politics*. Champaign-Urbana: University of Illinois Press.

Ellinwood, DeWitt C. and Cynthia H. Enloe, eds. 1981. *Ethnicity and the Military in Asia*. New Brunswick, N.J.: Transaction Books.

Enloe, Cynthia H. 1980a. *Ethnic Soldiers: State Security in Divided Societies*. Athens: The University of Georgia Press.

Enloe, Cynthia H. 1980b. *Police, Military and Ethnicity: Foundations of State Power*. New Brunswick, N.J.: Transaction Books.

First, Ruth. 1971. *Power in Africa*. Baltimore: Penguin.

Heeger, Gerald. 1977. "Politics in the Post-Military State: Some Reflections on the Pakistani Experience." *World Politics* 29, 2 (January), 242–62.

Horowitz, Donald L. 1980. *Coup Theories and Officers' Motives: Sri Lanka in Comparative Perspective.* Princeton, N.J.: Princeton University Press.

Hrebenar, Ronzld J. and Ruth K. Scott 1982. *Interest Group Politics in America.* Englewood Cliffs, N.J.: Prentice-Hall, Inc.

Huntington, Samuel P. 1968. *Political Order in Changing Societies.* New Haven: Yale University Press.

India, Lok Sabha. Estimates Committee. 1983. 49th Report on the *Ministry of Home Affairs: Police (Including CBI).* New Delhi: Lok Sabha Secretariat.

India, Lok Sabha. Public Accounts Committee. 1974. *133rd Report of the Public Accounts Committee 1973–1974.* New Delhi: Lok Sabha Secretariat.

India, Lok Sabha. 1977. *Lok Sabha Debates,* 6th series, 2nd session 4, 28 (July 13). New Delhi: Lok Sabha Secretariat.

Johnson, John J., ed. 1962. *The Role of the Military in Underdeveloped Countries.* Princeton, N.J.: Princeton University Press.

Kearney, Robert. 1978. "Language and the Rise of Tamil Separatism in Sri Lanka." *Asian Survey* 18, 5 (May), 521–34.

Leites, Nathan and Charles Wolf, Jr. 1970. *Rebellion and Authority: An Analytic Essay on Insurgent Conflicts.* Chicago: Markham.

Leys, Colin, ed. 1969. *Politics and Change in Developing Countries.* Cambridge: Cambridge University Press.

Lofchie, Michael P. 1972. "The Uganda Coup–Class Action by the Military." *Journal of Modern African Studies* 10, 1 (May), 19–35.

Qureshi, Sameel Ahmed. 1979. "An Analysis of Contemporary Pakistani Politics: Bhutto vs. the Military." *Asian Survey* 19, 9 (September).

Phadnis, Urmila. 1979. "Ethnicity and Nation-Building in South Asia: A Case Study of Sri Lanka." *India Quarterly* (July–September), 329–50.

Praval, Major K. C. 1987. *Indian Army After Independence.* New Delhi, India: Lancer International.

Rajagopal, P. R. 1987. *Communal Violence in India.* New Delhi: Uppal Publishing House.

Richter, William E. 1978. "Persistent Praetorianism: Pakistan's Third Military Regime." *Pacific Affairs* 51, 3 (Fall), 402–26.

Roberts, Michael, ed. 1979. *Collective Identities, Nationalisms and Protest in Modern Sri Lanka.* Colombo: Marga Institute.

Thomas, Raju G. C. 1986. *Indian Security Policy.* Princeton, N.J.: Princeton University Press.

Thompson, William R. 1973. "The Grievances of Military Coup Makers." Beverly Hills: Sage Professional Papers, Comparative Politics Series no. 01–047.

Veliz, Claudio, ed. 1967. *The Politics of Conformity in Latin America.* New York: Oxford University Press.

von der Mehden, Fred R. 1973. Comparative Political Violence. Englewood Cliffs, N.J.: Prentice-Hall, Inc.

Weiner, Myron. 1978. *Sons of the Soil: Migration and Ethnic Conflict in India.* Princeton, N.J.: Princeton University Press.

Wolf, Eric R. 1969. *Peasant Wars of the Twentieth Century.* New York: Harper, Row.

4

Ethnicity, Nationalism, and the Role of the Intellectual

Anya Peterson Royce

Whether one speaks in terms of the cultural properties of nationalism or the political perquisites of the state, the role of the intellectual in multiethnic populations is a critical one. The intellectual, whether writer, artist, or politician, is the one who articulates grievances, formulates nationalistic statements, and translates popular belief into a coherent ideology (Royce 1982, 106). It is the same individual who mediates local, ethnic, regional political, and economic concerns between local constituencies and the state. This role becomes even more significant in contexts where the state, rather than being a promoter of equality, functions as a distributor of privilege and a promoter of uneven development among regions, classes, and ethnic groups (Brass 1985, 3).

Throughout most of its history, Mexico, a nation of fluent ethnic diversity, has been a distributor of privilege. This is not to say that, confronted by threats from the outside world, it has not demonstrated a vital and coherent unity. Nor that it has been unsuccessful at generating moments of genuine nationalistic feeling across its distinctive classes and ethnic groups. These have been, however, momentary crystallizations of feeling that dissipate in the reality of day-to-day existence where one group's gain is another's loss.

103

The Zapotec of the Isthmus of Tehuantepec, especially those of the city of Juchitan, offer excellent material for a discussion of the role of intellectuals in mediating local, primarily ethnic concerns and the political dispensations of privilege on the part of the nation.

After Nahuatl and Maya speakers, the Zapotec represent the third largest indigenous group in Mexico. Of all the indigenous peoples, the Isthmus Zapotec have been the most successful in achieving a firm economic position within both the local and national contexts while maintaining a strong presence as Indians within a largely non-Indian nation. Rejecting a purely local identity, they have sought and won positions of political prominence at the regional and national levels. This appetite for participating as Indians within the larger Mexican sphere has characterized them throughout all of their recorded history. Recently, however, the emergence of the COCEI (Coalición de campesinos, obreros y estudiantes del Istmo [farmers, worker, students and independents]) as a major opposition party to PRI (Partido de la Revolución Institutional) has catapulted them onto the international scene. Newspapers, television documentaries, books, and magazines have carried the story of COCEI around the world.

COCEI and other populist parties, despite their broad base among farmers and workers, have been defined at crucial moments by Zapotec intellectuals. Carlos Monsivais and Rafael Doniz described the meeting of 4 August 1983 in which Cesar Agusto Carrasco G. was installed as leader of the Ayuntamiento Popular of Juchitan:

> Toda la información, leida a saltos y del modo discontinuo a que nos acostumbra la prensa nacional, no previene para esta vision fulgurante de un pueblo volcado en la adhesion, en la corporeización de lemas, rechazos y aceptaciones. Se inicia el mítin. Se pasa lista a los miembros del presidium: el escritor Fernando Benitez, la senora Rosario Ibarra de Piedra, del Frente Nacional contra la Represión, el rector de la universidad Autónoma de Guerrero, Enrique Gonzalez Ruiz, el antropólogo Arturo Warman, los pintores Francisco Toledo y Felipe Ehrenberg, el poeta Oscar Oliva. Por primera vez en mucho tiempo, se oye gritar en una plaza pública "Vivan los intelectuales! Vivan los artistas!" (16)[1]

Juchitan has always depended on the work and recognition of its intellectuals and its artists for its status as a special city, a preeminently Zapotec city. The creation of a unique Zapotec style began in earnest in the last half of the nineteenth century when the construction of the trans-Isthmian railroad brought a new kind of economic opportunity to the cities along its route. Throughout its history, Juchitan based its economy on the combination of agriculture and fishing and local and regional marketing. The early entry into commercial activity allowed the Juchitecos to accumulate both property and capital. Prior to the mid-nineteenth century, property was primarily agricultural land and capital took mainly the form of gold jewelry. The coming of the railroad provided Juchiteco men the opportunity for wage labor in addition to their traditional roles as farmers and fishermen. More importantly, it stimulated new entrepreneurial activity on the part of both women and men. Controlling as they did the property within the city, Juchitecos invested in small businesses—hardware stores, cantinas, restaurants, dry goods stores, and so forth, that served the transient population attracted by the railroad. Serving as fluid capital, gold became transformed into income property (Royce 1981).

The coming together of an augmented economy and the influx of non-Zapotec gave rise to the elaboration of Zapotec style. On the objective or observable side of this style were ranged the elements of dress, language, music, dance, food, and fiestas. These were complemented by fundamental Zapotec values, the most important of which is embodied in the word *guendalisaa,* meaning the sense of kinship, relatedness, and cooperation.

Two points are important to make in the discussion of Zapotec style. One is that it is eclectic and flexible; the second is that it was developed and is maintained by the cultural and economic elite. Taking the observable elements of style in turn, we are confronted by the melding of cultural elements that they represent. Zapotec dress, while based on a ubiquitous indigenous model, represents the influence of Philippine embroidered silk and French ball gowns. The former dates from the period when Spain was engaged in the silk trade, the latter from the period in the late nineteenth century when Maximilian and Carlota brought the French court and customs to Mexico. Juchitan was not immune to the French influence both because there was a French garrison in nearby Ixtepec and because Porfirio Diaz brought the still-powerful French influence with him when he visited his Zapotec mistress in Tehuantepec.

Zapotec music and dance draws heavily upon Spanish tradition. The music, with the exception of the indigenous flute and drum, follows Spanish melodic patterns and uses Spanish and generally European instrumentation. The words to these Spanish melodies are frequently Zapotec, however. The dance, *son,* is an amalgamation of a fandango and a waltz. The woman's part in particular shows nothing of the more typical Mexican Indian *zapateado* pattern or posture.

The food ranges from Isthmian specialities of armadillo, iguana, turtle eggs, and shrimp to crustless chicken sandwiches and chocolate cakes.

Language is one of the most important markers of identity and undergoes periodic cleansings of Spanish loanwords. Over 75 percent of the population of Juchitan is bilingual in Zapotec and Spanish but, in the game of ethnic politics, Zapotec holds sway. An active literary movement began in the 1930s and a journal devoted to it, *Neza* (The Road) sprang into existence, the product of a band of Juchiteco writers living in Mexico City. After a gap in publication, it reemerged as *Neza Cubi* (The New Road). It has been joined by the successful *Guchachi'reza* (The Split Iguana) published in Juchitan and featuring the work of local writers and artists.

Visual art was a relative latecomer in terms of a Zapotec identity but it has flourished since the 1950s. The best-known artists include Damaciano Orozco whose famous drawings now provide big business for a burgeoning T-shirt industry and Francisco Toledo, an artist of international reputation who has recently established a gallery and a museum in Oaxaca City. Images out of Zapotec legend and myth abound in Toledo's work—iguanas, toads, the *bere lele* (a kind of water ouzel), women who are part bird, part toad. These artists have influenced a new generation of young artists who are producing first-class work that is still distinctively Zapotec in content.

The institution that nominally oversees the cultural activity of the city is the Casa de la Cultura (House of Culture). It produces publications by the dozens, posters, radio programs; it sponsors performances of music and dance and lectures; it provides classes in drawing, the Zapotec language, music and dance; it houses a museum with rotating exhibits and a permanent collection of pre-Columbian artifacts; it has the only public library in the city and a collection specializing in the Isthmus. The Casa de la Cultura (in Zapotec *Lidxi guendabianni*) has waxed and waned in its role of purveyor of Zapotec culture. For the most part, this has had to do with the playing out of local politics and the relationships between families. Under the last municipal administration, for example, it has been relegated to a minor role while the authorities have taken the burden of promoting Zapotec culture onto themselves.

The success of the current municipal government and that of the COCEI government between 1980–83 in promoting a vital Zapotec identity has been limited. Both of those bodies have consciously sought the participation of that segment traditionally alienated from the political process except as dependents of the old families —the subsistence farmers, the fishermen, the unskilled workers. It is a laudable political aim but in doing so they have just as consciously rejected the participation of the old families whose elite status can be traced back to the earliest extant parish records (1743).

While numerically less important today, these families are essential to the definition and presentation of Zapotec identity. For every component, from language to dress to dance and music, they are the expert guardians and promoters. It is they, not the campesino or the fisherman, who have had the wherewithal, the knowledge and the inclination to take the bare elements of Zapotec identity and elaborate them into a style of great prestige.

The new lower class participants in the political process share many of the defining features—they speak Zapotec; they eat the indigenous fare; they wear a version of the traditional dress. They do so, however, not as a matter of choice but out of necessity. When these features are displayed to signal a preferred identity, they assume a shape that goes far beyond that dictated by necessity. The language then shines in all its power—it becomes poetical; it plays with tone and homophones to create sophisticated puns and double entendres; it creates rousing and complex political speeches. Traditional foods are consumed alongside items of international cuisine. The local costume is commissioned and its cost goes well beyond the budget of a lower class family. The aesthetics of dance and music are hotly debated and anything that does not adhere to those standards is roundly criticized.

Zapotec style, in its fullest form, requires leisure, money, and knowledge. The old elite have these three essential ingredients. While consumers of all that the Western world has to offer, they nonetheless maintain a commitment to a Zapotec identity.

Those families and within their ranks, the writers, poets, intellectuals, have provided the leadership for the city. It is they, often in collaboration with political figures not of their ranks, who have propelled the image of Juchitan beyond the boundaries of the city and the region. And it is they who have articulated the images of the world beyond to the bulk of the city's population. It is precisely this mediating function that has allowed Juchitecos to incorporate those aspects of non-Zapotec culture in a positive fashion. The result has been a bicultural stance that gives strength to both traditions.

In one of the region's earliest published manifestos, *Vindicación de la Conducta Política de los Tehuantepecanos* (Oaxaca, 1847), the citizens of Tehuantepec and Juchitan protested the imposition of an unpopular and unsympathetic governor by the state militia. It is a remarkable document for the logic and erudition of its argument. It quotes sections of the federal constitution in order to demonstrate the illegality of the imposed state government and the corresponding legality of the local opposition. It quotes from de Toqueville and Montesquieu on democracy and the legitimacy of authority. In one telling passage, the authors describe the governor, Don Joaquin García, as a man without culture and without learning.

This 1847 manifesto was neither the first time nor the last that Juchiteco intellectuals would find themselves on an opposition course to those in power at levels outside the Isthmus of Tehuantepec. It does set out the preferred tactic of the moral high ground based on a respect for law and learning.

Another common avenue for local nationalism was and is local history. One of the earliest, locally authored and widely distributed of this genre is Arcadio G. Molina's 1911 *Historia de Tehuantepec, San Blas, Shihui y Juchitán en la Intervención Francesa en 1864.*

Molina was the preceptor and a teacher at the school in San Blas. While a barrio of Tehuantepec, San Blas identified itself closely with Juchitan. Its population was primarily from Juchitan and, while the rest of Tehuantepec has gradually abandoned Zapotec as a language, the Blasenos maintain it as well as other aspects of Zapotec style.

As in the 1847 manifesto, Molina argues for the devotion of the local citizenry to Mexico as a nation. He documents in great detail the fratricidal battles between those from San Blas, San Pedro Shihui and Juchitan under the direction of Colonel Francisco Cortes and the local traitors led by Remigio Toledo. The battle of 5 September 1866 in which Cortes' ragtag army defeated the French army with its contingent of tehuanos under Toledo takes its place in Molina's account as one of many battles during that period of the French intervention. That battle has, however, assumed epic proportions for contemporary Juchitecos who celebrate it every 5th of September with speeches, poetry contests, bullfights, and a dance. The two French cannon, abandoned by the fleeing army, are the focal point of a monumental sculpture at the entrance to the city. It is an occasion to applaud the loyalty of the Juchitecos to Mexico and to remind the citizenry of the traitorous acts of those tehuanos who followed Toledo. The battle is also the subject of a *corrido* (narrative ballad), *5 de Septiembre,* written in Zapotec by Luis Sanchez (cf. *Corridos del Istmo,* Juchitan: Casa de la Cultura, n.d.).

Molina published other works equally nationalistic *(The Zapotec nation)* in content — a Zapotec grammar and syllabary, an account of Zapotec songs with words and music, a work called the *Rose of Love* for young people, and left a number of unpublished works as well. He was a firm believer in the importance of biculturalism and education. Almost all his works appear in both Zapotec and Spanish and he wrote a number of self-help books on conversation, writing, grammar, mathematics, anthropology, the solar system, and geometry. As we shall see, the pattern set by Molina has been followed by each succeeding generation of Zapotec intellectuals.

The love of learning and advancement through education has deep roots in this Zapotec community where neither was easy to achieve. One nineteenth century figure who exemplifies the desire to excel in the national arena without abandoning his Zapotec roots is Rosendo Pineda. He was born in 1851, the natural son of Teofilo Delarbre, a French engineer, and Cornelia Pineda, a Juchiteca. Opportunities for schooling beyond the primary level were limited in the Isthmus. Rosendo had exhausted them when Porfirio Diaz, then president of the Republic, visited Juchitan in the aftermath of the battle of the 5th of September 1866. As a reward for the support of Juchitan in that battle, Diaz chose six young Juchitecos to be educated in Mexico City and in Oaxaca. Rosendo Pineda was one of the three who went to the Instituto de Ciencias y Artes del Estado in Oaxaca. Under the supervision of Felix Diaz, governor of the state and brother of the president, Rosendo completed a law degree. He had already distinguished himself as a poet and an orator, talents that Juchitecos seemed to have in abundance.

On the basis of his continuing ties with the city of his birth, Rosendo was elected Diputado Federal representing Juchitan in the national assembly. This was the first of many positions he was to hold. He became an intimate of Porfirio Diaz holding the title of Chief of the Scientific Party. He was known in that role as the "Jefe del Diamante" (Diamond Chief). Diaz and all the intellectuals who surrounded him were advocates of French positivism, hence the prominence of the Partido Cientifico. It was a philosophy that extolled the virtues of reason and Diaz' passionate belief in it is one factor in his desire to remain in power. Despite the fact that he assumed the presidency committed to the notion that there should be no reelection, he stayed in power for thirty years believing that he and his advisors were the best suited to run the nation on a rational basis. Of his brilliant cabinet, Rosendo was a star and one of the few who exerted a balancing force. His "Jefe del Diamante" appelation was indicative of this role. The source of it comes from the use of diamond balance wheels in watchmaking that provide the most delicate balance possible.

That character and the basic liberal mentality that has characterized Juchitecos throughout their history gradually left him more and more disenchanted with Diaz who, for Rosendo, had abandoned the liberal ideology that had swept him into office in exchange for the power of a dictator. When Diaz asked his advice on the eve of being elected for yet another term, Rosendo told him that the best thing he could do would be to decline the nomination. When Diaz fell and Francisco Madero came into power, Rosendo was invited to join the maderistas. Though sympathetic to the revolutionary ideology of that party, Rosendo refused, remaining loyal to his own sense of duty. It exemplifies the kind of independence of thought and action that is so characteristic of Zapotec intellectuals. He died in September of 1914, having seen Madero brutally assassinated in 1913 and his country plunged into an internecine revolution that would pit Mexican against Mexican and that would divide his own beloved city.

His fate was kinder than that of another Juchiteco intellectual, Adolfo C. Gurrión, who would be killed in part for his attempt to heal the devisiveness in Juchitan. Gurrión was born in 1879 of humble parents. Through the sacrifice of parents and siblings, Gurrión graduated from the Escuela Normal para Profesores (the Normal School for Teachers) in Oaxaca in 1902. Like Juchitecos before and after, Gurrion, in his position as a writer for *El Estandarte* of Oaxaca, took a position against the reelection of Governor Martín Gonzalez. When Porfirio Diaz imposed Emilio Pimental as governor, Gurrión spoke against that act because it defied the laws of the nation. His liberal beliefs took him beyond state and local politics when he became the Oaxaca correspondent for *Regeneración,* the revolutionary newspaper published in St. Louis by the Flores Magon brothers.

Because of his activities, Gurrión was persecuted by Pimental and his followers. Having returned to the Isthmus in 1905, he was unable to find work because of Pimental's influence and, in fact, was arrested in Tehuantepec by one of Pimental's supporters. He returned to Oaxaca where he and a fellow istmeño, Plutarco Gallegos, published *La Semecracia,* a newspaper that spoke out against corruption. His fiery pieces once again aroused the ire of Pimental who imprisoned him in Oaxaca. After long court battles, Gurrión was finally released and went to Tepic where he was an influential member of its literary society. In 1908 he was named inspector of the Zona Escolar in the southern district of Baja California and for the next several years devoted himself to improving the educational climate throughout Mexico.

In the pattern typical for Zapotec intellectuals, Gurrión was elected Diputado Propietario for the District of Juchitan in 1912. And also in the pattern, the election was contested by other Juchitecos. His supporters among the Madero followers in Mexico dominated the dispute. In 1913, impelled by a desire to heal the wounds caused by bitter factionalism, he came to Juchitan to urge peace and a common cause between the Reds and the Greens. Neither side was at a point to listen to reason and Gurrión managed to return alive to Mexico City despite attempts to assassinate him.

Like many Madero supporters, Gurrión was left without a leader in 1913 when Madero and Pino Suarez were killed. He had made up his mind to go north and join the forces of Carranza in August of that year but returned to Juchitan to see his mother. It was a fatal decision. He was arrested in Juchitan and was shot by his escort on the way from San Jerónimo to Chihuitan. A year later, his family and friends had his body exhumed in Chihuitan and brought back to Juchitan. He was buried in a ceremony that brought the entire city out in mourning (cf. Gurrión 1987).

The Zapotec language, far from losing its importance as a defining feature of Zapotec identity, has been even more consciously elaborated as other indigenous languages disappear under the growing domination of Spanish. Its rhetorical use for speechmaking has long been a strategy of intellectuals and politicians. It has also, however, been recognized as a talent to be cultivated among the population in general. One of the oldest uses of carefully crafted Zapotec has been the speeches on the occasions of marriages given by those repositories of elegant Zapotec, the xuanna' (the person in charge of delivering the sermon and the nuptial benediction). Xuaana' are in particular demand even today by those who want a traditional wedding.

Another avenue for showing one's command of the language is the verbal punning engaged in by married women. Zapotec as a tonal language with different vowel lengths and homophones is well suited for punning. Women make use of these features as well as incorporating bilingual puns. This kind of verbal facility brings status to the women who practice it and there is a well-defined aesthetic that governs it.

In the 1930s Zapotec language and culture was extolled in the form of a regularly published journal called *Neza* (The Road). It was published by the Sociedad Nueva de Estudiantes Juchitecas in Mexico City, first on a monthly basis under the direction of Andres Henestrosa then bimonthly under Gabriel Lopez Chiñas. The first issue under Lopez Chiñas laid out the goals of the journal—to make available to Spanish-speakers the unique contributions of Zapotec history and culture. Because the journal also had a large local readership and because its writers wanted the Zapotec language to be more widely appreciated, every issue had its share of pieces in Zapotec, from poetry to legend.

Once again, we can see the attachment to local culture combined with the need to promote it beyond the local setting. At the same time, Lopez Chiñas strikes a note already familiar to us from the examples of Gurrión and Pineda, men who spoke out and remained true to their beliefs even at great cost. After a quotation from Father Gay that praises the importance of history and before the short Spanish forward comes a page that has the following Zapotec phrase: *"Zaa guiniccalii; qui zialu."* A free translation of this is "it does not matter that they speak ill of you; you will not dissolve." It sums up what has always been Juchitan's political strategy. As a city, Juchitan regards itself as a fiercely loyal contributor to the Mexican nation (when that nation has been on the correct path). Its people are used to others speaking ill of them, questioning their motives, distorting what they have done. And yet, Juchitan and its Zapotec culture have survived, an extraordinary accomplishment in the larger Mexican context where most Indian cultures are marginal.

While the stated mission was to promote a wider understanding of Zapotec culture, the students who organized and wrote the early *Neza* did not avoid what were political issues. They formed an Academy of the Zapotec Language to rationalize the alphabet and to encourage literacy; they wrote about the problems of a Juchitan confronting commercialization and industrialization; they took local authorities to task for providing inadequate facilities for the education of girls; they spoke of the dangers of malaria; they succeeded in getting ten scholarships to an industrial school in Mexico City which they offered to needy children from Juchitan.

Local attitudes toward the two men who were the earliest promoters of the journal reflect very strongly held Zapotec principles.

Juchitecos acknowledge the recognition that Henestrosa brought to Zapotec culture through his publications but they see it as indirect. They regarded his preference for living in Mexico and in France as an indication that he had forgone his Zapotec roots for the attraction of a life on the international literary circuit. Lopez Chiñas, on the other hand, was beloved by the Juchitecos throughout his life and, even now, in death where his tomb attracts Juchitecos who include it on their weekly visits to the tombs of relatives. However lauded he was, he never forgot Juchitan.

Neza reappeared in 1968 as *Neza Cubi* with the subtitle *Revista Literaria y de Cultura.* It was still published in Mexico City and its original vision remained. While Gabriel Lopez Chiñas contributed articles and poems as well as money, the journal was now under the direction of Macario Matus and Victor de la Cruz Perez.

The first issue carried a poem from the editors that sets out a problem and the direction Juchitan must take to address it. Juchitecos have lost the way, become confused, fallen into deviseness. The solution is crystallized in the last lines of the poem:

> Es necesario entonces
> un alto en nuestra marcha.
> Preguntarnos por donde
> y como caminaron los abuelos.
> Buscar el eco de sus voces
> dispersas por el viento.
> Buscar las huellas que dejaron
> y reconstruirlas
> para poder seguir la ruta
> y despues caminar, hermanos,
> los Zapotecas
> hacia la senda iluminada del progreso.
> Salud, hermanos y padres.[2]

The message is clear and it is the same one that Juchitan has followed for as long as anyone's memory can document: the strength of Zapotec culture lies in its ability to remember the achievements of previous generations. It is a message that embraces the notion of progress and change but one that cautions against abandoning the brilliance of the past.

It is difficult to give concrete figures on the readership, either for

Neza Cubi or for *Guchachi' reza.* The former was available from the beginning in Mexico City and in the isthmian cities of Juchitan, Espinal, Tehuantepec, Salina Cruz, Ixtepec, and across the Isthmus in Miniatitlan. The latter has been available primarily in Juchitan. In recent years, however, it has featured articles on the political scene, sometimes commissioned from well-known writers and that has increased its visibility. Both publications are common in the homes of middle- and upper-class Zapotec. Juchitecos living in Oaxaca and Mexico City also buy issues as they are published. The painter Francisco Toledo sells through local individuals a packet of journal issues and monographs on the Zapotec of the Isthmus so that latecomers to Zapotec culture can read those works that have been important in defining the nature of Zapotec history, society and culture. The packet is expensive, well beyond the means of most Juchitecos.

The written word, however, is just one of many avenues for the expression of Zapotec identity. The same messages have been given through verbal elaborations, music and song, dance, and visual art. And those media are accessible to everyone.

It is difficult to imagine a Juchiteco past childhood who does not know the name and the music of Cenobio Lopez Lena. Don Cenobio was a blind, self-taught musician whose virtuosity on the Isthmus variant of the flute brought him renown far beyond the confines of his native city. As important as his musicianship were his compositions that embodied in music fundamental aspects of Zapotec culture. The *bere lele* (alcarabán in Spanish, water ouzel in English) is a multivocalic symbol for the Zapotec, immortalized in poetry, the visual arts, and in at least one composition by Don Cenobio that mimics the bird's song. The *bere lele* is a bird whose characteristics mirror those qualities that the Zapotec value most. It is part wild and part domestic; it is fiercely loyal to those to whom it gives its affection; it languishes when it is removed from its native land. I witnessed just those qualities some years ago when a friend lay dying. Don Silayn was a frail old man who had outlived all but a daughter-in-law who lived across the isthmus in Coatzacoalcos. His constant companion was a *bere lele.* He contracted pneumonia and lay in the altar room of his house for five days, the focus of a constant stream of friends. The *bere lele* guarded his bed refusing to eat or to drink. When he died, it broke into a keening song that sent chills through all of us who were there and those who had resigned themselves to Don Silayn's death found themselves nonetheless moved to tears by the despair of the bird. It took its place under the bier set up in front of the house altar still refusing the solicitations of everyone. The daughter-in-law took it with her to Coatzacoalcos where it died a scant few weeks after its master. It is that song that Don Cenobio captured. The playing of it brings out all the associations that Juchitecos have, reminding them of the unchanging values of Zapotec society.

While corridos, those songs that immortalize important bits of history, have not been the major mode of commentary in Juchitan, their scarcity has been amply compensated for by a strong song tradition in both Zapotec and Spanish. Unlike the flute and drum tradition, the melodic lines and instrumentation are European. The sentiments and the language, however, are Zapotec and the songs are the property of humble and prosperous alike. Some of the local groups have achieved recording success at the national level which has underscored the Zapotec sense of the value of their identity.

Dance has long been an integral component of Zapotec identity and is displayed with pride each summer at the Guelaguetza in Oaxaca City. This is a gathering of groups representing all the indigenous peoples of Oaxaca who perform their distinctive dances for crowds numbering in the thousands on two successive Mondays in July. The Zapotec delegation has traditionally been the last but one in recognition of the exceptional style of its music and dance (the last group is a professional troupe from Oaxaca City).

Dance is an indispensable part of local celebrations as well, a fact reified in the Zapotec word *saa* which means music, dance, and fiesta. While everyone dances, not everyone does so in accordance with the aesthetic standards of the traditional style. This ability has been the domain of the elite families. In the past, it has been those families who have set the standards and provided the dancers who perform outside the region. One of the by-products of the increased political force of the COCEI has been the neglect of these families in favor of the larger mass of the population. This has had the effect of promoting less able dancers. That they represent the city now to the outside world is a source of concern for the old families. It is also recognized as a problem by the political leadership who have been its authors, cognizant as they are of the very real political value of a vibrant Zapotec identity.

The visual arts have become increasingly important as vehicles for the expression of Zapotec identity. That this has been a strategy at the national level is apparent to anyone familiar with the great Mexican muralists Diego Rivera and David Siquieros. We could go back even further to the rich inventories of indigenous culture represented in the pre-Colombian codices, some aspects of which have been incorporated in contemporary textiles and pottery to represent a link with the glories of the indigenous past.

Francisco Toledo is probably the best known of the Zapotec painters. His international reputation has made it impossible for most Juchitecos to buy his work in today's market. He has periodic expositions in the Casa de la Cultura in Juchitan, however, and has recently opened a museum in Oaxaca City where one can see his work and the work of other artists both native, Mexican and international. He has also encouraged younger Juchiteco artists many of whom are superb technicians and some of whom will surely establish reputations far beyond the region.

Although Toledo does not reside in Juchitan, he maintains an active interest in the affairs of his native city and is regarded by Juchitecos with pride as someone who carries their message to the widest possible audience. His Ediciones Toledo is an outlet for local writers as well as a vehicle for the resurrection of important documents of Zapotec intellect that have fallen into obscurity.

One medium that has attained wide currency in the last ten years is that of photography. The Casa de la Cultura has published a collection of photographs taken in Juchitan in the 1930s by Sotero Constantino Jimenez whose Fotoestudio Jimenez captured for posterity much of the local population. Individual Zapotec have taken advantage of the photograph since it became available as a way of recording important events and the images of family members. When cameras became a consumer good, the snapshot soon reached endemic proportions. The publication of photographs from the Jimenez studio as a book and in the form of postcards signifies an importance beyond that of individual families. It is yet another voice of Juchitan to the world outside the city and the region. There are other collections of photographs, those documenting the COCEI and one on the women of Juchitan, that are national bestsellers. On the local level, many of these photographs have been exhibited in the rooms of the Casa de la Cultura.

Whatever the medium of expression, the product and its author have to meet the exacting standards of the Juchitecos. A common thread running through all the examples I have given is the respect for the cultured individual. *Binni guendabianni,* the Zapotec gloss, is one of the highest accolades and, conversely, to be described as "without culture" one of the most devastating insults. "Culture" is not exclusively the property of those individuals who have had formal education. It means more broadly someone who knows, either through formal training or through experience and native talent. General Heliodoro Charis Castro is a wonderful example. Charis was born the son of a man who supported his family by hunting and selling iguanas. He was monolingual in Zapotec for most of his youth and had no formal schooling until he joined the revolutionary army. Through force of personality and his ability to think through complicated political and military strategies, he became a general in the Mexican army. He was Juchitan's leader for thirty years during which he articulated the needs of his city to the nation and got from that nation what Juchitan desperately needed. His highest priorities were schools, then clinics, bridges and basic infrastructure necessary for any city making its way in the modern world. He was and is regarded twenty-five years after his death as a man of culture, "un hombre preparado."

When Juchitecos have rejected leaders, one of the paramount factors has been their lack of culture, of preparation. When they have supported leaders who have spoken for them at the highest levels, it is because they have acknowledged them as cultured. Rosendo Pineda and Heliodoro Charis are but two examples.

The other factor which is crucial in getting the support of the people of Juchitan is whether or not an individual is seen as a Juchiteco. That means not merely the artifact of birth which is necessary but not sufficient. It means that that person understands Zapotec culture and is prepared to be its spokesperson. The rhetoric surrounding the 1989 municipal elections illustrates both these factors. In the summer, PRI announced that its candidate would be Jose Ramon Caraveo Molina. That announcement led to a march of some three thousand Juchitecos, most of them staunch priistas, denouncing Caraveo's selection. Nominally, Caraveo was claimed as a relative of the local Lopez Lena family. He was seen, however, as an intruder from Chihuahua. The local papers went further asking readers to reflect on what the Lopez Lena family had ever done for Juchitan, characterizing the family as commercial entrepreneurs who cared only for their own profits and not for the city, as a family that sneered at local customs and people. Caraveo was seen at best as an outsider and at worst as a member of a family that held Juchitan in contempt. Critics have also characterized him as a man of no culture.

That these notions of who is and is not an accepted political leader run deep in Juchitan is exemplified by the political campaign of Manuel Musalem Santiago (Tarú) in 1971. Tarú was the son of Lebanese immigrants to Juchitan and one of the old Zapotec families. He had been educated outside the city and had lived for some years in Guadalajara. Despite what might have been negative factors in his background, he came into the municipal presidency with the popular support of most of the city. Unlike his PRI opponent who was considered an outsider (even though he was born in the District of Juchitan), Tarú manipulated Zapotec identity. He gave rousing speeches in Zapotec. He used his connections with the old monied commercial and landed families, the newly rich entrepreneurs, and the campesinos. He created a platform of Juchitan for the Juchitecos. He was swept into office on a tide of popular sentiment and his campaign represented one of the first successful moves away from PRI since its establishment as *the* party of Mexico.

Tarú was removed from office before the end of his presidency by means of long-practiced PRI political tactics. His removal illustrates one of the difficulties that any spokesperson for Juchitan, whether intellectual or political, faces. One of the great strengths of Juchitan has been its promotion of a powerful regional identity. This is also its greatest weakness. The natural inclination of most Juchitecos has always been toward localism or the "patria chica." Leaders have to recognize this at the same time that they must understand and support national concerns if they are to be successful in that arena. In earlier times, Juchiteco leaders could make the balance. Mexico was developing as a nation and it took its leaders from those individuals who could think and fight regardless of class or ethnic origin. Charis is perhaps the best example of this. The national stamp of approval for "indigenismo" (Indianness) in the thirties and pre-war forties meant that Zapotec leaders did not have to abandon their native identity to be accepted at the state and national levels.

The political and cultural climate has changed, however, and local would-be leaders are often forced to choose between what are often quite different strategies and concerns. It is a new bureaucracy in which force of personality and "personalismo" are increasingly less effective in a system that distributes the power of leadership among elites trained in technical specialities in settings far removed from the experience of most of Mexico's people.

Zapotec intellectuals must be mediators in the most fundamental sense of the word, translating to the local scene the national ideology and serving, in Emerson's words, as the "crystallizing center" for the sometimes inchoate feelings of the Juchitecos (1960, 44). Theirs has always been an activist role rather than a more passive assessing and reporting of values.[3] They, like all Juchitecos, have thrown themselves passionately into their particular role. That they are so frequently at loggerheads with state and national levels and at times with their own city has as much to do with this style of thinking as is does with the issues themselves.

The present situation is volatile. The mutability is not new. What will demand accommodation is the very different nature of the national context. The tightrope that Zapotec intellectuals have always walked is more slippery now than ever before. Perhaps the qualities outlined to me last April by Cesar Agusto Carrasco Gonzalez, a former municipal leader and an intellectual, will become even more important. To understand and resolve issues, he said, one must have a very cold head and a very ardent heart.

The Juchitecos are unshaken in their belief that Juchitan can progress while remaining fundamentally a Zapotec city. What is certain is that, whatever the shape of leadership may be, if it is to last more than the brief span of individual influence, the values that have guided the Zapotec throughout their history will have the lion's share in its creation.

My association with the Zapotec of Juchitan began in 1967. This paper reflects much of what I have come to understand of Zapotec values in the intervening years. Profa. Delia Ramirez Fuentes has been a most able guide as well as a wonderful friend. On my last visit in April of 1989, the following individuals were generous with their time and reflections, especially with regard to political processes: Lic. Teodoro Altamirano, Lic. Cesar Agusto Carrasco Gonzalez, Dip. Enrique Martinez Hinojosa, Prof. Abel Trejo, Lic. Felipe Martinez. My family, Doña Rosinda Fuentes de Ramirez, Jesus Ramirez Escudero, Vicente Fuentes Pineda and the rest of the extended household, as always, provided a loving home and stimulating conversation. My husband, Ronald R. Royce, with his intimate knowledge of Zapotec language and ethnography, let my imagination roam where appropriate and kept it in check when it defied the evidence.

Notes

1. "All the information, read in fits and starts as we are accustomed to with the national press, did not prevent this image of a town charged with the spirit of closeness discussing problems, denials and acceptances. The meeting began. A list of members of the presidium was passed: the writer Fernando Benitez, Senora Rosario Ibarra de Piedra of the National Front against Repression, the Rector of the Autonomous University of Guerrero, Enrique Gonzalez Ruiz, the anthropologist Arturo Warman, the painters Francisco Toledo and Felipe Ehrenberg, the poet Oscar Oliva. For the first time in a long time, one heard in a public plaza the cry "Long Live the intellectuals! Long Live the artists!"

2.
> A stop along the way
> is necessary then.
> To ask ourselves where and how
> our ancestors walked.
> To find the echo of their voices
> dispersed by the wind.
> To look for the footsteps they left
> and to reconstruct them
> in order to follow the path
> and then to walk, brothers,
> the Zapotec
> toward the illuminated path of progress
> Greetings, brothers and fathers.

3. It is interesting here to speculate about the relationship of the Zapotec word for culture/intellect, *guendabianni,* and the kind of activism practiced by intellectuals. The phrase *bianni* means "light." The addition of the prefix *guenda* gives the word the meaning of making or creating light.

References

Brass, Paul, ed. 1985. *Ethnic Groups and the State*. New Jersey: Barnes & Noble.

Casa de la Cultura. nd. *Corridos del Istmo*. Juchitan.

Emerson, Rupert. 1960. *From Empire to Nation: The Rise to Self-Assertion of Asian and African Peoples*. Cambridge, Mass.: Harvard University Press.

Gurrión, Adolfo. 1987. *Biografía de Adolfo C. Gurrión*. Oaxaca: Ediciones Toledo.

Molina, Arcadio G. 1911. *Historia de Tehuantepec, San Blas, Shihui y Juchitan*. Oaxaca: Tip. de San German Hermanos.

Royce, Anya Peterson. 1981. "Isthmus Zapotec Households: Economic Responses to Scarcity and Abundance." *Urban Anthropology* 10 (3):269–86.

———. 1982. *Ethnic Identity: Strategies of Diversity*. Bloomington: Indiana University Press.

Tehuantepecanos, Los. 1847. *Vindicación de la Conducta Política de los Tehuantepecanos*. Oaxaca: Imprenta de Juan B. Carriedo.

<h1 style="text-align:center">5</h1>

Ethnicity and the State in Northern Ireland

Joan Vincent

It seems likely that no political unit has ever been so misunderstood, or so badly misrepresented, as the six counties that make up Northern Ireland. Some political scientists, who should surely know better, have even compared the civil unrest currently experienced there with ethnic and religious strife in Cyprus, Lebanon, or Sri Lanka. Yet Northern Ireland is not a state; it is a component part, a province or, at best, a region within the monarchical state of the United Kingdom of Great Britain and Northern Ireland. Minimally, therefore, the United Kingdom context of its regional politics must be retained and, in this era of submerged nationalisms and ethnic resurgences throughout Europe and the Soviet Union, the time is ripe to consider ethnicity in Northern Ireland in relation to the British state.

A caveat is in order, however. In recent months, cursory analyses have been made of Azerbaijan as the Soviet Union's Northern Ireland. This might suggest to the uninitiated that the present conflict in Northern Ireland revolves around ethnic violence. It does not. A more apt parallel in the very recent troubled history of Eastern Europe might be the Soviet republic of Lithuania or the Ukraine—except that their origins lie in settlements following World War II, whereas that of Northern Ireland lies in those re-

123

shaping Europe after World War I. Inasmuch as all came about with the break up of empires, they have in common an ethnic dimension.

Northern Ireland came into being as a temporary measure on the occasion of the secession of southern Ireland from the United Kingdom of Great Britain and Ireland. The way was paved by the passage of the Government of Ireland Act of 1920 that bestowed legislative devolution on Northern Ireland. A tripartite agreement between London, Dublin, and Belfast (thereafter represented by a parliament at Stormont Castle) recognising this new political arrangement was signed in December 1925. Since that time, political historians and commentators have adopted a multitude of terms to describe Northern Ireland, among them "a one-party statelet" (Bulpitt 1983, 145).

Ethnicity and the Traditional Divide: A Statelet in the Making

Two considerations underlay the work of the Boundary Commission which carved six counties out of the historic northern nine-county province of Ulster to form the new statelet of Northern Ireland. One was a reflection of postwar Europe and its minority problems. In the north of Ireland, it was believed, a religious minority, Protestants, had to be protected from assimilation into the theocratic Roman Catholic Irish Free State centered on Dublin. A second consideration was economic inasmuch as a viable hinterland had to be constructed politically behind the two dominantly Protestant northeastern counties of Antrim and Down. Four counties west of the River Bann (a river flowing into Lough Neagh) were therefore included. The grounds on, and the manner in which this was done, in spite of their nationalist political majorities and divergent economic interests makes a sorry story (Vincent 1988) and within Northern Ireland today, the distinction between Antrim and Down and the four western counties—Armagh, Fermanagh, Londonderry, and Tyrone—has intense cultural and political resonance.

It is common local knowledge within the border counties of Northern Ireland that the emphasis on religious and economic factors in the construction of the statelet hid a very significant *political* reality. Here, perhaps, Sir Winston Churchill was less to blame in 1922 than those who have quoted his words ever since, sometimes to propound what Tom Burns has called a "myth of atavism" (1977, 222–25) but more frequently to suggest that Northern Ireland's crisis is primarily religious. What Churchill said was:

> Then came the great war. Every institution, almost, in the world was strained. Great empires have been overturned. The whole map of Europe has been changed. . . . The modes of thought of men, the whole outlook on affairs, the grouping of parties, all have encountered violent and tremendous changes in the deluge of the world. But as the deluge subsides and waters fall short we see *the dreary steeples of Fermanagh and Tyrone* emerging once again. The integrity of their quarrel is one of the few institutions that has been unaltered in the cataclysm which has swept the world. (Churchill 1922, 1270, emphasis added)

Many who quote Churchill's words take him to have been speaking figuratively, understanding Fermanagh and Tyrone to stand for Protestant Ulster. I would suggest, rather, his particular vision of "dreary steeples" has misled those who have quoted him. Placing his comment again within the political context in which it was uttered, it is clear that it was a *political* quarrel, a quarrel *specifically* of Fermanagh and Tyrone, *a specific electoral outcome,* if you will, *and an electoral outcome repeated on many occasions between 1880 and 1920* of which Churchill quite deliberately—and not at all figuratively—spoke. For the electorate of Fermanagh and Tyrone, Protestant and Catholic alike, had consistently voted for Irish Home Rule. I have discussed the politics of the matter elsewhere in delineating the invention of what has been called "the traditional divide" in county Fermanagh (Vincent 1989a) and cannot give more space to it here in spite of its importance in showing how sectarian ideology replaced the struggle for Irish nationalism in the north.

It did so in a context of ethnic nationalist resurgence throughout England's periphery in these years. Plaid Cymru was founded in Wales in 1925 and the National Party of Scotland in 1928. By 1932 the Dublin government was actively pursuing a policy of gaelicization, a "special position" for the Catholic church, trade war with Britain, and neutrality in the world war. In 1949 the character of Northern Ireland changed irrevocably when the Irish Free State left the British Commonwealth and declared itself a republic. At this point, one ethnic solution to the Irish problem, reunification, would seem to have been set aside.

Today, the constitutional position of Northern Ireland rests on nine acts (Hull 1976, 91–104). The first was passed in 1800 and referred to Ireland as a whole. The three following (the Government of Ireland Act 1920, the Irish Free State [Consequential Provisions] Act 1922, and the Ireland [Confirmation of Agreement] Act 1925) were enacted to ratify the independence from Great Britain of the twenty-six southern counties and the dependent status within the United Kingdom of the six counties of Northern Ireland. The fifth act, the Ireland Act 1949, was introduced on the occasion of the south's declaration of its republican status and its quitting the British Commonwealth. Four more acts were introduced after 1973 when devolved government was withdrawn from the north and Direct Rule again imposed. These were the Northern Ireland (Temporary Provisions) Act 1972, the Northern Ireland Assembly Act 1973, the Northern Ireland Constitution Act 1973, and the Northern Ireland Act 1974. By these enactments, the six counties that made up Northern Ireland were returned to their pre-1920 political condition. Finally, in November 1985 negotiations began between the British and Irish governments aimed at constructing a new political status for the six northern counties. This, in the guise of the Anglo-Ireland Agreement, once again gave full recognition to a specifically Irish ethnic dimension in northern affairs.

Premises about Politics

The analysis of ethnicity that follows rests on four premises. First, as suggested above, it is necessary to treat Northern Ireland not as an independent national state but as a region, the politics of which can only be understood by asking where sovereignty lies. It is argued that political violence in Northern Ireland is engendered by its formal constitutional dependence on Great Britain and its international relations with (among other countries) the Republic of Ireland to the south.

This leads to the second premise: political violence in Northern

Ireland does not occur within a closed system but is both contextual and contingent in nature. The question then arises as to whether the current conflict is, indeed, primarily sectarian, a struggle between Catholics and Protestants as the postwar British settlement encouraged one to think. The population of Northern Ireland is almost wholly Christian (unlike that of Lebanon, Sri Lanka, or Azerbaijan!) 34.9 percent Roman Catholic and 58.2 percent Protestant. Nuanced analyses of geographers, ethnologists, and anthropologists, while recognizing that the conflict may have some sectarian aspects, nevertheless draw more attention to other forms of "imagined community" (Anderson 1983) including those of ethnicity, nationalism, "place" (locality), and class. Most people in Northern Ireland (with notable exceptions) insist that today's civil strife is not over religion but over sovereignty: not Protestantism but Loyalism; not Catholicism but Nationalism or Republicanism.

This emic observation leads me to my fourth premise: the equation of Catholicism with nationalism and republicanism, and Protestantism with unionism — the "traditional divide" — conceals the strengths of nonsectarian Ulster regionalism. What, then, encourages the persistence of the equation? Field research was carried out in Fermanagh, the most westerly of the six counties and, clearly, certain unique features of Fermanagh may have shaped my perspective. What these are will become apparent in the specifics of the discussion that follows. They certainly lead me to contend that many generalizations about Northern Ireland, not simply those figuring the "traditional divide," reflect a particular northeastern counties bias. This hegemonic Antrim/Down perspective requires not only rebuttal or modification, but explanation. Here I address the ethnic element in this hegemonic perspective by exploring the place of a new Ulster-Scots nationalism. This requires that I specify my assumptions about the nature of ethnicity and the conditions under which it is likely to be practiced.

Assumptions about Ethnicity

A processual and contextual definition of ethnicity was first set out in a somewhat uncharacteristically casual fashion by Lucy Mair in 1965 when she wrote of the movement of Italian emigrants to other parts of the globe. "Ethnicity," she suggested (1965) usefully describes their articulation of Italian identity within their new social settings, in Australia, Brazil, and the United States, for example. Her emphasis on the movement of peoples from one political setting to another is particularly apt for discerning the origins of ethnicity among the population of Ulster where English and Scots settlers were planted (transplanted and implanted) among a subordinated Irish population. Historicizing the events that gave rise to Mair's perception, suggests that ethnicity is, peculiarly, a cultural construction within empires. These take two forms: (1) political empires, such as that of the Hapsburgs, Great Britain, or the Soviet Union; and (2) economic empires, such as that of modern, global capitalism.[1]

Processual questions about ethnicity address its salience; when and where does one status — ethnic, religious, class — become articulated rather than another? (Vincent 1974). The Northern Irish situation brings out most clearly, and over time, the ambiguities and anomalies involved in the articulation of both ethnic and religious identities by individuals and groups, and the ideological hardening that occurs in moments of political crisis. Here I suggest that the recently signed Anglo-Irish Agreement has brought to light two subterranean ethnicites: that of the Ulster Scot in Northern Ireland and that of the Irish in England. Here I deal only with the first.[2]

Ethnicity as an Imperial and Counter-Imperial Construct

A story is told that is almost certainly apocryphal. As a plane descends to land at Belfast airport, the air hostess makes an announcement over the public address system. "Please fasten your seat belts and prepare for landing. To adjust to local time, all watches should be put back three hundred years."

This, although its raconteurs don't realise it, is a very *colonial* joke. It expresses a bias towards seeing the north of Ireland through the lens of British conquest, taking the listener back to the Plantation of Ulster at the beginning of the seventeenth century. Another tradition, another historiography, would have put time back eight hundred years, not three, tracing England's colonization of Ireland to 1155 A.D. when Pope Adrian IV (an Englishman) bequeathed Ireland to the English crown.[3]

Recourse to history both by the Northern Irish themselves and by those who seek to explain the modern conflict is a device born of despair. To suggest that ethnic reaction in modern Europe is revolutionary (Hechter 1975; Nairn 1977) is not readily accepted by the layman. That it is "directed against the basis of exploitation and domination in a specific form of social system, i.e. one characterised by cores and peripheries" (Kahn 1981, 48) and is thus not a legacy of the past but "a direct consequence of contemporary political and economic structures" (Hechter 1975; Kahn 1981, 50) tends to be denied[4] as the Northern Irish poet, John Hewitt found out when he attempted to explain the ongoing troubles in Ireland.[5]

> We tried to answer, spoke of Arab, Jew,
> of Turk and Greek in Cyprus, Pakistan
> and India; but no sense flickered through
> that offered reason to a modern man
> why Europeans, Christians, working-class,
> should thresh and struggle in the old morass.
>
> Failing there, we turned to history:
> the savage complications of the past;
> our luckless country where old wrongs outlast,
> in raging viruses of bigotry,
> their first infection.

Although history provides only an ideological, fall-back explanation of political behavior in the present, to historicize the Northern Irish, Christian, working-class Europeans of whom Hewitt wrote, and to historicize his selection of these statuses rather than others in his perception of the current crisis, is clearly necessary. For our present purposes, I must be brief.[6] Like the air hostess, I begin with the seventeenth-century Plantation of Ulster.

For the first two centuries of its existence the Plantation of Ulster was a plural society, its population was identified and identified themselves in ethnic terms. Different arrangements governed the Plantation in the various counties: Londonderry, for example, was colonized by the City of London; in Fermanagh an ethnic blueprint was adopted, some baronies being granted to English and others to

Scottish "undertakers." Not the Protestant religion but the oath of allegiance to the monarch was required of each. A few Catholic Irish, prepared to swear allegiance to the crown, retained their lands.

In county Antrim large estates were owned by Scottish Catholic nobles whose connections with Ulster pre-dated the Plantation by many decades. Indeed, Scots had colonized at least two counties of the six before the imposition of the English Plantation, a fact obscured by those who pay more attention to sect than to ethnicity. After the accession to the English throne of the first Stuart monarch, James VI of Scotland, the process of migration and settlement was simply more institutionalized.

The standard historiography of the Plantation (Robinson 1984) tends to aggregate its ethnic components in order to highlight its colonial character, presenting the population of Ulster in 1659 as follows:

TABLE 5.1

British and Irish in Ulster, c.1659

County	English and Scots	Irish	Total
Antrim	7,074 (45%)	8,965	16,039
Armagh	2,393 (35%)	4,355	6,748
Down	6,540 (43%)	8,643	15,183
Fermanagh	1,800 (25%)	5,302	7,102
Londonderry	4,428 (45%)	5,306	9,734

Source: Adapted from Robinson 1984, 105; figures are not available for County Tyrone.

An accompanying map (Robinson 1984, 110) shows the patterning of what Robinson calls Scottish and English settlement and cultural areas in present day nine-county Ulster (figure 5.1). I have added to his map the present international boundary between Northern Ireland and the Republic.

Contemporary Plantation sources suggest that ethnic identification was not as simple and straightforward as Robinson makes out. There is, for example, no indication on either map that a native Irish population exists. Yet Roy Foster has suggested (1988, 178) that "[T]hose who in the 1690s called themselves 'the Protestants of Ireland' or even 'the English of this kingdom' could see them-

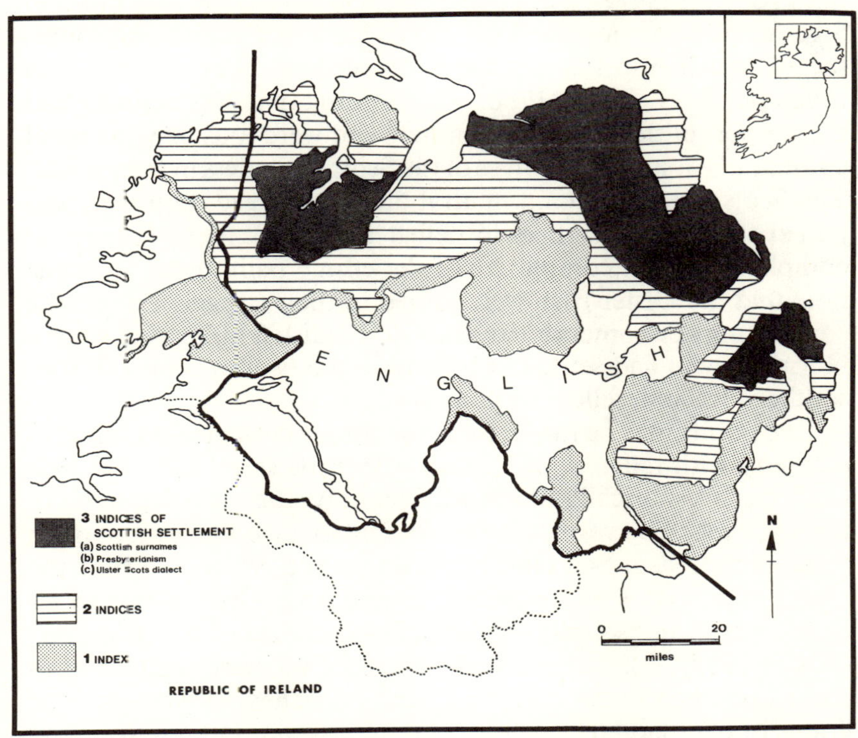

FIGURE 5.1
Cultural Areas in Modern Ulster (adapted from Robinson 1984:110).

selves as 'Irish gentlemen' by the 1720s." There was, he noted, some doubt as to whether they wanted to be *called* "Irish"; "but they increasingly felt that this was what they were, one way or another—a feeling solidified by various resentments. 'Tis hardly possible for anyone on your side', wrote Bishop Evans of Meath to Archbishop Wake in 1718, 'to conceive the general unaccountable aversion these people (tho lately come from England and Scotland) have to the English name' " (Foster 1988, 178).

County Fermanagh provides an excellent demonstration of the mythic fallacy of atavism and the recurrent need to question in every instance the salience of both ethnicity and sect. In 1641

Fermanagh's landed Irish gentry led a rebellion against their Plantation overlords even while professing a loyalty to the king himself. Significantly for our analysis, strategically for theirs, they massacred the English but not the Scots settlers. They did this with much publicity (Foster 1988, 87), claiming that they actually had the support of the Scots Covenanters and were thus obeying royal commands in sparing the lives of the Scottish settlers in their midst. The Scots did not remain neutral and disengaged, however, and joined their fellow settlers to defeat the Ulster Irish. Finally, to complete the rich complexity of the ethnic palimpsest, we must note that the Ulster Irish were joined in their struggle against the conquering newcomers by several Old English families (i.e. Anglo-Normans who had settled in Ireland in the twelfth century) from southern Ireland, fellow Catholics.

Two points may be made. First, the simple structural equating of ethnicity with religion, of English with Protestant and Irish with Catholic is historically unsound. Secondly, the historiography of the 1641 rebellion reveals the use by the English Parliament of an army recruited in Scotland but paid by the crown to crush the Ulster rebellion. This succeeded, as one Anglo-Irish historian recently put it, in "solidifying the Scottish nature of the province" (Foster 1988, 93). But, since the spoils of war were employed to make up arrears in the troops' pay and since these took the form of grants of Irish land, the success of the Scots did nothing to endear them to their Gaelic cousins.

An untangling of the threads of ethnic and sectarian alignments could be pursued almost indefinitely from the seventeenth century to the present but let me instead take a cultural shortcut by focusing on the figure and the event that loom so large in the popular iconography of Northern Ireland: William of Orange and the Battle of the Boyne. Alongside the sacred fervor of Ulster Loyalists live those who enjoy what can only be described as a profane ethnic joke. This takes the form of a doggerel about the Glorious Revolution of 1688.

> "King William was a Dutchman, same as Kruger, I suppose,
> He was married to a Papist, and had a Roman nose;
> Yet in yearly jubilation many Ulster people join,
> 'Cause a Dutchman beat a Scotsman at the Irish River Boyne;
> And we're told to keep the mem'ry 'green', or 'orange' fierce and hot
> Of this darling little hooley 'twixt a Dutchman and a Scot!"

Ethnic Ascendancy and the Failed Nation

As a result of this "darling little hooley" there emerged a consolidation of power in the hands of an ascendant ethnic group, whose component parts are not even mentioned in the doggerel—the Anglo-Irish. Their power had crystallized around 1775 (McCormack 1985), one expression of ethnic nationalism among many in an age when nation-states were coming into being throughout Europe. The construction of an Anglo-Irish ethnic community was shaped almost wholly by the antagonistic relations of the Irish-born ruling class with England, bearing in mind Daniel Corkery's admonition that "It would be well for all outsiders who would understand Ireland and its tragic history, or indeed any phase of it, always to keep before them the fact that the Ascendancy mind is not the same thing as the English mind" (1924, x).[8]

The political power of the Anglo-Irish "governing caste" (Foster 1988, 153) rested on its sectarian categorization of its own Ascendancy as one of Protestants of Irish extraction. Political exclusivity further required the continued penalization of dissenters against the established Anglican church, Roman Catholics and Presbyterians alike. It is useful, therefore, to view this event through Ulster Scots' eyes. Their historiographer, Rory Fitzpatrick, describes the new ethnic nationalism of the Anglo-Irish as follows:

> The idea of a united Ireland based on a triple partnership of Anglican, Catholic and Presbyterian had disappeared; the arrogance of the Anglicans, the selfishness of Catholics and the suspicions of the majority of Presbyterians had ensured that. From now on it was difficult for the middle-class Scots-Irish to think of their future in an all-Ireland context, so for the moment they turned from politics to something at which they were supremely good—the art of making money. (1989, 191)

Observe how Fitzpatrick tips his hand in that casual phrase "for the moment". He, like Robinson, is giving voice to an Ulster Scots nationalism resurgent today in Northern Ireland.

The political domination of the Anglo-Irish was short-lived. The British government bequeathed devolved government to them in 1775, establishing for the first time in its history an independent Irish parliament. In 1798, however, it was obliged to step in to crush a rebellion of the subaltern groups—Presbyterians and Catholics from the northeast and southeast, backed by the French—and to restore direct rule. The Union of Great Britain and Ireland, of which Northern Ireland is a relict, lasted from 1800 until 1920.

Northern Irish: Political Ethnicity and Nationalism in the Making

Given this first failure of Irish nationalism in 1798, led by Belfast business and Dublin intellectual interests, it took a long time for a distinct nationalism to rise again in the north. The Northern Ireland statelet constructed in the face of southern Irish secession from the United Kingdom was, as we have seen, shaped by externally imposed religious and economic constraints. Not until 1968 was it seriously challenged and then by a rebellious civil rights movement that cut across class, ethnicity, and sect. This was significant because it suggested that the existence of a specifically Northern Irish political community had been accepted by the population at large. Future discontents might, therefore, be settled through democratic challenges to the Stormont government.

This was not to be and, instead, dissident groups turned to violence. Shortly afterwards, in response to the Westminster government's inactivity in handling the crisis, a revolutionary call was made for UDI, a unilateral declaration of independence from Britain. This first attempt to build on the assumption of an independent national culture in the north was spearheaded by William Craig's Vanguard party. It, too, failed. Although both movements reflected a separate sense of Northern Irish cultural identity was in the making, the involvement of external interests in the civil unrest discouraged a coherent ethnic nationalism from taking shape and both movements proved premature. A further attempt is now underway, I suggest, grounded in a strategically constructed Ulster Scots ethnicity.

Ulster Scots Ethnic Nationalism

The form that a published work takes, and the timing of its appearance, have political significance. Rory Fitzpatrick's *God's Frontiersmen: The Scots-Irish Epic,* a coffee-table volume of shiny-leaved pages and numerous color photographs, was published by Weidenfeld and Nicolson of London in association with an independent television company (Channel Four) and Ulster Television (a BBC affiliate). The frontispiece showed an item of Belfast graffiti, a portrayal of William of Orange on his white charger; in the background, a cannon. Below, in dark letters, were the words "No Surrender"; faintly discernible against the bricks was the edict "No Pope here."

The Ulster Scots' "great ethnic adventure" (Fitzpatrick 1989, 52) took a familiar form. Fitzpatrick's language is that of the civilizing colonist:

> The ancestors of the Protestant population of Ulster arrived there in a series of immigrations during the seventeenth century, coming from the Scottish Lowlands and Borders and to a lesser extent from various parts of England, as far apart as Lancashire, Norfolk and Devon. Within a hundred years they had transformed the north of Ireland from a land composed largely of woods and swamps, interspersed with small areas of modest cultivation, into a province with roads, market towns and ports, supported by an increasingly arable system of farming, a thriving cattle trade and a domestic textile industry. Into a country where Catholic medieval values and an indolent pastoral economy pervaded, they brought Calvinistic protestantism and a stern work ethic. (1989, 1)[9]

Fitzpatrick then proceeded to account for the "evolution" of Ulster Presbyterians "as a distinct racial group" (1989, 3) by virtue of their middling position between "an aristocratic land-owning class, largely English in origin and allegiance and Episcopalian in religion, and a Catholic native Irish who feared and resented them" (Fitzpatrick 1989, 3). As for their civilizing mission, the words of no other than King James VI of Scotland (James I of England) are quoted: "The Scots are a middle temper, between the English tender breeding and the Irish rude breeding and are a great deal more likely to adventure to plant Ulster than the English" (Fitzpatrick 1989, 10). Thus was first formulated a familiar stereotype.

Within the framework of this Northern Ireland identity, historically constructed, Fitzpatrick claimed, in 1989, the political dominance of the Ulster Scots:

> Although they came into what was an English colony and many of them were originally part of the official settlement of Ulster by the English crown, the Scots so predominated in numbers, in the toughness of their culture and in the

> determination with which they acquired land, that *the whole Plantation enterprise took on Scottish characteristics and the name 'Ulster Scots' came in time to be applied to the entire non-Irish population of the Province.* (Fitzpatrick 1989, 1, emphasis added)

This is *not* the perspective of those west of the Bann in Northern Ireland today. Nor has it ever been even the thrust of earlier Ulster-Scots historiography. Responses to inquiries made in 1966, and again in 1978, run counter to any such hegemonic utterance.[10] The remainder of Fitzpatrick's theme, linking Presbyterianism, Orangeism, and Unionism, traces a religious-political, monarchical thread in Ulster history that he quite unrealistically ties to Ulster Scots ethnicity.

What was new was not the substance of Fitzpatrick's account, but its message: an implicit claim for the *identicality* of Ulster Scots, Presbyterianism, Orangeism and Ulster Unionism, and the suggestion that these — amalgamated as it were — comprised Northern Irish ethnicity. The book's political ideology looked backward to the Planter, the settler, the colonist on the moving frontier but it also reached out towards an Ulster Scots diaspora, expanding the frontier in Canada, America, Australia, and New Zealand. This is a point to which I shall return. First, however, it is necessary to account for this resurgence of Ulster Scots ethnic nationalism in Northern Ireland today? For this, we return to the state and to what Jim Bulpitt has called (1983) "territorial politics."

Thatcher's Britain: Ethnic and Territorial Politics

Territorial politics has been defined as "that arena of political activity concerned with the relations between the central political institutions in the capital city and those interests, communities, political organizations and governmental bodies outside the central institutional complex, but within the accepted boundaries of the state, which possess, or are commonly perceived to possess, a significant geographical or local/regional character" (Bulpitt 1983, 1). From this perspective, the making of the United Kingdom is equated with the anatomy of English imperialism.

In the twentieth century we have, perhaps, become accustomed to thinking of the world as made up of nation states, failing to appreciate that empire preceded nation. I have followed Leo Kuper in making this point with respect to ethnicity and multicultural states (Kuper 1983; Vincent 1984). For many in Northern Ireland the imperial army, colonial service, commercial and missionary opportunities throughout the empire have provided a considerable amount of the content as well as the context of their lives. They have created what Nairn (1977) calls a sense of "super-imperialism," a phenomenon I have described for colonial Uganda and South Africa, suggesting the importance of the monarchy for its legitimization (Vincent 1988).[11]

Variations occurred in the United Kingdom territorial political process. Ireland was not incorporated for nearly eight generations (between 1603 and 1800); Scotland between 1603 and 1707; Wales between 1284 and 1536. Wales and Ireland had never previously been united under one ruler; Scotland had. Wales never had had a parliament of its own; Scotland and Ireland had. Wales and Ireland were conquered by force of arms; Scotland was not. Indeed, there is a sense in which the north of Ireland, at least, was conquered by Scottish surrogate imperialism.[12] Ireland was a settler colony; Scotland was not (Wales fell somewhere between the two). This, then, was the territorial context of informal empire in which first Ireland from 1800 and then all that remained of it from 1920 — its relict six counties — operated. This is the regionalism of today's United Kingdom in which Scots regiments and prison warders are sent to Northern Ireland to maintain law and order and English members of the Westminster parliament are sent to Belfast to rule directly.

Unlike most European territorial states, the United Kingdom lacks a territorial department at the center, a Ministry of the Interior. There is a Scottish Office and a Secretary of State for Scotland; a Minister for Wales; and, since 1974, a Secretary of State for Northern Ireland. Legal institutions, currencies and educational and health institutions vary from region to region. Most importantly for Northern Ireland, the two major political parties, Conservative and Labour, do not contest elections within the province. Thus every election fought by a spectrum of Irish and Northern Irish parties becomes a virtual referendum on the constitution itself.

It is one of the ironies of political history — or, perhaps, one of the instruments of political economy — that the United Kingdom of Great Britain and Northern Ireland has never defined itself in *national* terms, as Benedict Anderson points out. It shares with the Soviet Union, he notes, "the rare distinction of refusing nationality in its naming" suggesting to him that "it is as much the legatee of the prenational dynastic states of the nineteenth century as the pre-cursor of a twenty-first century internationalist order." What nationality, indeed, would its name denote, he asks rhetorically: "Great Brito-Irish?" (Anderson 1983, 12)

Underpinning the territorial politics of the Westminster government lies what Bulpitt has called a Dual Polity the nature of which precludes active dominance over peripheral affairs.[13] The Dual Polity "was constructed to avoid problems, not solve them" (Bulpitt 1983, 165). Territorial conflict thus calls for the management of boundaries, not their change. And, within them, business as usual.

In 1973 what the center had designed as a self-contained statelet spilled over the edges to challenge Britain's sovereignty and cash the chips of ethnic solidarity overseas. In response, the Center went too far. It suggested a solution to the problem of what it saw as sectarian conflict in Northern Ireland. It proposed — and imposed — power sharing among party politicians who represented what they took to be Protestant and Catholic communities. For a few months, the solution appeared to be working and then a general strike was organized — "the most successful *political* action carried out by any European working class since the World War" (Nairn 1977, 242). In that strike, Robert Fisk has suggested, was germinated a new strain of Ulster nationalism since in future the government of the Republic "would have to deal with the Loyalists of Belfast as much as with the politicians at Westminster when they wanted to discuss both parts of their divided Ireland" (1975, 227). Fisk called his book *The Point of No Return: The Strike which Broke the British in Ulster.*

Who then were these Loyalists? Certainly not the remnants of Craig's Vanguard Party. Some who discuss the 1974 strike make much of the fact that the workers were Protestants and, for Marxist and socialist observers, there is something discomforting about this since most of their political leanings tend to support "Catholic" nationalism and republicanism. Here, like Fisk, I emphasize the workers' own expression of Loyalist identity and suggest that since the strike was initiated in, and organized from, Belfast and the industrial northeast, it may well have been at one and the same time an expression of Ulster Scots' militancy.

(I note in passing that the strike was not warmly and wholeheartedly supported by workers in county Fermanagh, where I was living at the time, and I believe that it is no coincidence that Fermanagh is the one county in Northern Ireland in which Anglicans [Church of the Ireland parishioners] outnumber Presbyterians and the descendants of English settlers outnumber Scots. See figure 5.1.)

Attention is thus drawn to class as well as ethnicity on the Northern Ireland frontier. The imposition of Direct Rule following the workers strike in 1974 was a class act that tested to its extremes Westminster's Dual Polity. The IRA's campaign to carry their "war of liberation" to the Center — London, Brighton, Birmingham, Guildford, Germany and Gibraltar — similarly challenges directly a sovereignty that rests on the controlled neglect of its peripheral domains.

Mrs. Thatcher's government came to power in 1979 with a middle-class mandate to curb unionism among the workers and, indeed, her regime has an excellent record in defeating strikers, from miners in 1980 to ambulance men in 1990. Most critically, however, her conservative regime's political economy rests on the enhancement of southeast England at the expense of the peripheral regions of Scotland, Wales, and Northern Ireland as well as the northern and southwestern counties of England itself. It is not without irony that this party led by Mrs. Thatcher, the Conservative and Unionist Party, is almost entirely supported by the electorate in the southeast (the most affluent part of Great Britain) and Northern Ireland (its poorest region.)

The *underdevelopment* of Northern Ireland is striking. Until 1974 when Direct Rule was reintroduced into the six counties, inadequate political representation, unemployment, and poor housing could be blamed on the Unionist dominated Stormont parliament, and characterized as anti-Catholic. It was also an inevitable result of the dialectical process whereby multinational capitalism had been welcomed into the province creating wealth for the few and impoverishment for the many. Since 1968 much of this capital has fled elsewhere.

Today Northern Ireland's population of 1,578,000 has the lowest percentage of over sixty-fives in the United Kingdom (14.4 percent) and the highest percentage under age 5 (8.7 percent). The birth rate at eighteen births per 1000 of the population is extremely high; the national average is 9.9 only. Given this large proportion of economically dependent citizens, it is not surprising that the provision of public services generates 35 percent of the gross domestic product (GDP); the national average is 23 percent. The GDP per head is the lowest in the United Kingdom. At the same time, the average gross weekly earning for males was also the lowest in the U.K. Between 1979 and 1987, Northern Ireland had the highest unemployment rate (31 percent for over 3 months) in the United Kingdom. Social security benefits accounted for around one fifth of average household income.[14]

Not for nothing did Mrs. Thatcher proclaim, a measure of reassurance to the Northern Irish people on the eve of the Anglo-Ireland Agreement. They had always been assured that no change in constitutional status could come about without the consent of the majority of its population. When she declared that "Northern Ireland is as British as Finchley" the Belfast city council and three Northern Irish borough councils took out a full-page advertisement in the *Daily Telegraph* to proclaim the fact. Two quotations from the prime minister in which she stated that matters affecting Northern Ireland were matters for Northern Ireland and Britain alone, were followed by a commentary:

Unfortunately the Prime Minister appears to have changed her mind.

The Anglo-Irish Agreement gives the Irish Republic a direct say in the government of part of the U.K. The people of Northern Ireland don't like it. But then, the people of Finchley probably wouldn't like it either.

The vast majority of the people of Northern Ireland still want to remain part of the U.K. Is that so wrong? (*Daily Telegraph* 1 May 1987)

The question has to be raised as to whether a very real sense of relative deprivation has begun to foster anew a distinctively ethnic Northern Irish identity and, if so, what relation this bears to other earlier constructed communities.

The signing of the Anglo-Irish Agreement in 1985 provided a turning point in Northern Ireland's ethnic politics. On this occasion, and unlike 1922, the agreement was signed by the Westminster and Irish governments alone, there being no parliament in Belfast to permit the fashioning of a tripartite concordance. The Agreement thus restored a specifically *Irish* ethnic dimension to Northern Ireland's political future. It also left the Loyalists with the sure knowledge that Westminster was not unambiguously in favor of close ties. If territorial distancing could not be maintained, closer union was not to be fought for. Perhaps Northern Ireland was not, after all, as British as Finchley.

Conclusion

This, then, is the current ambiguous political situation in Northern Ireland. Border Polls, secret negotiations with the IRA, above all the acceptance of the Irish dimension in their affairs, have brought Loyalists daily closer to the realization that they might have to go it alone. Can they in any way remain British? And, if so, what might be the content of their Britishness? What is their place in the larger scheme of territorial politics? And will they remain content with that place?

When Northern Ireland could *not* be kept at a distance, when troops had to be despatched there, and when the secretary of State for Northern Ireland had to be taken into the cabinet, Westminster's Dual Policy was clearly at risk. The continued economic growth of southeast England balanced by the privatization of panregional resources (British Airways, natural gas, water, aspects of the national Health service) suggest that the risk has been contained. But the accumulation of wealth in southeast England has been accompanied by the increasing underdevelopment of Northern Ireland.

If the Loyalists of Northern Ireland are not prepared to be nationally Irish, then to be Northern Irish has to be given both cultural and political content. It is in this context that the revival of Ulster-Scots ethnicity becomes significant. Within four years of the signing of the Anglo-Irish agreement, Rory Fitzpatrick, his publisher and British television networks have launched a campaign of ethnic politics. Their choice of labels has been particularly significant. In effect, they downplay the confessional basis on which, as the polity of a religious minority, Northern Ireland was supposedly established in the 1920s. They adopt an American religious terminology, replacing Anglican (the Church of Ireland) with Episcopalian, a term rarely used in Britain itself.

There is meaning, too, in the use of the American term Scots-Irish, rather than the vernacular Ulster Scots, to label the new ethnic nationalism. Ever since its founding as the first new nation (to use Lipset's phrase) United States' antipathy to English imperialism has permitted, even encouraged, the use of armed political force against it. The shaping of Ireland's politics by American interests has been continuous, at least since the formation of the Irish Republican Brotherhood (now the IRA) in Boston and New York in 1858. An appeal to Scots-Irish ethnic nationalism broadens the arena in which future confrontations may take place.

This is a strategic gambit but one that has its dangers. It seems likely, for example, that some artisanal construction work will have to be done in the forge of cultural hegemony if the newly constructed ethnicity is to be accepted by all elements within the Northern Irish population. Antipathy to and dissent from England may not be enough, although, as we have seen it has existed in the north since the seventeenth century. It provided the basis for the first independent Anglo-Irish parliament and for revolution against it in the eighteenth century; and, not without bloodshed and civil war, it brought the Irish Free State into being in the twentieth. The new historiographers will have to reconstruct the old linguistic argument pitting Celts (the Irish and Scots) against Anglo-Saxons (the hated English). The Anglo-Irish would then become a small ethnic minority in Northern Ireland as they are in the Republic. They will have to reconstruct the ancient population flows of Gaelic-speaking peoples to and fro across the narrow waters between Ulster and Scotland from time immemorial. They will certainly have to rethink Fitzpatrick's perceptions of pastoralism and Catholicism, providing, perhaps, a modern contestation of that enlightenment thinking so divisive for an earlier generation of highland and lowland Scots.

This seems an unlikely political scenario. Ethnic nationalisms have not met with much success in Ireland — even in the south. A much more likely future would seem to lie in the recovering and restoring of a Northern Ireland political culture and nationalism such as were beginning to emerge by 1968.

Finally, with precedents all around, in Eastern Europe now as well as in the West, the likelihood of at least a temporary collapse of British territorial politics and the emergence of ethnic nationalisms — Scots, Welsh, and Scots-Irish — within a federalizing Europe seems less remote. The poet, remember, who failed to convince his listeners with analogies to Arab, Jew, and Turk and Greek also spoke of Europeans — Christian, working class, modern men — in Northern Ireland. Certainly ethnic revolutions and the break-up of Britain are less remote than one might have thought before Mrs. Thatcher's Tory party came into power. There is an irony in that, too, if the jingoism of her Falklands War and the utilitarian political economics of her regime, have bred within the historic domestic imperialism of Great Britain the ultimate ethnic nationalisms that call it into question.

Notes

1. Elsewhere I have explored ethnicity as the subaltern side of the political economy of capitalism in the United States (Vincent 1979, 1989b). The relation of capitalism to the colonial state is historically variable and I distinguish the two forms of empire categorically as a matter of convenience.
2. At the moment this paper is being written, correspondents to the *Daily Telegraph* are suggesting (1) the reunification of Great Britain and Ireland and (2) the expulsion of Northern Ireland from Great Britain, thus leaving its people to fight the matter out for themselves. The first letter (from Cornelius O'Donaghue of Blackpool) suggests that recent correspondence and articles about reunification "follow the classic pattern of ignoring the million or so Irish-born and educated people living in Britain." Furthermore, O'Donaghue suggests, if people in the Republic were asked by referendum their opinion on unification, they would support it. "One step the Dail [the Irish government] could take which would help ease the fears of our Northern cousins," he suggests, "would be to rejoin the Commonwealth" (*Daily Telegraph* 14

March 1990). This is an expression of what I have elsewhere termed ultra-montane ethnicity (Vincent 1979). The second letter (*Daily Telegraph* 19 March 1990) assumes the existence of a distinctive Northern Irish ethnicity. The extent to which this has, indeed, come into being is the subject of a current report for HRAF (Vincent, forthcoming).

3. These two paragraphs are taken from a paper on *The Categories of Colonialism* presented at the Spring meeting of the American Ethnological Association, San Antonio, Texas, 2 May 1987. That paper went on to make an ethnographic and analytical point about colonial categories and internal divisions among the practitioners of colonial rule. It raised questions about the global processes engendering local colonial communities. Here I take these processes for granted in order to concentrate exclusively on the meaning and relevance of sectarian and ethnic categories in Northern Ireland in 1990.

4. Kahn elaborates on Hechter's observation: "However the ethnic supremacy of the core culture was not asserted in Machiavellian fashion to obscure the *real* forms of capitalist observation. It was on the contrary part and parcel of a form of economic control and exploitation that rested on what has been loosely termed unequal exchange." (1981, 51)

5. Hewitt's poem, "Conversations in Hungary," is quoted in Nairn 1977, 224.

6. My ten-chapter *Dragon's Teeth: Seeds of Discord in the North of Ireland* (a work in progress) provides the longer account.

7. This is not the place for a critique of Robinson's methodology but it should be pointed out that the measures chosen tend to inflate the "Scottish" presence, e.g., in rural districts where more than 50 percent of the British surnames in the electoral lists are Scottish and in baronies where more than 50 percent of the Protestant population is recorded as Presbyterian. For a full discussion of his techniques see Robinson 1982, 19 where he argues that "To understand why, and how sub-regions with differing cultural identities have developed within Northern Ireland, it is essential to gain an historical perspective, both of the cultural landscape and of the often over-simplified relationships between religious denomination, ethnic origin and political affiliation." My own work using family surnames in an analysis of marriage, religion, and class in county Fermanagh (Vincent 1983) suggests a much more complicated picture. Clearly there is a need for comparative studies east and west of the Bann.

8. Anglo-Irish ethnicity in the making is to be found in Maria Edgeworth's *Castle Rackrent* (1800) and *The Absentee* (1812) describing the Anglo-Irish of county Longford, another Plantation county. Today it is more familiar to us, perhaps, from the novels of Molly Keane.

9. I am, of course, quoting the passage for its tone and content and not for its historical accuracy. It should be pointed out, perhaps, that only the Scots immigrants could be called Calvinistic Protestants; the English immigrants were anything but Calvinistic.

10. See Vincent, forthcoming. Unfortunately the questionnaire inquires (Rose 1971; Moxon-Browne 1983) were directed almost entirely to relating religion and nationality, meaning by the latter, degrees of Britishness and Irishness. It was found that, for most of the population Irishness and Britishness were not mutually exclusive categories but matters of sentiment and conviction. In 1966, 15 percent of the Catholics and 39 percent of the Protestants gave as

their national identity British, while 76 percent and 20 percent respectively said they were Irish. In 1978, after nine years of political violence and civil unrest, the number of Catholics asserting British identity remained at 15 percent but that of Protestants had risen to 67 percent. Of the Catholics in 1978, 69 percent said they were Irish, but only 8 percent of the Protestants— an indication of the decline in the ethnic option for settling the conflict. Nevertheless, in the population at large, 62 percent considered themselves more similar to people in the Republic of Ireland than to people in England —an indication, I would suggest, of the emergence of a distinct Northern Irish ethnicity, a Celtic fringe ethnicity similar to that of the Scots and the Welsh, that has come into being as a counter-imperialist reaction to British rule.

11. Nairn notes (1977, 235–36) the British government's successive attempts to solve its Irish problems through some sort of Home Rule between 1880 and the 1920s, suggesting that it would thus "assimilate the island by more rational and modern means," i.e., through economic rather than political imperialism. Protestant Ulster, as Nairn calls it, resisted these moves, not in "the assertion of its own distinct identity and rights, its own capacity for national self-determination in a separatist sense. Instead it was fought as a desperate battle for the frontier: for imperialism, 'British Ireland' in the old sense, Protestant Ascendancy over the 'natives,' civilized settler values, and so on. This kind of over-compensation," he notes, "was not peculiar to Ulster. One can (e.g.) perceive many elements of it in the super-imperialism which also characterized Scotland and Wales in the 19th and early 20th centuries. However, in Irish conditions these traits were magnified to maniac proportions" (1977, 236).

    It should be noted that Nairn slips in his writing throughout his chapter on Northern Ireland in *The Break-up of Britain* (1977) from a delineation of "the Scotch-Irish" (233) "Crofter-Crofton-Crawford Scotch-Irish Protestantism" (following James Joyce) in "the North-East" (229) with its "four-county industrialization" (236) to the aggregate concepts of "Protestants" on the one hand and "Ulster" on the other. He thus provides a trajectory for a revisionist argument, without seeming to be aware of it.

12. Much as Teso was conquered by the Baganda!

13. Bulpitt's argument is similar to that which explains why advanced modern capitalism *needs* a peasantry (Carter 1979; Vincent 1980, 1990) and it is surely no coincidence that Britain's longest surviving peasantries were, indeed, to be found in Scotland and Ireland.

14. The statistics throughout this paper are taken from government publications, Year Books and the like, used in connection with my forthcoming encyclopaedia article on "The Northern Irish" to be published by HRAF.

References

Anderson, Benedict. 1983. *Imagined Communities: Reflections on the Origin and Spread of Nationalism.* London: Verso.

Bulpitt, Jim. 1983. *Territory and Power in the United Kingdom.* Manchester: Manchester University Press.

Carter, Ian. 1979. *Farm Life in Northeast Scotland 1840–1914: The Poor Man's Country.* Edinburgh: John Donald.

Churchill, Winston. 1922. Speech in the House of Commons, 16 February 1922. Irish Free State (Agreement) Bill. Second reading. *Hansard,* 1270. London: Hansard.

Corkery, Daniel. 1924. *The Hidden Ireland: A Study of Gaelic Munster in the Eighteenth Century.* Dublin: Gill.

Fisk, Robert. 1975. *The Point of No Return: The Strike which Broke the British in Ulster.*

Fitzpatrick, Rory. 1989. *God's Frontiersmen: The Scots-Irish Epic.* London: Weidenfeld and Nicolson.

Foster, Roy F. 1988. *Modern Ireland 1600–1972.* London: Allen Lane.

Hechter, Michael. 1975. *Internal Colonialism: The Celtic Fringe in British National Development, 1536–1966.* London: Routledge and Kegan Paul.

Hull, Roger H. 1976. *The Irish Triangle: Conflict in Northern Ireland.* Princeton, N.J.: Princeton University Press.

Kahn, Joel S. 1981. "Explaining Ethnicity: A Review Article." *Critique of Anthropology* 4:43–52.

Kuper, Leo. 1984. "International Protection Against Genocide in Plural Societies." In *The Prospects for Plural Societies,* edited by David Maybury-Lewis. Washington, D.C.: American Ethnological Society.

Mair, Lucy. 1965. *An Introduction to Social Anthropology.* Oxford: Clarendon.

Moxon-Browne, Edward. 1983. *Nation, Class and Creed in Northern Ireland.* Aldershot: Gower.

Nairn, Tom. 1977. *The Break-up of Britain: Crisis and Neonationalism.* London: New Left Books.

Robinson, Philip. 1984. *The Plantation of Ulster: British Settlement in an Irish Landscape, 1600–1670.* Dublin: Gill and Macmillan.

Rose, Richard. 1971. *Governing Without Consensus.* London: Faber.

Vincent, Joan. 1974. "The Structuring of Ethnicity." *Human Organization* 33:375–79.

———. 1984. "Cultural Minorities." *Science* 226, 4675:683–84.

———. 1988. "Sovereignty, Legitimacy and Power: Prologomena to the Study of the Colonial State in Early Modern Uganda." In Ronald Cohen and Judith D. Toland (eds.) *State Formation and Political Legitimacy.* Political Anthropology, Vol. 6:137–154.

———. 1989a. "Local knowledge and global processes in two border villages: political violence in County Fermanagh," in Chris Curtin and Thomas M. Wilson (eds.) *Ireland from below: social change and local communities.* Galway: University of Galway Press.

———. 1989b. "In the shadow of the armory: Capitalist production and the construction of ethnic culture." Paper presented at the annual meeting of the Society for Economic Anthropology, Mount Pleasant, Michigan, April 28–29.

———. 1990. *Anthropology and politics: Visions, traditions and trends.* Tucson.: University of Arizona Press. Forthcoming. "The Northern Irish," *Encyclopedia of world cultures.* New Haven: Human Relations Area Files.

6

Batak Heritage and the Indonesian State: Print Literacy and the Construction of Ethnic Cultures in Indonesia

Susan Rodgers

Since Leach's work on the Kachin (1954), Southeast Asian specialists have realized that ethnic categories throughout the region are situationally defined, politically labile, and often quite flexible in social scope. Mainland and island Southeast Asia have many hundreds of ethnic minority societies but drawing a simple, stable ethnic map of the location of these groups has proved impossible, for ethnic boundaries shift on the ground and in terms of group membership. In addition, at the level of the individual in these societies, men and women sometimes alternate between ethnic labels (going from one subtype of Karen, for instance, to another.) They do this according to their audience and according to complex social contexts, which reach from the village level to larger ethnically mixed regions. A typical situation is for a migrant who has moved to a foreign area to temporarily switch his or her original ethnic identity to the locally dominant one for the duration of his or her residence in the new area. Upon leaving the region, the person may shift identity once again. Sometimes the person will accomplish this change of ethnicity by entering and then later leaving a local clan. Religious affiliation is sometimes also used in Southeast

147

Asia in an ethnically loaded way. For instance, in early twentieth century Sumatra, highland Bataks sometimes "became Malay" by switching from their local village religions to Islam, the faith of the lowland populations.[1]

There are other ambiguities in Southeast Asian ethnic identity as well. As Leach, once again, points out (1954:1–17), seemingly separate groups may share the same languages and "village customs," while in other cases what seem to be single ethnic societies such as the Kachin may have access to a variety of quite contrastive political models for shaping social thought and action. Individuals and sometimes whole villages in such societies can shift from one political model to another according to historical circumstances, and according to the categories of people with whom they are dealing.[2]

This deeply interactive aspect of Southeast Asian ethnicity is not limited to relations between ethnic minorities such as the Kachin or the Batak and their neighboring societies, however; the interaction between minority societies and the nation states that now encompass them also shape group identity in important ways. An example of this interaction is the topic of this chapter. I shall focus on ideas of Angkola Batak culture (the Sumatran society in question here) as propounded on the one hand by certain Angkola writers and on the other hand by authors working for the Indonesian national government. My special concern will be the role of the print media in constructing such notions of "Angkolaness." The two sets of writers promote strikingly contrastive visions of Angkola, as a people and a set of ethnic customs and traditions. This situation makes the printed media a volatile realm of political discourse in modernizing Indonesia. For this reason it merits attention from anthropologists, historians, and political scientists interested in charting the process of Indonesian national state formation in microlevel terms, as minority societies come to discover themselves (and be discovered and redefined by their national governments) through the public media.

The Creation of Ethnic Cultures in Indonesia

In contemporary Southeast Asia, most nations are well into their fourth decade of postcolonial independence and have become increasingly successful at extending state ideology to ethnic minorities in their hinterlands. In this political context, interaction between small ethnic societies at the nation state's periphery and national governments at the center is probably the major social mechanism today for defining ethnic categories in the region. This process of ethnic group definition is being pursued with particular vigor in present-day Indonesia, a nation which includes over 300 ethnic societies.[3] Many of these have separate languages (generally spoken in addition to the national tongue, Indonesian) and maintain distinct "village customs." The latter are often spoken of in Indonesia as *adat*. This word, which derives from Arabic, implies conformity to supposedly ancient, prototypically correct patterns of behavior and speech, said to have been bestowed on humans by distant ancestors. This is the folk view, but it is important to note that many of these "ancient village heritages" for the various ethnic societies are constantly being reconfigured—and at times forthrightly invented—in dialogic relationship with the ideology and political agenda of the Indonesian national state.[4] This is not a fundamentally new circumstance for these minority societies, for notions of peoplehood and history in these cultures have long been defined in relation to the large traditional state societies that border the highland groups. Adat has also developed in dialectical relationship with Islam and Christianity (the country is about 90 percent Muslim and 5 percent Christian).[5] During the Dutch colonial period *adat* in the various ethnic home regions was also reshaped in relation to the Dutch legal code.

Given this historical complexity, a comprehensive account of minority society ethnic identity concepts in Indonesia is beyond the scope of this chapter. Thus, I have taken this case study approach to Angkola Batak social thought, as it can be examined through their print literature. I shall concentrate mostly on texts from the 1970–1989 period, although valuable work could also be done for the 1920s and 1930s, when Angkola society interacted with the Dutch colonial state, and with the early nationalistic movement.

The Angkola Bataks' rural rice-farming home region is located in South Tapanuli, North Sumatra. These last two designations are administrative units of the national government that administers the area, runs the public schools there, and controls the entire area politically through the national military. The mountainous region around Lake Toba includes some six to seven Batak home regions. The borders of most of these are roughly coterminous with the government's subprovincial borders (and both were strongly shaped by the old Dutch colonial administrative units for the Bataklands.) The population of each of these home regions is predominantly Batak, mixed with small numbers of Javanese, Minangkabau, and Indonesian Chinese.

In addition to the several societies of rural Bataks living in North Sumatra there are also many thousands of Batak migrants residing in multiethnic cities outside Tapanuli and Karo. Migration began in the 1890s, as newly literate southern Bataks from Angkola and Mandailing moved to the East Coast Deli plantation belt for salaried jobs as clerks and low-level government officials for the Dutch. Once Indonesian national independence was secured in the 1945 – 49 revolution, the urban migration process continued and expanded to include members of all other Batak societies. Second- and sometimes third-generation city migrant Batak families now reside permanently in densely multiethnic cities such as Medan, Palembang, and Jakarta. Today, Angkola Batak are a strikingly well-educated and relatively prosperous minority society both in the ethnically mixed urban centers and in their ethnically homogeneous South Tapanuli home region.

What the categories "Batak" and "Angkola" mean are much at issue for both home region and city people. Recent research on the construction of ethnic cultures in other parts of Indonesia and the Pacific Basin provides a useful background here for understanding Angkola social thought on the point.

The situation in Outer Island Indonesia in general is similar to that described by Linnekin (1983) for Hawaii. In both cases, ethnic peoples are engaged in a constant project of inventing traditions for themselves, which they then present as ancient, unvarying customs, passed down from the ancestors. These old ways, however, must also be presented to the public and to the national government as strikingly compatible with modern life and national existence. Importantly, Linnekin finds that rural populations and city residents construct histories and cultures for themselves in a quite self-conscious and politically astute way. This is certainly the case for Angkola, where all print authors are well aware of the history of the Indonesian nation, know its political power in North Sumatra, and know Angkola's effective political vulnerability within the nation.

Atkinson (1983) documented another crucial aspect of ethnic culture construction in Outer Island Indonesia in her article on Wana efforts to rethink their ritual traditions in light of the national government's promotion of monotheistic religions, and particularly Islam, as the proper faith for a respectable ethnic society to profess. Atkinson reviews a variety of Wana strategies for recasting their village rituals into a new form that allow them to present these activities as part of a proper *agama,* or world religion (the sort of religion the national government decrees is a necessary component of a civilized human society. Peoples without a god and a holy text are defined by the Jakarta government as pagan and backward, and suspected of being disloyal to the nation.) The Wana are by no means passive partners in this cultural redefinition dialogue with the national government. Rather, they are extremely cagey political operators who first learn what the national government officials demand in the way of a local ethnic culture and then set about repackaging their culture (in the Wana case, their rituals) into what might be called a marketable form. As we shall see, some Angkola Batak writers take a somewhat different approach, by pointedly ignoring the sort of reconciliation the central government seeks between national government and local ethnic culture.

Volkman finds another form of political resourcefulness on the part of another Sulawesi society, the Sa'dan Toraja, in her study of Toraja revisions of their rituals as the area has become a target of the international tourist trade (1984). She notes that Toraja ethnic identity and their sense of their heritage has been shaped by two main forces: out-migration of youth to cities (where they meet members of other ethnic societies and confront strong nationalist imagery) and international tourism, which brings European and American vacationers to the Toraja highlands in search of spectacular funeral rituals. The Toraja have begun to "put on" the sort of large-scale village rituals that international tourists seek. Volkman points out that this process of cultural redefinition cannot be seen in stark terms simply as the crass exploitation of Toraja villagers by outsiders. Rather, members of the society are themselves active participants in marketing their culture to various audiences, in ways politically helpful to themselves.

Hoskins (1987) documents a similar situation for the Kodi of West Sumba. In a fascinating account of local Kodi attempts to create a historical past for themselves given the political constraints of the Indonesian nation's powerful history-creating institutions (the public school system, national holidays, a roster of National Heroes), Hoskins finds that the Kodi have fixed on a headhunter named Wona Kaka who attacked Dutch forces in 1911. They use this fact to place him within nationalist history, and to give him a venue out of local Kodi myth. The national government (loath to admit any "uncivilized" practice such as headhunting in its past) demands proper Revolutionary War credentials and proper anti-colonial sentiments from its constituent ethnic societies. The Kodi redefined Wona Kaka in this light, gaining a certain measure of political legitimacy for themselves in the process.

Negotiations of this sort along the border between local ethnic myth and nationalist history are occurring throughout the archipelago. In many areas, such as Angkola, print literacy is central to these processes.

Print as a Forum for Constructing Ethnic Identity

In much of their public culture since 1910 Angkola Batak have endeavored to do two things at once: on the one hand they have tried to be faithful to supposedly ancient Angkola traditions, while on the other they have striven to be "progress-minded," or *maju*. They often invoke the latter orientation as their rationale for their general support for Indonesian nationalism. Indeed, with the one major exception of an unsuccessful separatist movement in 1957–59 (North Sumatra's PRRI Rebellion, directed against the central government in Jakarta), the southern Batak societies have generally acceded to national government control of South Tapanuli over the last forty years. With only minor Muslim-led criticism of the national government (and with virtually no Communist resistance in the area) Angkola Batak today accept an overall consensus that their land and people are part of Indonesia. Along with this, though, they have taken great pains to glorify their "ancient village heritage" as a morally excellent and specifically Angkola tradition whose distinctive character and content should be maintained within the larger nation.

National and local systems of mass communication have been crucial to Angkola efforts to define their group identity, and to the national government's own efforts to define and control the Angkola. During the national period following the Revolution, such print media forms as books, pamphlets, newspapers, and government documents have served as a sort of grand concourse for writers speaking for the nation to interact with ethnic minority group authors. In Angkola (introduced to print literacy starting in the 1850s and a center for newspaper and book publishing by the 1920s), print has provided a forum to two major, differing constructions of Angkolaness and its linked concept, the Angkola past.

Firstly, South Tapanuli-based Angkola writers have constructed a generally flattering portrait of local ethnic traditions, in their abundant printed works about their customs and history.[7] Their stress has typically been on Angkola cultural excellence and on Angkola political autonomy. In these works, village society is generally portrayed as a self-contained social world answering only to itself. Villages are presented as human entities organized in accord with the cosmology of the universe itself (a scheme of thought that omits mention of the nation.) In these same locally authored works, Angkola's marriage alliance system and its ideology of patrilineal clan descent (both similar to that reported by Leach for the Kachin) are lauded as the fundamental "support stones" (a local phrase) of Angkola's political life. Angkola's particular alliance and descent traditions are portrayed as the major source of the "moral excellence" and purported peaceable character of the farm villages.

In contrast to this is a second view of Angkola, promoted in national government publications and in the works of certain Angkola authors seeking government subsidy for their books.[8] The central government is now publishing several series of descriptive, documentary, and often quite self-consciously ethnological books and pamphlets about this part of Sumatra. The books in this series have titles[9] such as *Children's Games of North Sumatra, Proverbs in the Angkola-Mandailing Language, Traditional Ceremonies in the Area of North Sumatra,* and *Traditional Sayings as a Source of Information on the Culture of the Area of North Sumatra.* These works are written predominantly in the national language, Indonesian, except for such things as the original texts of local proverbs, which are in the ethnic tongues. In these books, Angkola emerges as a small, politically dependent minority society within a nation whose official motto is Bhinneka Tunggal Ika, or "Unity from Diversity." In some of these government publications, Angkola's clan-based history has been subsumed into national, secular history, with an emphasis on the centrality of Javanese history in the nation's past. Java has the largest population of any Indonesian ethnic society and its court culture dominates the national agenda of what a proper high civilization should be.

In government publications of this sort, Angkola's ideology of ranked marriage alliance and clan descent from founding ancestors has been effectively shorn of its political connotations, to emerge (in the social science-like jargon of Jakarta's government publications) as a "system of family relationships."

This strategy of reducing politically loaded systems of village thought such as Batak marriage alliance and descent constructs to comfortably nonpolitical subsystems of "ethnic culture" such as family relations illustrates, I think, the larger process at work here: the national government is apparently trying to extend its control throughout the archipelago by redefining its constituent ethnic minorities in a social science-like rhetoric that essentially trivializes them. An important component of this process is the government's practice of describing local ethnic cultures in an old fashioned folkloristic style that transforms village systems of political thought into quaint customs of minor antiquarian interest.

This process of culture definition can best be understood by examining some actual texts. My first examples will be drawn from the works of Angkola authors who promote a politically robust version of their culture. After looking at that sort of text we can turn to excerpts from the Indonesian national government's ethnic cultures series.

Southern Batak Writers Define Angkola

In the textual analyses that follow, Angkola authors eulogize Angkola society as a freestanding polity based in the *dalihan na tolu.* This phrase can be translated as the "three support stones on the hearth"; folk exegetes say that when the stones are placed equidistant from each other they serve to support a cookpot. Angkola commentators[10] go on to say that the three support stones of Angkola *adat* are *kahanggi* (a man's lineagemates), *anakboru* (that first group's wife-receivers) and *mora* ("wealthy," the first group's wife-givers.) Wife-receivers are said to be perpetually indebted to their "superior, holier" wife-givers, who shower them with blessings. *Mora* in its turn, though, cannot exist without the support and financial help of their wife-receivers. The close cooperation and mutual indebtedness of these three fundamental "stones" of Angkola society are said to underlie good social order and peace in villages. Relations between rajas, or chiefs, and between nobles and commoners are also thought to derive from this fundamental three-stones-on-the-hearth base. Village government, too, is explained in this alliance and descent idiom. Local custom handbooks eulogize these notions at length, uniformly placing kinship relations at the center of human social life.

Before looking at several examples of texts which do this, several ethnographic and historical observations can be made about Angkola political structure and the culture's experience with print. Angkola's political status vis-à-vis the other Batak societies has long been ambivalent. This is a situation that colors custom handbook literature. In addition, as noted, Angkola is located in South Tapanuli, which has a dual identity as both a subprovince on the national maps and the ancestral Angkola home region. It is structural ambiguities of this sort that provide an opening for different sorts of writers to discuss Angkola ethnic identity in different voices.

With regard to the Angkola's relationship with other Batak societies, and to Angkola understandings of the category, 'Batak,' Angkola villagers and townspeople generally know little about the *adat* or mythic history of the other Batak peoples, although some will say that their clan ancestors (eleven to thirteen generations ago) migrated southward from the "older" Toba home region near the time the clans were being founded. This is certainly the version of the past the Toba themselves hold and branches of some of the major Toba clans are indeed found in the "outlying" Batak home regions far from the lake. However, in general, the Angkola pay little attention to the Toba past and its supposed ancestral relationship to Angkola. In fact, the Angkola tend to disparage other Batak societies as being "less refined" and civilized than they are. A particular point of pride is the Angkola language, which is held to be especially mellifluous and subtle. Marriage to Tobas is discouraged in many Angkola families, because Toba brides and grooms are feared as brusque, overbearing, uncooperative, and dirty. By contrast to this, Angkola often see the Mandailing to their southern border as a particularly close and compatible society. The Mandailing dialect of Batak is thought to be even more refined and beautiful than Angkola, and Mandailing ritual practices, oratory, and village political positions are thought to resemble Angkola ones closely. Mandailing, strongly Muslim and strongly influenced by Minangkabau culture, has sent many migrants to the East Coast plantation belt of Sumatra's Deli coastline. In the early decades of this century Mandailing migrants found themselves stereotyped as "Batak," which in the migrant areas meant either heathen, or Christian. In heavily Muslim East Sumatra, the association with pork consumption was a distinct disadvantage. Most Mandailing were in fact Muslim by this time. Large numbers of them simply dropped their diagnostically Batak clan names in the 1900–1930s period and blended in with Malay Muslim society in East Sumatra. They "became Malay," or "masuk Melayu" (entered Malay), as the local phrase has it. Today, Mandailing migrants are in the process of rediscovering themselves as members of a Batak society, now that many of their number hold prominent positions in the government, in universities, in publishing, and in law. Some are beginning to use their clan names again, and to form Mandailing clan history clubs in cities.

Angkola have generally considered the Batak label to be less problematic. Not all will forthrightly state they are Angkola *Batak* (some associate Batakness with Tobaness and an uncouth character) but many do use the word; this is particularly true of Christians. In interaction with Toba, Karo, and Mandailing people, residents from throughout the northern part of South Tapanuli will often tag themselves "Angkola," if not Angkola Batak. At the more local, village level, in areas such as Sipirok (an *adat* domain within Angkola), people will often say they are "Sipirok people." In this case, the operative social unit is the *harajaon,* or *adat* chieftaincy domain.

This is generally a loose cluster of some ten to fifteen villages, focused around a "bamboo stem" founder village, which is occupied by the descendants of the domain's high rajas. The *harajaon* is the fundamental political unit of Angkola, within *adat* thought. The chiefs of each of the *harajaon'*s constituent villages will either claim descent in the area's major lineages, or descent in one of that line's long-established wife-giver lines or wife-receiver lines. Angkola as a whole has about ten such chieftaincy domains, each identified with a core lineage of one or the other of the region's several major clans, or *marga.*

The chiefly house of each of the domain's village clusters will typically be linked to a large number of other ancestral noble houses of other clans, through ranked marriage alliance ties. For instance, House 1 of Lineage A of the Pane clan will have Houses 2, 3, 4, and 5 of other clans as their traditional "inherited wife-receivers." House 1 will have given its daughters and sisters to these other houses as brides over a number of generations. As is the case with the Kachin and a number of eastern Indonesian societies (Leach 1954; Fox 1980; Van Wouden 1933; Hicks 1979; Forth 1981), this "bride gift" sets up a political relationship of superordination and subordination; tight bonds of indebtedness cement the partners together as superiors and inferiors, with each *anakboru* receiver group acting as the subordinate, beholden partner to its *mora* wife-givers.

In this scheme, (lauded in Angkola's elaborate ritual oratory delivered at adat ceremonies), the wife-givers are associated with certain cosmological correlates, such as the sky, an upper spirit kingdom of supernatural rajas, and the ability to "shower blessings" and supernatural protection and good luck on their wife-receivers. The latter are the mundane, this-world partner to their *mora,* protecting them from physical harm and acting as their spokesmen and bodyguards in ceremonies.

House 1 in this scheme will not get its own brides from any of its receiver houses. The marriage system is rigidly asymmetrical at the level of houses, and, ideally at least, at the level of the localized lineage. So, House 1 would have its own set of beneficent wife-provider houses, who will shower House 1 in turn with blessings, supernatural protection, luck, fertility powers, and so on. Thus the whole system, in the ideal, works as follows:

A.   — Wife-givers (*Mora* to B.)

brides
fertility powers
luck, blessings
advice, knowledge
spiritual care   livestock gifts, brideprice payments
Upperworld, Sky   physical protection of mora
Right side   labor services in *mora's* field, *adat*
rituals
physical height   Lowerworld, Earth
                                        left side
                                        shortness
B. Wife-receivers (Anakboru to A.)

In practice, each major house would have a large number of wife-giver partners in its own village and in several outlying ones. It would also have a plethora of *anakboru* all over the local and regional countryside, throughout the *harajaon* domain. In colonial times, in fact, chiefs built up a support base by maintaining the two sorts of alliance ties with as large a range of powerful outside villages as possible. Today, villagers still talk of village social order in these descent and alliance terms. However, they well recognize that each settlement has a second and effectively more powerful level of government: the bureaucracy of the Indonesian national government.

As a province of the nation, North Sumatra has an appointed governor (a military officer), a representative assembly, and a number of *bupati,* or subprovincial heads. Each ancestral Batak land is roughly coterminous with one of these *kabupaten,* or subprovincial units. Officials are generally Batak men, though often they are from different areas than the ones they administer. Each subprovince is divided into a number of *kecamatan* (county districts) and these too are headed by central government officials, also usually Batak men. North Sumatra also has a number of high military officials from Java, as well as Acehnese and Minangkabau in the educational bureaucracy.

At the village level a dual governmental structure is also found. In the *adat* chieftancy system of each *huta* or village there will be a head raja, his Council of Village Rajas, the Council of Village Elders, and the raja's main public spokesman, or *Orangkaya*. The positions of all of these men will be determined by their clan and marriage alliance relationships to the founder lineage of the village. Parallel to their ceremonial administration of the village (indeed, they are concerned mostly with ritual life) will be the government-appointed Village Headman. He will report to the Kacamatan district head, called the *Camat*. In practice, some Village Headmen are young people with little traditional prestige in the settlement, among the rajas. In other villages, the rajaship councils may have one of their own number (usually a relatively well-educated younger man) in the Headmanship position. So, the administrative situation is mixed, although it is safe to say that the central government officials generally control the domains of formal schooling, national development projects such as roads and clinics, business law, and criminal law. The rajas and their alliance partners dominate the village ceremonial sphere as well as much of marriage and inheritance law. They share this latter area with the Islamic courts.

In the ritual oratory of the life crisis ceremonies, *anakboru* wife-receivers and *mora* wife-givers are eulogized in large-scale, deeply political terms, as the partners who must work together for human society to endure and prosper. In the higher oratory, cooperation among alliance partners is also said to be necessary to good cosmic order, and for the assurance of good harvests from the fields. The rajas and their supporters such as the *Orangkaya* are described in similar terms: as part and parcel of the basic order of things in the universe, and as demonstrations of the beneficent powers of the smoothly functioning "three support stones."

This strong reliance on ideas of clan founders, ancestral houses, powerful heirloom treasures (seen as power objects of the rajas), ranked marriage alliance relationships, and ranked leagues of beneficent rajas is also found in much Angkola printed literature on their society. This is especially true of those local Angkola writers who choose to publish much of their work in the Angkola language as opposed to the Indonesian national language. Such authors generally see their audience to be the group of Angkola young people they deem in need of instruction in the old customs; also included in their audience are old people in South Tapanuli towns, interested in ancient ceremonies.

The 1970s and 1980s saw a boom in *adat* handbook publishing on the topic of ancient Angkola ways. This is perhaps tied to the relative prosperity of the 1970s period, when the country was enjoying an oil boom. That decade also saw an increase in the number and size of *adat* ceremonies held in South Tapanuli. These rituals were generally founded by rich urban migrant families who apparently wished to increase their prestige by holding large weddings, funerals, and house dedications back in their lineage's home villages. At such three-day-long feasts of merit, a household could pay off a large number of ceremonial debts to *mora,* thus increasing their store of luck powers. City people would often come to these rituals as lineagemates or alliance partners of the hosts, but often they would not understand the subtleties of the ritual speeches, or in fact even the basic rationales for the oratory and the various ceremonial processions, animal sacrifices, and gift exchanges. Thus the *adat* guidebooks, to explain the ceremonial minutiae to city folk, or to record it for rural adat aficionados.

Generally, these small volumes[11] provide descriptive accounts of highly idealized life crisis rituals, of the sort once performed by the rich old rajas in colonial times. The authors often give sample orations, which use especially elegant phrases. The guides also explain marriage alliance and even kin term usage in elaborate detail. Other, related books recount Angkola lineage histories.

Now we can consider several texts, for their portrayal of Angkola as a culture. The Padangsidimpuan newspaperman and Muslim school principal G. Siregar Baumi has written a series of eight *adat* guides (Rodgers 1990a) and what he terms "Culture Guides" that are representative of this entire range of literature. Some of his books are in Angkola while others are in Indonesian. He runs one school in Medan and a second one in Padangsidimpuan, dividing his time between the two places. While not a raja in a strict sense, Sutan Tinggi (his honorific title)* is an accomplished orator with an encyclopediac knowledge of *adat* lore from his area of Angkola, called Marancar. As is common practice in this type of *adat* literature, Sutan Tinggi devotes many pages to small ceremonial details (e.g., how to construct a mound of ritual foods, how to deliver the different types of blessing speeches, how to arrange betel leaves during a brideprice presentation ceremony.) Beyond this, though, he often describes Angkola society in discursive terms. He stresses the importance of the Three-Support-Stones-on-the-Hearth as the fundaments of village life. The following, from his book "Ancient Leaf Letters" (or secret lore) shows the thorough penetration of alliance and clanship imagery into Siregar Baumi's vision of Angkola. Note also his self-confident tone in setting out his social world. Neither the realm of national life nor Java appear in this passage. Excerpts from one central chapter read as follows:

Society and Social Life

South Tapanuli society is mainly based on family relationships, which themselves derive from blood descent through the father's side (patriarchat). All of this carries the following philosophy: the Three-Support-Stones-on-the-Hearth. That in itself involves adat's social ties, which are based on three fundamental family relationships: *kahanggi, anakboru,* and *mora*. . . . The closeness or distance of family relationships is based on blood ties. It is only a small portion of the population, near Natal, where things are based on ties through mother's blood (matriarchat). Society consists of big families and little ones. We can portray the family ties as follows:

1. Family ties start out with but a single family, which then goes on to become a whole *suku* (marga, clan).
2. The single family goes on to become a group of adat elders, who are called the Group-Who-Are-of-a Single-Council-of-Adat-Elders. [Note: this section goes on to list the family group that holds a sacrificial meal together, then the whole village, then the larger chieftainship domain.]

In society, there are certain people whose function it is to maintain good social order. These consist of:

1. The Raja as the leader of adat society.
2. The Orangkaya as the secretary, or Spokesman.

---

* His full title means "Sutan Exalted and Bold, Upholder of World Affairs."

3. The Council of Rajas, who are the representatives of the descendants of rajas.
4. The Council of Village Elders, the representatives of adat society (these must be mature, married men).
5. Hulu Balang, the military commander and defense minister of the Raja and society.
6. The Hatoban slaves, the people who are the slaves and task-doers of the Rajas and descendants of rajas (Nowadays there aren't any of these anymore.)

The writer then goes on to list and briefly define six different types of rajas, four types of Orangkaya spokesmen, and three varieties of *anakboru*. The latter are described as follows:

5. Anakboru, or the group we marry our daughters to. Each household or family has its anakboru, who are normally called their Anadboru-Who-Guard-the-Door-Against-Dangers, guarding the door with a hardwood crossbar.
6. Yes-Saying Anakboru, who are longtime anakboru and who already have several generations of our daughters who have gone and married them.
7. Inherited Anakboru, which according to memory started with our ancestors, and now it has been so very many generations like that it cannot be counted anymore how long our daughters have been married to them. Now the relationship can't be broken off. Several titles or names have become customary ones to say to anakboru:
   1. Anakboru.
   2. Hardwood-Bar-Guarding-the-Door . . . [Note: the writer continues this list of eulogistic titles, including ones such as Cane-Over-the-Slippery-Spots, Augmenter-of-What-Lacks, Subtractor-of-Excess. All of these phrases refer to anakboru's value in supporting mora.] (Siregar Baumi 1984a, 58–63)

Siregar Baumi concludes this chapter by discussing anakboru-of-anakboru and the wife-givers-of-wife-givers. With that his discussion of society ends.

Several points are worth mentioning here, in searching for Siregar Baumi's views of Angkola as a political entity. First, as noted, Indonesia is simply absent, as a social place or even an abstract idea. This is true throughout the book, except for a few token acknowledgements in the introduction. There, the author alludes to the importance of documenting local cultures, in books, as part of Indonesia's national development efforts. After noting this need the writer no longer mentions the point. The rest of the volume (all 294 pages of it) concerns Angkola as an independent entity, unmoored to any larger social world. From interviews with Siregar Baumi in 1987, it is clear that he is quite aware of the actual Indonesian national administrative control of Tapanuli; in his portrayal of Angkola in his books, though, he is unintimidated by that larger political entity and chooses to omit mention of it.

Second, Siregar Baumi presents his readers with a strongly stratified society, divided into a noble class, a commoner class, and even a group of slaves. He does write, as an aside, that this last class no longer exists, but in other parts of the book he describes the *hatoban* slaves' role as servants to the rajas and as marriage exchange "goods" without apology. Such forthright attention to class stratification is quite in line with local Angkola thought (dominated by concern with social location) but flies directly in the face of nationalist ideology, which is explicitly democratic and egalitarian. Siregar Baumi simply avoids mention of this alternative social world.

Third, he places alliance and descent at the center of social life, and at the center of a village's social organization into levels of rajas, councils, Orangkaya spokesmen, and so on. These men get their positions by being "inherited anakboru" to their village rajas and so on through various kinship-based devices. He ends the section by borrowing some common oratory phrases to eulogize the wife-receivers. In ritual speech, these are power-filled words whose pronunciation invokes the cosmological conjunction of complementary opposites such as *mora* and *anakboru,* Upperworld and mundane world, and so on. By including this rush of esoteric oratory here, the writer may be trying to lend an air of ancientness and authenticity to his text.

Fourth, and rather paradoxically, Siregar Baumi draws on Western social science terms (patriarchat, matriarchat, borrowed from colonial-era Dutch ethnographies) and on an expository form typical of schoolbook prose (his outlines and numbered lists.) Batak writers often use such terms and styles to impart an aura of modernity and seriousness to their works, rather as if they were decorating a tree with ornaments. In Siregar Baumi's work, he has juxtaposed these progressive-sounding touches with exceedingly parochial, traditionalist images of village life. It could be that he is employing all available rhetorical strategies to lend luster to his presentation of Angkola society and daily life. His approach here also implies that serious, modern readers should pay attention to such an Angkola world.

Fifth, Siregar Baumi does not attempt any political exegesis to try to convince his readers that the Angkola class system, or marriage alliance system, or Angkola clan loyalties are compatible in some way with the Indonesian nation. He simply presents Angkola in straightforward, descriptive prose, with an air of confidence and pride. He even turns the tables on the national culture a bit by appropriating such governmental terms as "representative" and applying them to the old Angkola chieftancy positions.

A second of the same writer's publications, on bridewealth negotiations, portrays an even more unabashedly class stratified Angkola. In the sixty-three-page *Mangampar Ruji, Mangkobar Boru* (1978), *Figuring the Marriage Payments, Negotiating the Brideprice* the author details the different types of brideprices, according to the rank which a young woman's father's lineage occupies. Each variety of bride is assigned an appropriate cash and livestock brideprice. The writer goes on to note that transfers of slaves and personal attendants accompany the marriage of a raja's daughter (13). Siregar Baumi occasionally reminds his readers that slaves existed only in "the Feudal Age," back in colonial times, but such points are downplayed. Rank-conscious, fully stratified Angkola chieftaincies are the predominant social image throughout the small *adat* guide. The author also notes regretfully, in introducing the book, that Angkola people today have fallen away from the old bridewealth customs and no longer negotiate nor pay the full roster of fourteen marriage debts. This casts the modern age as a time of relative cultural impoverishment, predated by a fuller, older Angkola world.

Two additional custom guides also picture Angkola as a free-standing polity, drawing its strength from ancient alliance and clanship traditions. Baginda Marpaung, a Padangsidimpuan teacher and folklorist, published a superb proverb sampler called *Pundjut-pundjutan* ("Wallet of Memories") in 1962. He followed this in 1969 with *Joy in Common Meeting* (in Angkola, *Djop ni Roha Pardomuan*), a prose narrative on a family's progress through all of Angkola's major *adat* ceremonies. *Joy in Common Meeting* speaks of diligent *anakboru,* beneficent *mora,* and generous rajas who rule over orderly villages. Society is portrayed in chart form as follows (11):

Raja Panusunan Bulun ("Raja-Gatherer-of-Leaves")
Raja Pamusuk (another high chief)

Council of Elders
Home Household

Anakboru   Mora
Anakboru-of-Anakboru   Mora-of-Mora.

Baginda Marakub goes on to exult, "When we carefully take all this into consideration, within adat, our hearts are astounded at the goodness of our first generation ancestors' agreement on all of this. There are no words of dissension from any of them: all wish to bring the ritual to completion" (11). He goes on to reiterate how "extremely good" the *adat* of the earlier generations was. Passages of this sort, which recur throughout the book, gently disparage "this present age of progress," which is clearly identified with national life. Things are "less complete" nowadays, and the social world is given to disagreement and disorder.

Baginda Marakub's proverb sampler *Pundjut-pundjutan* provides an extended exegesis of some 740 Angkola *adat* sayings. Like his narrative of ceremonial life just discussed, this proverb volume also maintains a steadily eulogistic tone when dealing with adages about rajas, alliance, or clanship. In the following passages, wife-givers and wife-receivers and their close relationship of mutual indebtedness is placed at the center of village life (16–17):

Proverb no.39: The Support Beam at the Center of the Roof.
   The 'bungkulun' is the part at the top of the house. All the roof pieces of the house meet there. If that top support beam is aligned correctly, the house won't fall down. The 'support beam at the center' is the support beam where all the parts of the mid-section of the house and the kitchen meet.

This central support beam is given to anakboru wife-receivers as a name for them, for they are always the peacemakers in their mora's house. If there might happen to be a disagreement or an argument in their mora's house, it will be the anakboru who will bring peace and who will resolve it. . . . And whoever might happen to be at fault, it is always the anakboru who must take the blame. So, anakboru like this are the Central Support Beam, whom mora fears.

In this explanation, *anakboru's* mystical abilities to heal *mora's* disputes are stressed; this is a core theme as well in ritual orations. In such statements, the wife-receivers must be catered to, lest they bring supernatural dangers down on village society. A second saying deals with another, related phrase for *anakboru:* they are said to be their wife-givers "Cane Over the Slippery Spots, Their Lamp Showing the Way in the Night Darkness" (246–47). The *anakboru,* Baginda Marakub says, prop up their *mora* when the latter undergo difficulties, and light their way through gloomy periods, so that society as a whole can prosper. The book as a whole has many more exegitical passages of this sort, all claiming that good wife-giver/wife-receiver relations are crucial to village social order. Numerous other passages (e.g., proverbs nos. 19, 20, 31) praise the generosity and magical protective powers of rajas. The latter are always treated respectfully and in detail throughout the book.

In sum, this sort of folklore book places alliance and descent and the leagues of chiefs at the center of Angkola society. Alliance and descent images are explained at length, without apology. The same forthright pride in local traditions attaches to presentations of Angkola class stratification. But, the government's own folklorists writing for the Ethnic Culture series fire a volley in the other direction, systematically culling all serious references to the political implications of Angkola *adat* from their discussions of ritual, oratory, and village life.

Angkola in the National Government's Ethnic Culture Series

Starting in the 1970s, increased government revenues from oil taxes were used to fund a variety of national development projects, such as paved roads, irrigation systems, and new schools and clinics. The central government's Ministry of Education and Culture used their new funds in part to finance several series of publications on the ethnic cultures of the archipelago. Sometimes these books were based on new studies, done by research teams of provincial government civil servants. In a few cases, the Ministry simply reprinted folklore collections first published in the 1930s, under Dutch auspices.

These government publications were intended for distribution to public libraries and schools throughout the country. The books were to be used as source material for children in the different ethnic home regions to use in learning about their own cultures. Further, the books would introduce peoples like the Bataks to readers in other ethnic regions of the nation. The series included a local history project, for each province (with titles devoted to the history of the local struggles against the Dutch, and to the history of education in each province.) There was also an ambitious ethnic language dictionary project and a series of folklore texts (myths, chants, sample orations.) A separate series was devoted to folktales. Another dealt with children's games and other forms of public entertainment while another series focused on "traditional ceremonies." Many of these books were sponsored by a ministry project called the *"Proyek Inventarisasi dan Dokumentasi Kebudayaan,"* or the Culture Inventory and Documentation Project. A late offshoot of this endeavor, in 1983 and 1984, was a series of books (one for each province of the country) under the rubric, "Traditional Sayings Which Have a Connection with the Principles of the *Pancasila.*" The latter is the five-part, motto-like national ideology of Indonesia: Belief in God, National Consciousness, Humanism, Social Justice, and Sovereignity of the People. President Soeharto's New Order regime invokes the Five Principles at every opportunity, in all ethnic home regions, as the unifying philosophy of the nation and as a bulwark against the central government's three great fears: a Communist resurgence, ethnic fragmentation, and Islamic fundamentalism. Soeharto's administration has seized on the motto with particular fervor as their rationale for maintaining a relatively secular regime in an overwhelmingly Muslim society. The *Pancasila* is also being used to legitimate the government's many economic development efforts, in the name of national progress and *"Pancasila* Democracy."

The volume from this *Pancasila* series for North Sumatra is a telling if heavyhanded example of the government's attempt to reinterpret ethnic folk traditions in nationalist terms. A particularly vapid version of Angkola culture emerges from this volume in the series. The book, published in Jakarta in 1984, was written by a committee of Toba Batak government officials, all with advanced academic degrees (one author was a lawyer and the other four had the equivalent of master's degrees.) Selected for reconciliation with the Five Principles were traditional sayings from the Toba Batak, the Karo, and the people of Nias (a non-Batak people, located on an offshore island.) The choice of ethnic cultures to represent North Sumatra to the rest of the nation is significant in itself: the national government in general seems to have acceded to the Toba claim that they are the aboriginal, "most genuine" Batak society from which all the others have descended. Associated with this notion is the idea that Toba has the "purest" and oldest Batak culture.

The book proceeds via a series of *explication de texte* commentaries on familiar proverbs and *adat* sayings from each ethnic area, in much the same format used by Baginda Marakub. However, here the lengthy commentaries inform readers what the old Batak and Niassian sayings are "really about" the abiding Indonesian core values set out in the Five Principles. These eternal verities were always there in these local proverbs, readers are led to believe; the handbook will simply draw these truths out. Here is an example from the Toba section showing this technique. Most of the Toba proverbs used in the volumes are quite similar to Angkola ones and easily intelligible in the southern region. Indeed, the two Batak dialects at issue are almost fully intelligible with each other.

Saying no. 6:
Balintang ma pagade
Tumandakhon sitadoan
Arimuna ma gabe   The thread-separator, the cloth-
Molo masipaolo-olan.   holder,
                      Stepping upon the weaver's foot-pedal;
                      Your good fortune will pass on through
                          many generations,
                      If you just respect and honor one
                        another.

So, the advice contained her in this saying advises us that people who are siblings to each other or who are a married couple will always love each other and will always be-of-a-single-word-and-agreement.

This proverb is normally said to newlyweds who are just starting out their life together in their house, or it is said by the *hula-hula* (the side which gives women) and the *boru* (the side which receives women) at the *adat* wedding ceremony.

At *adat* weddings, old people often say this proverb when it happens that there is a disagreement between the *hula-hula* and the *boru*, when they disagree about how to carry out the *adat* (that is, when one side hasn't provided enough financial aid for the ceremony). So, it will be hoped that one side will just forgive the other side for that deficiency. The hope is: that a large deficit might be made smaller, that a tiny deficit of money might simply be eliminated.

And the same is true of the young man and the young woman, the newlyweds. It is hoped that they will always sail their prow so that they will always be 'saying-yes-to-each-other.' That is, always following along one after the other, always helping each other, so that they might prosper together. It is only through such a yes-saying mode of lie that they can live together as man and wife and that their wishes may be attained—that is, that they might attain prosperity. That means having descendants who live in a state of happiness and prosperity, prosperous in material as well as spiritual things.

This saying shows the great importance of living together in a state of agreement with each other, always valuing each other, full of tolerance for each other—and always ready to forgive each other should there happen to be any deficiency. So, this saying has a close connection to the Principle, 'Indonesian Unity.' (23–24, my translation)

The stress here is on the household, the married couple, and the adat ceremony. Omitted entirely are any references to the ways in which *anakboru/mora* ties structure village society in a political sense, or to the relationship of the exchange of gifts and financial support among alliance partners and the rajaship councils. Rather, alliance becomes a matter of the domestic economy, and the ritual obligations of the marriage ceremony itself. This commentary and others like it throughout the book also have a treaclely quality to them, with their optimistic passages about tolerance and peaceability. This is a main stress also in the national government's presentation of its hopes for a united Indonesia, free of ethnic or religious strife.

A second government publication, also about traditional sayings and this time about Angkola and Mandailing examples, shows the same processes at work. *Sayings in the Angkola-Mandailing Language* (1980) is an anthology of southern Batak proverbs with Indonesian language translations and short commentaries. These explanations frequently reduce the larger political dimensions of alliance and clanship to family matters. For instance, the fourteenth entry in the volume is a saying about the wife-receivers' duty to protect their wife-givers from physical harm. As noted earlier, in village thought this assertion has deep social and cosmological reverberations. In the government volume the proverb emerges as follows:

> Middle-Rafter-Holding-Up-the-House-Roof—that is, the good *anakboru* who is always ready to do *mora's* bidding, in such cases as putting an end to fighting within the mora group. In such cases, they wouldn't want to give more weight to one side or another.
>
> That is, a son-in-law or a brother-in-law who is a good follower. Whenever you order him to go off and do something for you, he will never refuse. Moreover, he can be used as a go-between (a peacemaker) for the family. (10–11, my translation)

Again this exegesis reduces the larger political dimensions of *anakboru* and *mora* relations to domestic matters and arguments within the household. In village thought, the very order of the cosmos is dependent on *anakboru's* peacemaking efforts.

Another government volume on southern Batak proverbs, called *Proverbs in the South Tapanuli Batak Language* (1982) trivializes Angkola *adat* oratory and its alliance and clan descent ideas in another way. The major part of the book (sixty-two pages of the total of eighty-three) consists of an alphabetically arranged series of Angkola language sayings, followed by paragraph-long explanations of them, also in the Angkola language. These commentaries concentrate on the literal meaning of the phrases in the proverbs, and on what each saying means in its most general sense. These explanations tend to omit most discussions of *anakboru* and *mora* relations (in contrast to Baginda Marakub's lengthy commentaries on the subject.) The last part of the book delivers an even more powerful political message about the status on Angkola thought in relation to the Indonesian nation. Each of the 232 Angkola proverbs discussed earlier in the book are listed once again, followed this time by one-sentence Indonesian-language translations. But, these translations butcher the literal meanings of the original Angkola, reducing them to ridiculously oversimplified catch phrases. For instance, the 220nd entry reads:

Angkola:	Indonesian:
220. Siala ulu mangimpal tala palu2, magulang rap margulu, malamun saulak lalu.	Be of-a-single-word, of-a-single agreement.

> The *Siala* plant's knobby head of fruit all joins together its work as a hammer; put it in a wallowing hole and it all gets equally muddy; when it ripens it ripens all at once.

To readers from other Indonesian ethnic groups who might come across this entry, the metaphorical richness of the Angkola botanical phrases would be invisible.

As a genre, then, such government publications on the nation's minority societies work to define a people such as the Angkola Batak in several key ways. First, the Angkola are presented as one small subsociety of a larger, vaguely defined ethnic unit (the Bataks), who are themselves presented as a small constituent part of a huge multiethnic nation. Each small society is given its own set of small volumes, in the various ethnic culture series. Second, the Angkola culture emerges as a collection of ceremonies, family rules, and old sayings, none of which are seen to have much political content and none of which allow for themes of social conflict. Third, Angkola culture is second-guessed, so to speak, at every turn, with each Angkola *adat* sayings or social practice translated into a "larger" Indonesian context. The latter is identified with modern life, while the ethnic culture is shown to derive from the past (more specifically, the hoary past.) Fourth, Angkola marriage alliance uniting ancestral houses disappears, in favor of an emphasis on the marital pair themselves. Finally, Angkola clans and their ancient origins are eclipsed in favor of a stress on the living members of a household and village, and the present period of modernizing Indonesia.

Conclusions

Efforts to define ethnic cultures in contemporary Indonesia are obviously intensely competitive endeavors, pitting representatives of various visions of the social community against one another in a variety of arenas: print publications, tourism promotions, and such media forms (not discussed here) as ethnic culture theme parks and ethnic culture shows on the national television station. At present, for North Sumatra, there is no resolution to the conflict between the two sets of images of Angkola presented on the one hand by Angkola custom book authors and on the other hand by government committees working for the Ethnic Culture series. Neither side's views of the Indonesian social world has eclipsed the other; a multiplicity of visions of Angkola are available for public consumption. It may not be too much to say, in fact, that Indonesian printed media presentations of minority cultures are one of the most active and combative parts of Indonesian political discourse today, since these negotiations about what constitutes a proper ethnic minority culture have not yet been resolved.

This Batak case has shown that this one ethnic culture in Indonesia is being defined along several dimensions: in terms of its history (clan-based and mythic, or secular and nationalist), its kinship ideology, and its ceremonial life. Writers working to promote a strong, autonomous Angkola culture politicize all of these domains, while national government committees translate the Angkola past, its alliance and descent ideas and its *adat* rituals into folklore. It would be intriguing to discover whether or not government publications series in other developing Third World nations are attempting to transform the political ideologies of their minority societies in similar ways. It would be equally interesting to see if these ethnic societies are able to resist government redefinition efforts in ways as imaginative and resilient as those marshalled by the Angkola.

Notes

1. On ethnic identity in Southeast Asia see Moerman 1965; Lehman 1967; Lebar et al. 1964; Keyes 1981, 1984; Friedman 1975; Rosaldo 1978; and Nagata 1981. On Batak ethnicity see Bruner 1961, 1973, 1974; Liddle 1967, 1970, 1972; and Kipp 1983. Rodgers 1990b includes a short discussion of ethnic identity and gender symbolism in Angkola.
2. See especially Bruner 1973 and Kipp 1983 on this point in relation to the Toba and Karo Batak.
3. On Indonesian nation state formation in relation to ethnic minorities see Davis 1979. On the role of the communication media in this process see Jackson and Pye 1978.
4. On this point see especially Hoskins 1987 and Atkinson 1983.
5. Volkman's *Feast of Honor* (1985) provides an excellent ethnographic case study of this process.
6. For background material on Angkola and issues of cultural change as the society becomes more thoroughly integrated into the nation, see Rodgers 1978, 1983, 1984, and 1986.
7. Typical works include Marpaung 1962 and 1969, Dalumante and Pohan 1985, Sutan Pargarutan 1984, Siregar and Siregar 1974 and Harahap 1986.
8. Typical books in this series include Arrasjid and Sutan Keadilan 1982 and Hanafiah 1980, as well as the booklets published by the Indonesian govern-

ment's Departemen Pendidikon don Kebudayaan, listed in the reference section.

9. The original titles here were *Permainan Anak Anak Daerah Sumatra Utara, Parumpamaan di Hata Angkola-Mandailing,* and *Ungkapan Tradisional Sebagai Sumber Informasi Kebudayan Daerah Sumatera Utara.*
10. Such commentators include regular villagers and townspeople as well as adat chiefs. I base this comment on my 1974–77, December 1980, and October 1986–March 1987 ethnographic fieldwork in the Sipirok area.
11. *Adat* guides include Marpaung 1969, Dalimunte and Pohan 1985 and Harahap 1986. There are many more such guides, most published in the last fifteen years.

References

Arrasjid, Harun and Sutan Keadilan. 1982. *Umpama-umpama Hata Batak Tapanuli Selstan.* Jakarta: Departemen Pendidikan dan Kebudayaan, Proyek Penerbitan Buku Sastra Indonesia dan Daerah.

Atkinson, Jane M. 1983. "Religions in Dialogue: The Construction of an Indonesian Minority Religion." *American Ethnologist* 10(4), 684–96.

Bruner, Edward M. 1961. "Urbanization and Ethnic Identity in North Sumatra." *American Anthropologist* 63: 508–21.

Bruner, Edward M. 1973. "Kin and Non-Kin." In A. Southall (ed.), *Urban Anthropology,* London: Oxford University Press.

Bruner, Edward M. 1974. "The Expression of Ethnicity in Indonesia." In *Urban Ethnicity,* Abner Cohen (ed.), London and New York: Tavistock. 251–80.

Dalimunte, Abd. Rachman and Sondat Pohan. 1985. *Adat Daerah Tapanuli Selston: Surat Tumbaga Holing.* Medon: Privately published.

Davis, Gloria, ed. 1979. *What is Modern Indonesian Culture?* Athens, Ohio: University Center for International Studies, Southeast Asia Series No. 52.

Departemen Pendidikon and Kebudayaan. 1981–82. *Permainan Anak Anak Daerah Sumatera Utara.* Jakarta. Proyek Inventarisasi don Dokumentasi Kebudayaan Daerah.

Departemen Pendidikan don Kebudayaan. 1982. *Sistim Kesatuan Hidup Setempat Daerah Sumatera Utara.* Jakarta: Proyek Inventarisasi dan Dokumentasi Kebudayaan Daerah.

Departemen Pendidikan dan Kebudayaan. 1983–84. *Ungkapan Tradisional yang Berkaitan dengan Sila-Sila dalam Panca Sila.* Jakarta: Proyek Inventarisasi dan Dokumentasi Kebudayaan Daerah.

Departemen Pendidkan dan Kebudayaan. 1984. *Sejarah Sosial Daerah Sumatra Utara Kotamadya Medan.* Jakarta: Proyek Inventarisasi dan Dokumentasi Sejarah Nasional.

Departemen Pendidikan danKebudayaan. 1984-85. *Arti Lambang dan Fungsi Tata Rias Pengantin dalam Menanamkon Nilai-Nilai Budaya Daerah Sumatera Utara.* Jakarta: Proyek Inventarisasi dan Dokumentasi Kobudayaan Daerah.

Departemen Pendidikan dan Kebudayaan. 1984. *Ungkapan Tradisional Sebagai Sumber Informasi Kebudayaan Daerah Sumatera Utara.* Jakarta: Proyek Inventarisasi dan Dokumenasi Kebudayaan Daerah.

Departemen Pendidikan dan Kebudayaan. 1985. *Upacara Tradisional Daerah Sumatera Utara.* Jakarta: Proyek Inventarisasi dan Dokumentasi Kebudayaan Daerah.

Friedman, Jonathan. 1975. "Tribes, States, and Transformations." In *Marxist Analysis in Social Anthropology,* Maurice Bloch (ed.), New York: Wiley.

Hanafiah, Ali. 1980. *Parumpamaan di Hata Angkola Mandailing.* Jakarta: Departemen Pendidikon dan Kebudaaan: Proyek Penerbitan Buku Bacaan dan Sastra Indonesia dan Daerah.

Harahap, T. Mr. Tigor. 1986. *Pastak Pago-Pago.* Padangsidimpuon: Privately published.

Hoskins, Janet A. 1987. "The Headhunter as Hero: Local Traditions and their Reinterpretation in National History." *American Ethnologist* 14(4), 605–21.

Jackson, Karl D. and Lucien Pye, eds. 1978. *Political Power and Communications in Indonesia.* Berkeley: University of California Press.

Keyes, Charles F., ed. 1981. *Ethnic Change.* Seattle: University of Washington Press.

Keyes, Charles F. 1984. "Tribal Ethnicity and State in Vietnam." *American Ethnologist* 11 (February 1984), 176–82.

Kipp, Richard. 1983. "Fictive Kinship and Changing Ethnicty among Karo and Toba Migrants." In Kipp and Kipp 1983, 147–54.

Kipp, Rita S. and Richard Kipp, eds., 1983. *Beyond Samósir: Recent Studies of the Batak Peoples of Sumatra.* Athens, Ohio: Ohio University Center for International Studies, Southeast Asia Series No. 62.

Leach, E. R. 1954. *Political Systems of Highland Burma.* Boston: Beacon.

LeBar, F. M., G. Hickey, and J. K. Musgrave. 1964. *Ethnic Groups of Mainland Southeast Asia.* New Haven: HRAF Press.

Lehman, F. 1967. "Ethnic Categories in Burma and the Theory of Social Systems." In P. Kunstadter (ed.), *Southeast Asian Tribes, Minorities and Nations.* Princeton: Princeton University Press, 93–124.

Liddle, R. William. 1967. "Suku Simalungun: An Ethnic Group in Search of Representation." *Indonesia* 3(1967), 1–30.

Liddle, R. William. 1970. *Ethnicity, Party, and National Integration: An Indonesian Case Study.* New Haven: Yale University Press.

Liddle, R. William. 1972. "Ethnicity and Political Organization: Three Sumatran Cases." In *Culture and Politics in Indonesia.* Cornell University Press.

Linnekin, Joyce. 1983. "Defining Tradition: Variations on the Hawaiian Identity." *American Ethnologist* 10, 241–52, May 1983.

Marakub Marpaung, Baginda. 1962. *Pundjut-Pundijutan.* Medan: Islamiyak.

Marpaung, Bgd. Marakub. 1969. *Djop ni Roha Pardomuan (Paradaton Tapanuli Selatan).* Padangsidimpuan: Pustaka Timur.

Moerman, Michael. 1965. "Ethnic Identification in a Complex Civilization: Who Are the Lue?" *American Anthropologist* 67, 1215–30.

Nagata, Judith. 1981. "In Defense of Ethnic Boundaries: The Changing Myths and Charters of Malay Identity." In Keyes 1981, *Ethnic Change,* 87–116.

Partgarutan, Sutan. 1984. *Menulis dan Membaca Hurup Batak bahasa Tapanuli Selatan.* Medon: Privately published.

Rodgers, Susan. 1978. "Angkola Batak Kinship through its Oral Literature." Ph.D. Dissertation, Department of Anthropology, University of Chicago.

Rodgers, Susan. 1979a. "Advice to the Newlyweds: Sipirok Batak Wedding

Speeches—Adat or Art?" In Edward M. Bruner and Judith Becker (eds.), *Art, Ritual, and Society in Indonesia*. Athens, Ohio University Papers in International Studies, Southeast Asia Monograph Series 53, 30–61.

Rodgers, Susan. 1979. "A Modern Batak *Horja:* Innovation in Sipirok Adat Ceremonial." *Indonesia* 27, April 1979. Ithaca, N.Y.: Cornell Modern Indonesia Project, 103–28.

Rodgers, Susan. 1983. "Political Oratory in a Modernizing Southern Batak Homeland." In Kipp and Kipp (eds.), 1983, 21–52.

Rodgers, Susan. 1984. "Orality, Literacy, and Batak Concepts of Marriage Alliance." *Journal of Anthropological Research* 40, 3, Fall 1984, 433–50.

Rodgers, Susan. 1936. "Batak Tape Cassette Kinship: Constructing Kinship through the Indonesian National Mass Media." *American Ethnologist* 13, 1 February, 1986, 23–42.

Rodgers, Susan. 1990a. "A Batak Antiquarian Writes his Culture: Print Literacy and Social Thought in an Indonesian Society." *Steward Journal of Anthropology* 17, 1–2, "Conversations in Anthropology: Anthropology and Literature."

Rodgers, Susan. 1990b (forthcoming). "The Symbolic Representation of Women in a Changing Batak Society." In Shelby Errington and Jane M. Atkinson (eds.), *The Paradox of Power: Gender in Southeast Asia*. Palo Alto, Cal.: Stanford University Press.

Rosaldo, Renato. 1978. "The Rhetoric of Control: Ilongots Viewed as National Bandits and Wild Indians." In *The Reversible World: Symbolic Inversion in Art and Society,* Barbara Babcock (ed.), 240–57. Ithaca, N.Y.: Cornell University Press.

Siregar, O. Gorga Torsana, and Sutan Habiaran Siregar. 1974. *Toga Siregar.* Medan: Privately published.

Siregar, Baumi G. Gelar Sutan Tinggibarani Perkasa Alam. 1978. *Mangampar Ruji/Mangkobar Boru (Musyawarah Perhitungan Mas Kawin Menurut Adat Tapanuli Selatan.)*. Tapanuli Selatan: privately published.

———. 1980. *Methode Baru pelajaran membaca dan menulis huruf-huruf*

———. *Batak Tapanuli Selatan. Aksara Batak Tapanuli Selatan.* Padangsidimpuan: privately published.

———. *Horja Godang Mangupa di na Haroan Boru, Horas Tondi Madingi Sayur Matua Bulung.* Padangsidimpuan: privately published.

———. 1984b. *Seni Budaya Tradisional daerah Tapanuli Selatan Suku Batak Angkola-Padanglawas-Mandailing dan Pesisir.* Padangsidimpuan: privately published.

———. 1984a. *Surat Tumbag Holing, Adat Batak Angkola-Sipirok-Padangbolak-Barumun-Mandailing-Batang natal-Natal.* Padangsidimpuan: privately published.

———. 1986. *Pabagas Baru.* Padangisimpuan: privately published.

Sutan Tinggibarani Perkasa Alam and Dra. Rukiah Siregar, Paruhumon Harahap. 1977. *Burangir na Hombang: Buku Pelajaran Adat (Tap Sel) (Tapanuli Selatan) Siulaon Sapanjang Adat Dipersembahkan untuk Masyarakat dan Naposo/Naulibulung.* Padangsidimpuan: privately published.

Sutan Tinggibarani Perkasas Alam, Dra. Rukiah Siregar, Drs. Bahasan Siregar Bgd. Mulia. 1981. *Bona-Bona ni Partuturan (Cara-Cara Bertutur Sopan san-*

tun dalam Hubungan Kefamilian Menurut Adat Tapanuli Selatan. Padangisi-dumpuan: privately published.

Volkman, Toby A. 1984. "Great Performances: Toraja Cultural Identity in the 1970s." *American Ethnologist* 11(1), 152–69.

Volkman, Toby A. 1985. *Feasts of Honor: Ritual and Change in the Toraja Highlands.* Urbana: University of Illinois Press, Illinois Studies in Anthropology, no. 16.

7

Ethnicity and State-Building: The Case of the Palestinians in the Middle East

Emile Sahliyeh

The literature on ethnicity reveals the presence of two perspectives for the explanation of the phenomenon of group ethnic identity. The first perspective posited several features required for the formation of ethnicity. A group's collective identity is based upon ascriptive and primordial relationships.[1] The presence of a common culture and a distinct social origin, race, and region are deemed essential for the rise of communal identity and the differentiation among assorted social collectivities.

In addition, language, a shared religious belief system, territory, and legal political entity are viewed as essential requisites for the rise of ethnicity.[2] In this context, the proponents of this perspective argue that language, as a communication device, discriminates against the non-natives, while religion serves as an important foundation for communal identification and the emergence of a separate tradition. It suggests to its adherents a world perspective and an encompassing social character. The definition of ethnic identity also includes the presence of territory and a sovereign state. The presence of a territorial homeland provides the groups with a reference point and helps to draw the boundaries between it and other

177

ethnic communities, while the state furnishes the institutional framework within which the interests of an ethnic community are protected. The nation-state reflects the collective will of the populace and their common heritage. Such an ethnic national device lessens the anxieties and the uncertainties of the individual and the social collectivity alike. These attributes offer a point of reference and a locus for political allegiance.

Other advocates of this approach contend that educational achievement is also an important aid for the survival of the group. The political weight of a particular community depends upon the strength of its educated elite. Indeed, the expansion of education is the driving force behind the emergence of a class of intelligentsia.

These variables combined are not, however, always relevant or sufficient to the explanation of communal identity formation. For instance, while language and religion are pertinent to the formulation of the ethnic identity of some groups, class, race, social origin, or region may be more salient in other cases. Still in other instances, ethnicity requirements may go beyond the aforementioned primordial attributes. Aside from the influence of language, race, and religion, ethnicity involves a common historical experience as well as a group belief in a shared destiny and the presence of common symbols and grievances that tie the members of that social collectivity together. Communal passions and self-esteem may also arise from the interaction of a certain group with other outside rival people.[3] In this connection, external dangers and strains to the security and the survival of the group will reinforce the feelings of ethnic solidarity among the members of that community.[4]

The second perspective attributes the emergence of ethnic feelings to instrumental considerations.[5] The proponents of this perspective argue that ethnic identity serves the practical needs and interests of the members of the community. The durability of the ethnic identity is contingent upon its ability to provide security, social status, and economic benefits for its members more than do other existing alternatives. Thus, the presence of appealing opportunities outside the native circle for an individual's economic and social advancement can lead to the decline of ethnic solidarity. As a consequence, the members of such an ethnic society can modify their identity to suit the new rising conditions. Finally, in view of the effectual nature of this perspective, ethnic identity is not a closed system as outsiders can be incorporated in the ethnic group.

Such theoretical pronouncements do not explain accurately and completely the rise of modern Palestinian nationalism. First, the limited usefulness of the instrumentalist perspective is evidenced in the emergence of Palestinian nationalism itself. Despite the presence of numerous opportunities for some of the Palestinians to assimilate into other societies, the vast majority of the Palestinians did not abandon their quest for an independent state and a distinct national identity.

Second, some of the core features of the primordial perspective on ethnicity do not fully qualify the Palestinians to be a separate ethnic community. In particular, language, religion, race, and social origin do not entitle the Palestinians to a discrete national identity. The Palestinians share these features with the rest of the Arabs.[6] Islam and the Arabic language, for instance, are insufficient indexes for the rise of a separate Palestinian identity. Arabic is the language of all the Arabs and, as such, is not a differentiating feature of the Palestinian people. Moreover, many of the Palestinians converse with the local dialects of their country of residence.

Islam is the religion of most Arabs and, as such, is not exclusive to the Palestinians. Islam also provides a religious reference point to some of the Palestinians who happened to be Christians. Concerning their social mores, practices, customs, and conventions, the Palestinians are also analogous to the rest of the Arabs.

Finally, the emergence of a Palestinian ethnic identity presents another challenge for the primordial perspective. The Palestinians have not converged in a single country. Instead, they live in different regions including the Middle East, Europe, and the United States.

Yet, despite their physical dispersal, the oneness of language, race, religion, and common political aspirations that the Palestinians share with the rest of the Arabs indicates that a discernable Palestinian national identity appeared. The Palestinians do not deny their attachment to the Arab world, they nevertheless recognize themselves as a distinct national group.

The Evolution of Modern Palestinian Nationalism

The growth of modern Palestinian nationalism as distinct from Arab nationalism can be attributed to the crisis milieu that the Palestinians lived through and to the efforts of mobilizational agents. The crisis milieu refers to the Palestinians' deep sense of deprivation and grievance, as manifested in the physical dispersal of their society, their attachment to the land, and the Israeli presence in Palestine. These attributes, more than the central features of the primordial perspective, illustrate the rise of an exclusive Palestinian nationalism and the development of communal solidarity.

Since the early days of the twentieth century, the Palestinians have experienced an ongoing crisis atmosphere.

Prior to the World War II, the Palestinians witnessed the placement of Palestine under British mandate with its declared goal of helping in the formation of a state for the Jews in Palestine, and the facilitation of Jewish emigration and the transfer of land to them. The Arab defeats of 1948 and 1967, the subsequent dispersal of the Palestinians from their homeland, and Israel's occupation of the West Bank and Gaza, further compounded the suffering of the Palestinians. Moreover, the memories of the massacres at Dar Yasin, Sabra, Shatilla, and Tal al-Za'tar are at the core of the Palestinians' collective agony.[7] The Palestinians have also endured pain at the hands of some of their fellow Arabs, including Syria and Jordan. Finally the harsh living conditions inside the refugee camps contributed further to the anguish of the Palestinians.[8]

The net effect of these crises was the rise of a Palestinian national identity and communal solidarity. The right of return and the creation of a Palestinian state were at the core of Palestinian nationalism. For some time, the aim of Palestinian nationalism was the liberation of all of Palestine. However, since 1977, and more explicitly since 1988, the establishment of a West Bank and Gaza independent state, where Palestinian traditions and cultural heritage can be preserved, has become the core objective for the Palestinians. The ubiquitous appeal of these goals explains why the majority of the Palestinians did not seek incorporation in the societies of their host states, nor did they strive to create an alternative homeland for themselves outside Palestine. Instead, the Palestinians remained loyal to Palestine and maintained their separate existence and formed their autonomous political organizations and institutions.

Aside from the impact of the crisis milieu and the collective historical experience, Palestinian nationalism resulted from the presence of a number of mobilizing agents. These include the Palestinians' traditional elite, militant counterelite, mass organizations, and PLO with its various factions. The self-conscious Palestinian traditional elite, drawn mostly from well-to-do families, sought to promote Palestinian nationalism prior to 1967. Following the formation of the PLO in 1964, however, Palestinian nationalism was further accelerated at the hands of the Palestinian counterelite who were mostly drawn from lower-income backgrounds and who espoused a more militant form of Palestinian nationalism. The new leadership took control of the PLO in 1969 and initiated the military struggle as a primary means to liberate Palestine. The PLO and its political programs provided the exiled Palestinians with a point of reference and loyalty.

Until the 1980s, the collective historical experience and the attachment to the land rather than to religion furnished most Palestinians with the base for nationalism. Yet, starting in the 1980s, loyalty to Islam and the Arabic language have assumed special saliency to an increasing number of Palestinians within the occupied territories and inside Israel. The prolongation of Israel's military occupation of the West Bank and Gaza, the rise of Jewish fundamentalism, the construction of Israeli settlements on Arab lands, and the provocation of the Israeli settlers to the local Palestinians made Islam and the Arabic language important elements in the ethnic chart of the indigenous Palestinians. Both Islam and the Arabic language symbolize the Palestinian collective identity vis-à-vis Israel and provide them with a strong feeling of ethnic purity, historical continuity, and sense of self-preservation.

In view of the exclusive nature of Israel's Jewish culture and the state's political identification with Zionism, the Israeli Arabs were not integrated into the Israeli society. This explains why many of them increasingly identified with the politics of Palestinian nationalism and later in the 1980s with Islam.[9] Following Israel's occupation of the West Bank and Gaza and the elevation of the PLO to the position of being the sole legitimate representative of the Palestinians, the Israeli Arabs viewed themselves increasingly as part of a broader Palestinian community.

Palestinian nationalism, as we know it today, has passed through a number of phases. The first such phase began before World War I and ended with the outbreak of the first Arab-Israeli war in 1948. This phase witnessed the emergence of early Palestinian nationalism. The second phase, 1948–1967, was marked by the Palestinians' relegation of the task of reconstructing Arab Palestine to the Arab armies. The third phase began in 1967 when the collective Arab armies were defeated. The Arab defeat allowed for the emergence of modern Palestinian nationalism.

The First Phase: Pre-World War I to 1948

Prior to World War I, the Arabs of Palestine extended allegiance to the Ottoman Empire. Their loyalty to the Ottoman state was based upon their belief in Islamic unity. The gradual unfolding of the long-term objectives of the Zionist movement of forming a Jewish homeland in Palestine, led the Arabs of Palestine to support the territorial integrity of the empire. It was assumed that the preservation of the Ottoman dynasty would ensure the Arab and Islamic character of Palestine.[10]

The outbreak of World War I and its developments ended the old order and witnessed the rise of early Palestinian nationalism. The initial signs of this new nationalism took the form of an Arab awakening against the Ottoman rule and the policy of Turkification of the non-Turkish subjects of the empire. The Turkification policy antagonized the Arabs who were proud of their ethnic background.[11]

Britain's undertaking during the war, to facilitate the establishment of a homeland for the Jews in Palestine and the placement of Palestine under the British mandate in 1919 as well as the subsequent Jewish emigration to Palestine, unleashed Palestinian nationalism and resistance during World War I and after. Between 1917 and 1920, numerous Arab political associations were formed in Palestine to protest British Zionist policy and the increasing

Jewish immigration to Palestine. Though these political organizations served as vehicles for the expression of Palestinian national interests, the local politicians were not united in their approach to resist the Zionist goals in Palestine. By the end of World War I, two trends were discernable. The proponents of the first trend believed that the political independence of Palestine would arrest the British and Zionist designs in the holy lands. Those politicians were older and came from socially prominent Palestinian urban families. Land possession, education, social preeminence, and wealth were the primary vehicles for the influence and legitimacy of the older politicians. Prior to the breakup of the empire, those politicians were members of the Ottoman civil service system.

The seasoned politicians formed several political societies known as the Moslem Christian Associations (MCA) in the main cities in Palestine. Such societies, however, were not accessible to the average Palestinian Arab. Only individuals drawn from the leading families became members of the MCA.

Though the older politicians were strongly opposed to Zionism and Jewish emigration to Palestine, they did not try to bring about a showdown with it. Their age and conservative background led them to follow a low profile approach towards Britain. They were also anxious to maintain their access to the British local government. For this reason, those patriarchal politicians used persuasion and petitions as the primary means to convey their political demands.[12]

The older politicians opposed the merger of their country into Syria. From their perspective, the political independence of Palestine would eliminate the Zionist threat to their country. The opposition to a Palestinian-Syrian merger stemmed, in part, from their local patriotism and their antagonism to Syrian political hegemony. Their preference for Palestine's political autonomy was dictated by their fear that the unity with Syria would foil their privileges and foster the interests of their political rivals.

The narrow Palestinian focus of the conservative politicians contrasted sharply with the stands of the proponents of the second trend. Those politicians who were younger in age, wanted to unite Palestine with Syria under the leadership of Prince Faisal (the son of King Hussein, the Sharif of Mecca). They posited that such a unity would provide Palestine with sufficient protection. In their view, the incorporation of Palestine with Syria would not only promote the cause of Arab unity and contain Zionism, but would also strengthen their quest for local leadership.

Because of their young age, those politicians did not have the opportunity to assume high administrative posts within the Ottoman bureaucracy. However, in their effort to contain the Zionist threat to Palestine, the new politicians were more assertive in their dealings with Britain than their older counterparts. To achieve their goals, the younger politicians employed a variety of techniques including the submission of petitions to the British, demonstrations, and strikes. In addition, they formed two political organizations Al-Muntada Al-Adabi (the Literary Club) and Al-Nadi Al-Arabi (the Arabic Club). The membership in both clubs was confined to the sons of rich Palestinian families.[13]

The rise of early Palestinian nationalism. The goal of uniting Palestine and Syria ultimately failed. The placement of Palestine under the British mandate required that the Palestinians center their efforts upon narrow provincial issues including the opposition of British pro-Jewish policies and the Zionist plans to colonize Palestine. In addition, the division of Greater Syria between France and Britain thwarted the search for unity. The quest for Arab unity was also frustrated by the split within the ranks of the Arab nationalists. The local elite in each of Palestine, Syria, Lebanon, and Iraq reconciled themselves to the dictates of native politicians who were busy with issues pertaining to their individual countries. Finally, Prince Faisal's controversial dealings with the Zionists and his effort to win British support in his quarrel with France over Syria further alienated the politicians in Palestine.

In view of these developments and the mounting Zionist menace, the advocates of unity with Syria were swayed that the Palestinians' interests and wishes should assume primacy. Thus, the collapse of Faisal's government in Syria, in July 1920, was marked by making Palestine the locus for the local elite's loyalties and allegiance.

The fixation with Palestinian parochial interests was evidenced at the third Palestine Congress in December 1920. Irrespective of their former political persuasion, the Palestinian elite demanded the formation of a national government accountable to the parliament representing the Arab majority in Palestine. They also called upon Britain to terminate its mandate and to stop the implementation of the idea of a Jewish homeland in Palestine. These demands were put forward repeatedly during the interwar period and were behind several rebellions that occurred during the British mandate over Palestine.

In conclusion, the Zionist objectives of forming a state for the Jews in Palestine aroused the Palestinians to organize politically in order to defend their land. Likewise, the dereliction of efforts for Arab unity played a crucial role in the ascendancy of Palestinian nationalism.

The primary concern for the Palestinians during the interwar period, was the formation of an accountable government rather than the creation of a state. After all, the Palestinians were living on their own territory. The setting up of a sovereign government and the declaration of independence were the two missing elements.

The interwar period was also marked by the convergence of power in an authoritative national leader Haj Amin al-Husaini (the Mufti of Jerusalem) and the emergence of the Arab executive. The formation of national parties, committees, and unions also attested to the rise of Palestinian national awareness. The presence of such structures allowed for the gradual political mobilization of different social groups and their incorporation into the resistance movement against the British and the Zionists.

Yet, the Palestinian leadership was not able to achieve for the Palestinians their right for self-determination nor was it capable of stopping the process of creating a Jewish state. The local elite's search for political independence were hampered by the rivalries among the leading families, the lack of sophisticated political organization, and by the opposition of both Britain and the Zionists.

The Second Phase: The Arabization of the Palestinian Problem, 1948–1967

Following the formation of Israel, the Palestinian society was split into four main clusters: Israeli Palestinians, West Bank and Gaza Palestinians, Palestinians living in refugee camps in the neighboring Arab states, and Palestinians residing in the Arab world and the West. The physical dispersal of the Palestinians complicated the task of nation-building and the emergence of a separate Palestinian nationalism in the post-1948 era. In the 1950s and the early 1960s, Palestinian political activists opted for trans-national ideologies, movements, and parties. Some Palestinians joined the Ba'ath Party, others were enlisted in the Arab Nationalist Movement (ANM), some became communists, and still others were associated with the Moslem Brotherhood movement. West Bank notables backed the Hashemite regime in Jordan.

The net result of the political and physical dispersal of Palestinians was their predisposition to trust the task of liberating their land to the collective Arab will and armies. Arab unity was seen as sine qua non for the liberation of Palestine. Though the process of Arabizing the Palestinian question started earlier during a pro-longed strike in 1936, the Arab custodianship of the Palestinian question was accelerated in 1948 when the Arab states sent armies to Palestine to check the emergence of Israel. The Arabization of the Palestinian question was facilitated in the 1950s by the emer-gence of Nasser and his charismatic leadership, his espousal of Pan-Arabism, and the merger of Syria and Egypt in 1958. These events lessened the appeal of local Palestinian nationalism. Indeed, most Palestinians believed that Arab unity was capable of liberat-ing Palestine.

The primacy of Arab nationalism compelled the majority of Palestinians to subordinate their interests to the dictates of Arab nationalism. Moreover, rivalries among Arab countries and politi-cal territorial ambitions of Arab leaders hindered the development of separate Palestinian political institutions. In this connection, the Arab Higher Committee's request from the Arab League in 1948 to form a Palestinian government was foiled by the internal splits within the ranks of the Palestinians and the rivalry between Egypt and Jordan for the custodianship of the Palestinian problem.[14] Due to its interest in the annexation of the West Bank, Jordan was vehemently opposed to the formation of any Palestinian govern-ment.

In response to the establishment of the All Palestine Govern-ment (APG) in Gaza, King Abdallah convened four political rallies for West Bank notables between the fall of 1948 and the winter of 1949.[15] The participants landed backing for the king's plan to merge the West Bank with the East Bank and censured the formation of the All Palestine Government. Yet Egypt did not intend to make APG a viable political institution. The transfer of the APG's headquarters to Cairo, its replacement by a military administration in Gaza, Egypt's restrictions upon the political activities of APG's officials, Jordan's continued opposition, as well as the absence of any significant Arab support led, finally, to the collapse of the APG in 1963.

The Third Phase: The Emergence of Modern Palestinian Nationalism

A configuration of factors in the early 1960s paved the way for the gradual decline of the role of Arab nationalism and the rise of a separate Palestinian national identity. First, with the exception of Jordan, which granted the Palestinians citizenship, none of the Arab states integrated the Palestinians en masse in their societies. The nonassimilation of the Palestinians accorded them a distinct status and helped them to keep their grievances alive. The reluctance of the Arab countries to integrate the Palestinians stemmed, in part, from their desire not to jeopardize the Palestinians' right of return and compensation. Moreover, at a time of economic underdevelopment and political instability, many of these Arab states did not want to simply incorporate a large number of poor, unemployed, and politically volatile groups of individuals into their society.

Second, despite the Palestinians' reliance upon the Arab countries for almost two decades, the political divisions in the Arab world impeded the crystallization of a united approach for the resolution of the Palestinian question. The collapse of the United Arab Republic in September 1961 created serious doubt in the minds of many Palestinians about the feasibility of the dream of Arab unity as a vehicle for the liberation of Palestine.

Indeed, Israel's divergence of the waters of the Jordan River in 1964 demonstrated the inability of the Arab heads of state to respond militarily to such a challenge. The Arab armies' defeat in 1967 confirmed the inefficacy of the joint Arab approach to the resolution of the Palestinian question and shattered the confidence of the ability of Palestinians in the Arab countries to liberate Palestine. The failure of the collective Arab approach altered the Palestinians' outlook towards their own role. After the defeat, the ideology of Palestinian nationalism replaced Pan-Arabism as a rallying point and became an important resource for generating political support and defining goals for the Palestinian nationalist movement. Finally, the acceptance of both Egypt and Jordan of United Nations Resolution 242 that viewed the Palestinian question as a refugee problem swayed the Palestinians to rely upon themselves for the liberation of their homeland.

Third, an alternative to the Arab collective approach surfaced in the early 1960s. The Algerians' attainment of their independence in 1962, through the strategy of national liberation warfare, gave the Palestinians an alternative to the Arab collective approach. In particular, the Algerian model gave credibility to the ideas of a newly organized Palestinian guerrilla group (Fatah) in the mid-1960s. Fatah's leaders advocated a more active role for the Palestinians in the liberation of their land.

Fourth, despite their geographic dispersal, the Palestinian society was experiencing rapid modernization. This was evidenced in the increase of the number of educated Palestinians and their exposure to mass media. The process of education brought about political changes away from the traditional order and dominance of the conservative elite. The new generation questioned the legitimacy and the authority of the older politicians while at the same time became more receptive to the idea of Palestinian nationalism.

The rise of this new generation of Palestinian political activists in the 1960s accelerated the growth of a Palestinian separate identity. With the failure of the pre-1948 Palestinian leadership to navigate Palestine to political independence, an opportunity existed for the emergence of this group of younger and more militant Palestinians to gradually replace the patriarchal elite. In the late 1950s and the 1960s, this innovative leadership started to address issues relating to Palestinian nationalism. The 1967 war accelerated the demise of the traditional elite and their replacement by the more militant and nationalist leaders. The change in the leadership was completed in 1969 when the leaders of the resistance took over the PLO.

The role of mobilizing agents: The primacy of the outside.   These four factors constituted the appropriate contextual setting for the tale of modern Palestinian nationalism. The process of mobilizing the Palestinians occurred at different rates and at different times. Soon after the breakup of the Palestinian society in 1948, Palestinian organizational activism was slow to occur. The physical dispersal of the Palestinians to several Arab states made this task difficult to achieve. The provision of food, shelter, employment, and education were the immediate concerns for the Palestinians. Teachers, women, labor, and student unions, associations, and cooperatives were formed as well as health and child care centers to render services for their followers. Prior to 1967 the Palestinian activists established the General Union of Palestine Students (GUPS), the General Union of Palestine Workers (GUPW), the General Union of Palestine Women (GUPWM), the General Union of Palestine Teachers (GUPT), and the Palestine Red Crescent Society (PRCS). Later on, these institutions participated in the process of reviving Palestinian national consciousness.

The mass organizations availed the Palestinians of a medium for identity renewal, a mechanism for political participation, and a vehicle to meet the socioeconomic needs of the Palestinians. These organizations also represented an important communication channel between the national leadership and the mass public in various locations.

Most of the mobilizational efforts were conducted by the Palestinian activists in the refugee camps. The new political activists were drawn from middle- and lower middle-class families—a fact that made them more attentive to the needs of political organizing among the refugees than the older elite. The refugee camp dwellers were the first to respond to the mobilizational efforts of the resistance groups.

Four groups were active in the process of mobilizing the Palestinians during the 1960s and after.[16] The first of these groups—

established by Arafat and his associates in the early 1960s—was Fatah. The main preoccupation of Fatah's leadership was the nurturing of a distinct Palestinian national awareness and the mobilization of the Palestinian mass public.[17] In December 1964, Fatah's leaders introduced the concept of military struggle as a vehicle to liberate Palestine. Initially, the military activities of Fatah intended to force the irresolute Arab armies to engage Israel. Fatah also upheld the necessity of Palestinian autonomy and underlined their leading role in the fight for the emancipation of their land away from Arab custodianship. Fatah espoused Palestinian self-reliance rather than depending upon transnational Arab ideologies and organizations.

After the 1967 war, two new Palestinian commando groups were formed. The Popular Front for the Liberation of Palestine (PFLP) and the Democratic Front for the Liberation of Palestine (DFLP) advocated guerrilla warfare and class struggle as the only vehicles for the liberation of Palestine. They believed that the road to Palestine is an integral part of a social revolution in the Arab world. The engagement of both groups in international terrorism and their radical Marxist orientations confined their support to a small circle of students and intellectuals.

The third commando groups included al-Sa'iqa and the Arab Liberation Front (ALF) which were sponsored by Syria and Iraq, respectively. The growing popularity of the resistance groups after the Arab defeat of 1967 forced both countries to form their own organizations in order to influence the direction of Palestinian politics. Al-Sa'iqa and the ALF emphasized the Pan-Arab nature of the Palestinian struggle.

The fourth mobilizing group refers to the PLO which was created by the first Arab summit conference of 1964. Its formation came partly in response to growing Palestinian national sentiments and partly as an attempt to control the activities of the Palestinians. Until 1969, the PLO was not identified with military struggle. The organization was then dominated by the traditional notables. During that period, the PLO envisaged the Palestinians role in the liberation of Palestine as being corollary to that of the Arab armies. The prestige of the Arab sponsored PLO suffered as a result of the

1967 military defeat. By contrast, the resistance groups enjoyed mounting popular attraction. This was especially the case following the al-Karamah battle in which an Israeli military unit received relatively heavy casualties when it attacked a base for the resistance across the Jordan River in March 1968.

The mounting resistance popularity reached political fruition in February 1969 when the Palestinian commando groups led by Arafat took over the PLO. The new PLO was more effective in mass mobilization. It intensified its organizational vigor and hastened the growth of Palestinian national consciousness. The PLO's supportive mass organizations became more energetic in rendering social, educational, and health services to the refugees.

The PLO has all the signs of a government, including a cabinet, a parliament, and various social, economic, and cultural departments and agencies.[18] The PNC functions like a parliament in exile. Its members represent the interests of the various Palestinian constituents including the PLO factions, the popular organizations, prominent Palestinian individuals, and the Palestinian communities in different geographic regions.

In 1973, the PNC created the PLO's Central Council to oversee the implementation of its resolutions. In addition, the PNC elects the members of the executive committee which has sixteen members with several cabinet portfolios including the departments of military, planning, information, politics, the occupied homeland, education, social affairs, popular organizations, and the Palestine Fund. The composition of the executive committee reflects the political weight of the differing PLO factions including Fatah, the PFLP, the DFLP, al Sai'qa, the communists, and some independents. There is also the Palestine Red Crescent Society which serves as the department of health. It offers humanitarian and medical services to the Palestinians, especially in the refugee camps. It also operates a number of hospitals and clinics in some of the Arab countries.[19] The various PLO departments provided numerous employment opportunities for hundreds of Palestinians.[20]

The PLO offices in different Arab capitals function as embassies. They issue travel documents, marriage certificates, and extend financial aid to students and needy families. In addition, these offices provide a meeting ground for Palestinian political activities and for the celebration of national holy days.

The PLO military factions operate as political parties representing different ideological and political interests within the Palestinian nationalist movement. The competition among these factions was often violent and intense. By the early 1980s there were around thirty newspapers and magazines in Lebanon alone, attesting to the vigor of the political debate among these groups. The outcome of this competition was the increase in the political awareness of their constituents.

To broaden the support to the Palestinian problem, the PLO identified various national liberation movements and groups who were advocating a similar cause of self-determination and anticolonialism. The resistance groups viewed their struggle as being part of a larger anti-Western Third World drive. In the late 1960s and early 1970s, the radical factions of the PLO used violence and terrorism to publicize the Palestinian question.

By contrast, while using violence, the mainstream of the PLO began to focus upon political means to realize the national rights of the Palestinians. In particular, PLO leaders utilized their access to international organizations and movements to mobilize support for the Palestinian question. The PLO's diplomatic efforts bore fruits in the 1970s and the 1980s. In 1974, Arab heads of state passed a resolution recognizing the PLO as the sole legitimate representative of the Palestinians and acknowledged their right for self-determination. In mid-1970s, the United Nations granted the PLO an observer status in the General Assembly while the non-aligned movement admitted the PLO as a full member.

Many Third World and communist countries extended diplomatic recognition to the PLO. These diplomatic victories enabled the PLO to open political offices in different Arab capitals and its representatives were admitted to the Arab League. In response, the leaders of the PLO modified their goals and tactics.

The inclusion of the inside.   The PLO's early mobilizational efforts took place among the refugee camps. The Palestinians inside Israel, the occupied territories, and outside the Arab world were the last to be mobilized. Since 1973, the PLO started to pay more attention to the political mobilization of the Palestinians within the occupied territories. With the opening of the borders between Israel and the West Bank and Gaza, the political, social, economic, and cultural contacts and interactions were renewed among the Palestinians alongside the Green Line.[21] Such interaction accelerated the growth of Palestinian national consciousness and reduced further the appeal of Arab nationalism.

After 1973, the influence of the pro-Jordanian elite over West Bank local politics weakened. The drop in their power was, in part, caused by Jordan's defeat in the 1967 war and the Jordanian-Palestinian civil war of September 1970. Israel's political restrictions upon the traditional elite, the radicalization of the student movement, and the role of mobilizing agents including PLO factions, local communists, and the Islamic movement contributed to the demise of the older politicians. The ascendancy of Palestinian nationalism was further expedited by the decline of Pan-Arabism. The death of Egyptian president Gamal Abdel Nasser, the drop in Egypt's hegemonic leadership of the Arab world, and the profusion of local conflicts in the Middle East further reduced the political influence of local politicians.

In the summer of 1973, the pro-PLO Palestine National Front was formed (PNF). The PNF undertook the task of promoting allegiance to the PLO and the checking of Jordan's influence.[22] The PNF called for the formation of an independent Palestinian state in the occupied territories and advocated the right of the PLO to represent the interests of the Palestinians in any political talks.

The second half of the 1970s was marked by the increasing consolidation of Palestinian nationalism in the West Bank and Gaza. The conduct of municipal elections in 1976 gave an additional boost to Palestinian nationalism. During those elections, the conservative pro-Jordanian politicians were defeated. In March 1977, the PNC allocated financial assistance to the municipalities inside the occupied territories. The PLO's economic aid was significantly enhanced after 1978, when the Arab heads of state convening in Baghdad appropriated $150 million to be distributed annually inside the West Bank and Gaza. The National Guidance Committee (NGC) was formed in 1978 to oppose the Camp David accords.

Palestinian nationalism reached a climax in the West Bank and the Gaza Strip when a popular uprising (Intifada) erupted in December 1987. During the Intifada, numerous popular committees mushroomed throughout the occupied territories to render voluntary services to their members and to promote communal solidarity. In many respects, a parallel process of indigenous independent institution-building in areas of legislation, justice, trade, education, health, social welfare, and economic infrastructure is being formed within the occupied territories. Such activities have laid down the foundation of the future Palestinian State.

From total liberation through armed struggle to a West Bank-Gaza state through diplomacy: 1969–1989. With the ouster of the old PLO leadership and their replacement by more militant and younger leaders in the late 1960s, the overall goal of the Palestinian nationalist movement came to be the formation of a Palestinian State in all of Palestine. In 1968 and 1969, the Palestinians wanted to liberate all of Palestine without due regard to the interests of the Israeli Jews. Yet between 1969 and 1974, the Palestinians began to openly call for the formation of a secular democratic state in all of Palestine where Moslems, Christians, and Jews would live. The outcome of this shift was the PLO leaders' recognition of the presence of a national Jewish community in Palestine. In 1974, the Palestinians moved one step further when they endorsed the concept of creating a Palestinian national authority on any liberated part of Palestine. Three years later, the Palestinians gave a more explicit definition of the concept of national authority during the thirteenth meeting of the PNC in March 1977. The PLO supported the formation of an independent state in the occupied territories as the first stage for the total liberation of Palestine at a later period. This phased solution remained the PLO's formal position until November 1988 when the PNC in its nineteenth session declared the creation of a Palestinian State in the West Bank and Gaza with East Jerusalem as its capital.

The evolution of the PLO's political stands since the late 1960s resulted from the unfolding of a host of Palestinian domestic, Arab regional, and international factors.

During the decade of the 1970s, the primary constituency of the PLO was the exiled Palestinians who lost their land in 1948. The

PLO leaders were responsive to the wishes of those Palestinians and their desire to return to Palestine. Following President Sadat's political accommodation with Israel in the wake of the 1973 October war and the growing importance of the West Bank and Gaza as the future site for the Palestinian state, compelled the PLO leaders to endorse the concept of a national state on any liberated part of Palestine. This was the first step in the process of total liberation of the land. Such a phased solution sought to simultaneously accommodate two conflicting interests: the concept of an independent state was introduced to satisfy the needs of the Palestinians within the occupied territories whose immediate aim was the termination of Israel's military occupation. Those Palestinians were becoming increasingly the primary source of legitimacy for the PLO. The idea of a phased solution was also meant to appease the PLO hardline groups who continued to press for the liberation of all of Palestine.

In November 1988, the PLO accepted the 1947 United Nations partition resolution 181 which called for the formation of an Arab state and a Jewish state in Palestine. Such a step was dictated by the unfolding of developments in the Middle East, the world at large, and within the Palestinian community. In particular, three events compelled the leaders of the PLO to take this course. First, the Palestinians' political moves came in response to their recognition of the colossal gap between their capabilities and those of Israel. In addition to its massive conventional superiority, Israel has nuclear and chemical weapons and also possesses satellite capability and medium range missiles. By contrast, the Palestinians have light arms and hand grenades. In addition, the PLO's loss of its independent base of military operations in both Jordan and Lebanon in 1970 and 1982, respectively, cast serious doubts about the Palestinians' strategy of military struggle.

Second, the declining utility of military force in the 1980s bolstered the Palestinians' propensity to establish a West Bank State. After eight years of bloodshed, the outcome of the Iraq-Iran war was ambiguous. The declining usefulness of military force as an instrument for political influence has been also evidenced in the inconclusive outcome of Israel's 1982 invasion of Lebanon and the protracted nature of the Syrian involvement in that country.

The 1980s also witnessed another trend of finding political solutions to pending regional problems. This trend was evidenced in the Soviet Union's decision to withdraw its troops from Afghanistan, the independence of Namibia, and the political liberalization program within the Soviet Union and the far-reaching political change in Eastern Europe. These events combined to convince the PLO's aging leadership that time was not working on their side and that they needed to launch a major political initiative.

The developments within the Palestinian community reinforced the PLO's resolve to eventually declare political independence. The expulsion of PLO troops from Lebanon, in the wake of the 1982 war, was marked by the drop in the political influence of the hardline groups. With the withdrawal of its troops from Lebanon, the PLO leaders were not primarily responsive to the interests of the refugee camps in Lebanon. The West Bank and Gaza instead became the PLO's primary constituencies and its principal source of legitimacy. However, it was the uprising of the Palestinians within the occupied territories that made the most discernible impact upon the PLO's political orientation. The Intifada changed the Palestinian perceptions and attitudes and developed among them a strong sense of self-reliance and confidence.[23] Finally, King Hussein's decision to sever legal and administrative ties with the West Bank prompted the PLO leaders to declare the formation of a state.

Conclusions

This chapter has sought to explain the emergence of Palestinian nationalism. The previous analysis has indicated that the rise of a separate Palestinian nationalism and the setting up of Palestinian political institutions, passed through several stages. During the mandate period, the Palestinians opted for the formation of a government. The question of forming a state was inconsequential. With the loss of Palestine in 1948 and 1967, the Palestinians' overriding concern was the restoration of the Arab identity of Palestine. The formation of a state was therefore not an urgent issue. With the accelerated growth of Palestinian nationalism in the wake of the defeat of the Arab armies in the 1967 war, the question of establishing a state became a pressing issue. The Intifada was the catalyst that compelled the PLO to finally declare a state in the occupied territories.

Unlike many Third World states, Palestinian nationalism was well developed prior to the establishment of the state. To the Palestinians, the formation of a state is the requisite framework for the fulfillment of their political, social, cultural, and economic identity and existence. Political independence is the highest end of nationalism. Since the early decades of the twentieth century, Palestinian nationalism has been awaiting the formation of a state. As a result of their perceptions of rising Israeli threats to their physical presence, group solidarity among the Palestinians has intensified over the years.

The presence of a common language and historical experience and the belief in the just nature of the Palestinian cause strengthened the Palestinian cultural identity. Palestinian nationalism is also the byproduct of the Palestinians' common vision of a desired future. The experience that the Palestinians gained from the Intifada reinforced their sense of communal solidarity. These combined factors separate Palestinian nationalism from Arab nationalism.

Exposure of the Palestinians to advanced education and mobilizational efforts of the PLO and other mass organizations had an effect on Israel. Israel's military occupation of the West Bank accelerated the process of social mobilization and enhanced Palestinian national consciousness and communal solidarity. The outcome of these changes has been the consolidation of Palestinian nationalism and the quest for national identity and political independence.

The Intifada constitutes a turning point in Palestinian modern history. It increased the communal national awareness among the Palestinians within the occupied territories. It advanced the political weight of those Palestinians living in the West Bank and Gaza, and legitimized their role in the larger Palestinian nationalist movement. With the shift of the center of gravity of the Palestinian nationalist movement to the occupied territories, the PLO became more responsive to the interests of the West Bank and Gaza Palestinians.

Notes

1. See Charles Keyes, ed., *Ethnic Change* (Seattle: University of Washington Press, 1981); Fouad Ajami, *The Arab Predicament* (New York: Cambridge University Press, 1981); Joseph Rothschild, *Ethnopolitics: A Conceptual Framework* (New York: Columbia University Press, 1981); R. A. Schermerhorn, *Comparative Ethnic Relations* (New York: Random House, 1970); James McKay, "An Exploratory Synthesis of Primordial and Mobilizational Approaches to Ethnic Phenomena," *Ethnic and Race Relations* 5 (October 1982): 395–420; and J. Ross, ed., *The Mobilization of Collective Identities: Comparative Perspectives* (Washington, D.C.: University Press of America, 1981).
2. For more information, see Crawford Young, *The Politics of Cultural Pluralism* (Madison: University of Wisconsin Press, 1976), 23–55.
3. See Dov Ronen, *The Quest for Self-Determination,* 53.
4. See Jeffrey A. Ross, "The Mobilization of Collective Identity: An Analytical Overview," in *Mobilization of Collective Identity,* eds. Jeffrey A. Ross and Cottrell, 9–10.
5. For the instrumental perspective, see Abner Cohen, "Introduction: The Lesson of Ethnicity," *Urban Ethnicity,* ed. Abner Cohen (London: Tavistock Publications, 1974), ix–xxiv.
6. Laurie A. Brand, *Palestinians in the Arab World: Institution-Building and the Search for State* (New York: Columbia University Press, 1988), 10–12.
7. Ibid., 12.
8. For an assessment of the impact of refugee camp life, see Rosemary Sayigh, "The Palestinian Identity Among Camp Residents," *Journal of Palestine Studies* 6 (Spring 1977); Rosemary Sayigh, "Sources of Palestinian Nationalism: A Study of a Palestinian Camp in Lebanon," *Journal of Palestinian Studies* 6 (Summer 1977): 35–38; and Bassem Sirhan, "A Refugee Camp Life in Lebanon," *Journal of Palestinian Studies* 4 (Winter 1975).
9. Mark A. Tessler, "Ethnic Change and Non-assimilating Minority Status: The Case of Jews in Tunisia and Morocco and Arabs in Israel," *Ethnic Change,* ed. Charles Keyes (Seattle: University of Washington Press, 1981).
10. For a very useful analysis of the rise of Palestinian nationalism, see Muhammad Y. Muslih, *The Origins of Palestinian Nationalism* (New York: Columbia University Press, 1988). The discussion draws heavily upon that study.
11. William B. Quandt, F. Jabber, and Ann Lesch, *The Politics of Palestinian Nationalism* (Berkeley: University of California Press, 1973), 14; D. Gilmour, *Dispossessed: The Ordeal of the Palestinians* (London: Sphere Books, 1982), 143. For a detailed treatment, see ibid.
12. For a detailed treatment, see Muslih, *The Origins of Palestinian Nationalism,* 155–65.
13. See ibid., his chapter concerning younger politicians.
14. See Brand, *Palestinians in the Arab World,* 22–24.

15. Ibid.
16. For additional information, see Quandt, Jabber, and Lesch, *The Politics of Palestinian Nationalism,* Part II and Kirisci, *The PLO and World Politics,* chapter 4.
17. See A. Frangi, *The PLO and Palestine* (London: Zed Books, 1983), 94–96 and Quandt, Jabber, and Lesch, *The Politics of Palestinian Nationalism,* 55–56.
18. For more information, see Rashid Hamid, "What is the PLO?" *Journal of Palestine Studies* 4 (Summer 1975).
19. Brand, *Palestinians in the Arab World,* 39–40.
20. For additional information on the PLO, see Kirisci, *The PLO and World Politics,* chapter 4 and Helena Cobban, *The Palestinian Liberation Organization* (Cambridge: Cambridge University Press, 1984).
21. For additional information, see Emile Sahliyeh, "A Survey of the Political Attitudes of Palestinians in the West Bank and Inside Israel," *Palestinians over the Green Line,* ed. Alexander Scholch (London: Ithaca Press, 1983).
22. For a detailed discussion of political developments in the West Bank in the 1970s, see Emile Sahliyeh, *In Search of Leadership: West Bank Politics Since 1967* (Washington, D.C.: Brookings Institution, 1988), chapter 4.
23. See, for example, Graham E. Fuller, *The West Bank of Israel: Point of No Return?* (Santa Monica, Cal.: The RAND Corporation, 1989). This report was prepared for the Office of the Secretary of Defense.

References

Ajami, Fouad. 1981. *The Arab Predicament.* New York: Cambridge University Press.

Brand, Laurie A. 1988. *Palestinians in the Arab World: Institution-Building and the Search for the State.* New York: Columbia University Press.

Cobban, Helena. 1984. *The Palestinian Liberation Organization.* Cambridge: Cambridge University Press.

Cohen, Abner. 1974. "Introduction: The Lesson of Ethnicity." In Abner Cohen (ed.), *Urban Ethnicity.* London: Tavistock Publications.

Frangi, A. 1983. *The PLO and Palestine.* London: Zed Books.

Fuller, Graham E. 1989. *The West Bank of Israel: Point of No Return?,* Santa Monica, Cal.: The RAND Corporation.

Gilmour, D. 1982. *Dispossessed: The Ordeal of the Palestinians.* London: Sphere Books.

Hamid, Rashid. 1975. "What is the PLO?" *Journal of Palestine Studies,* Summer, 4.

Keyes, Charles, ed. 1981. *Ethnic Change.* Seattle: University of Washington Press.

Kirisci, Kemal. 1986. *The PLO and World Politics: A Study of the Mobilization of Support for the Palestinian Cause,* London: Frances Pinter.

McKay, James. 1982. "An Exploratory Synthesis of Primordial and Mobilizational Approaches to Ethnic Phenomena." *Ethnic and Race Relations,* October 5: 395–420.

Muslih, Muhammad Y. 1988. *The Origins of Palestinian Nationalism.* New York: Columbia University Press.

Quandt, William B., F. Jabber, and Ann Lesch. 1973. *The Politics of Palestinian Nationalism.* Berkeley: University of California Press.

Ronen, Dov. 1979. *The Quest for Self-Determination.* New Haven, Conn.: Yale University Press.

Ross, J. ed. 1981. *The Mobilization of Collective Identities: Comparative Perspectives.* Washington, DC: University Press of America.

Rothschild, Joseph. 1981. *Ethnopolitics: A Conceptual Framework.* New York: Columbia University Press.

Sahliyeh, Emile. 1983. "A Survey of the Political Attitudes of Palestinians in the West Bank and Inside Israel." In Alexander Scholch (ed.), *Palestinians over the Green Line.* London: Ithaca Press.

————. 1988. *In Search of Leadership: West Bank Politics Since 1967.* Washington, D.C.: Brookings Institution.

Sayigh, Rosemary. 1977a. "The Palestinian Identity Among Camp Residents" *Journal of Palestine Studies,* Spring, 6.

————. 1977b. "Sources of Palestinian Nationalism: A Study of a Palestinian Camp in Lebanon." *Journal of Palestine Studies,* Summer, 6: 35–38.

Schermerhorn, R. A. 1970. *Comparative Ethnic Relations,* New York: Random House.

Sirhan, Bassem. 1975. "A Refugee Camp Life in Lebanon." *Journal of Palestine Studies,* Winter, 4.

Tessler, Mark. 1981. "Ethnic Change and Non-assimilating Minority Status: The Case of the Jews in Tunisia and Morocco and Arabs in Israel." In Charles Keyes (ed.), *Ethnic Change.* Seattle: University of Washington Press.

Young, Crawford. 1976. *The Politics of Cultural Pluralism.* Madison: University of Wisconsin Press.

8

Jewish Ethnicity in Israel: Ideologies, Policies, and Outcomes

Herbert S. Lewis

*Twenty years ago, when we were young, we
knew just how it would be. It was clear that in a
generation there would be complete
assimilation. But it didn't happen that way. It's
amazing what is going on now (1989).*
—A university professor, raised in Israel

Introduction

This comment succinctly captures a major change in the view of
Jewish ethnicity in Israel — and perhaps of ethnicity in much of the
rest of the world. Israelis in general, and especially Israel's political
and intellectual leadership, expected to see the millions of Jewish
immigrants who came to Israel from all over the world rapidly
acculturate and assimilate to one another. They were expected to
become just "Israelis," "modern Jews," and to conform to an ideal
model of secularized citizens of a democratic country. In fact the
outcome to date has been much more complex and ambiguous.
This paper, in keeping with the theme of the volume, deals with the
relations between the Israeli state and Jewish ethnicity, and with
the transformation of Israeli attitudes and expectations regarding
it.

From the beginning of Israel's existence, the government of necessity, played an unusually important role in dealing with ethnicity. The first leaders and officials took over a new and unformed polity and were immediately faced with the necessity of dealing with an avalanche of immigrants that tripled the country's population within little more than a decade. All the institutions of the country had to be established *de novo* or adapted from preexisting ones, and the center was vital in this process. Many of Israel's villages, towns, and cities were created by central planners. So were the various industries, institutions, services, and educational and other systems that are required for social and economic life. Israel is a highly centralized state and its growth was controlled by the center to an unusual degree.

We may, therefore, speak of the importance of the state in dealing with ethnicity as well as with everything else. On the other hand I wish to avoid the imputation that "the state" may itself be an actor, above and beyond the individuals that compose its leadership and make decisions. To speak of states, as is often done, as if they had certain aims, demands, requirements, evolutionary trajectories, or directions involves unwarranted reification and, perhaps, teleology. The focus in this paper will be on the very human and fallible decision-makers and opinion-formers who influence the attitudes and actions of the government regarding Jewish ethnicity. It is their values, ideas, aims, knowledge, experiences, and sympathies that are reflected in the policies the leaders of the government implemented while trying to cope with the problems they perceived. In this paper we shall spell out what those values and ideas were and how they were affected by the changing realities of the situation as it developed.

The major arguments of the paper are the following: (1) the original insistence of the Israeli establishment on a policy of acculturation and assimilation for all Jewish groups might be said to have been "overdetermined." Everything in their experience directed them to that point of view. (2) Despite analyses, predictions, and policies aimed at "the fusion of the exiles", country-of-origin ethnicity continues to play a significant role in Israeli sociopolitical and cultural life. (3) Israeli leaders, with varying degrees of alacrity, responded to the evidence that significant elements of Jewish Diaspora ethnicity would have to be accommodated in Israeli society by changing their policies, even if not their ideology. (4) At present there is a developing pattern of pluralism among Jewish groups which features agreement about Israeli Jewish nationality and identity but tolerates, perhaps even fosters, complementary ethnic identities and the maintenance of *at least* "symbolic" ethnicity based on preexisting Diaspora affiliations.

The Background

Although a new Jewish society was in the process of formation in Palestine from the beginning of the twentieth century, the State of Israel was formally established in May 1948. At that time the leaders of the Jewish community were able to set up the institutions of a sovereign state: political and governmental structures, an educational system, a military, with all the associated powers and policies these institutions require.

In these first years, as a result of the government's new power to permit immigration to the country (which had previously been forbidden by the controlling British mandatory power), the population of the new state doubled from 650,000 to more than 1,340,000 within three years and trebled within thirteen. Jewish immigrants had come from more than fifty countries (Immigration and Settlement 1973).

In order to rescue Jews in dire need in Europe, to facilitate the immigration of Jews from Asian and North African countries, and to increase the state's population, the leaders of Israel proclaimed a policy of unrestricted immigration to Israel for all Jews. This was accomplished with The Law of Return promulgated on 5 July 1950. The impact of this decision was far-reaching indeed, for it changed the demographic and ethnic character of the developing Jewish society fundamentally.

Before 1948 the Jewish population of Palestine (known as the *yishuv*) consisted of a large majority of immigrants and the children of immigrants from Europe, and especially from East and Central Europe. (Perhaps 20–25 percent of the population of the *yishuv* was composed of Sephardi and Yemenite Jews but the preponderance of those in decision-making positions were of European origin.) The new mass immigration was divided almost equally into Jews coming from post-World War II Europe and those coming from North Africa and Asia, especially from Morocco, Tunisia, Libya, Egypt, Yemen, Iraq, Iran, Turkey, and India. By the 1980s more than half of the Jewish population of Israel traced its origins to North Africa and Asia. The founders of the Jewish state had not expected this, and the consequences of this remarkable cultural, social, and demographic change are still being worked out.

Jewish Ethnicity

Communities of people considering themselves to be Jewish, and recognized as such by the members of other similar communities, existed throughout most of the world in 1939. They were linked by a sense of peoplehood based on the idea of a shared historical past and by a common religious belief with its associated worship, laws, and practices. At that time the great majority of the world's estimated 15 million Jews lived in Europe and the Americas, above all in Eastern Europe (Russia, Poland), and the United States. (Most of the Jews of the Americas, South Africa, and Australia were immigrants and the descendants of immigrants from Europe.) But there were substantial populations of Jews in Asia and North Africa as well, especially in the countries noted above. And the lives and culture of these Jews were often quite different from those in Europe and America.

Although there had been a general tendency for Jewish communities everywhere in the world to remain endogamous, to live in communities separated from their non-Jewish neighbors, and to maintain their own worship and distinctive style of life and values, in all cases they came to resemble to some degree the people among whom they lived as well. This is especially true since the period of the Enlightenment in Western Europe, which offered to many Jews the chance to become very much like — if not identical with — their neighbors. But even where communities were kept separate from their Christian or Muslim neighbors they still partook of much of the material culture, the economic system, and expressive life of the people around them. It was inevitable that the differences between various Jewish communities would be even greater, in certain dimensions, than the similarities. And that the Jews would be more like their non-Jewish neighbors in some ways than like their fellow Jews from far distant countries. The cultural and social systems of a city like Fez or the villages of the Atlas mountains affected the Jew from Morocco just as surely as the life of a small town *(shtetl)* in Galicia or in Berlin, marked the Jews from Europe. And so Israel was populated, after 1948, by a far more complex melange of peoples than had previously been the case. This was a development that nobody had expected or planned for and one that was not considered in the ideologies of Zionism until that time.

The Aims and Ideology of Zionism

Zionism is the nationalist movement of the Jews that grew out of the experiences of European Jews in the nineteenth century. The Jews had endured various forms of persecution for well over a millenium in Christian Europe, and were once again experiencing major troubles in Eastern Europe in the late nineteenth century. A small group of Jewish intellectuals came to the conclusion that the only way for the Jews to be secure, to live in dignity, to avoid injury and insult was to become a "normal people," with a homeland of their own (See, for example, Hertzberg 1960; Halpern 1969; Laquer 1972).

These early Zionist thinkers were, of course, influenced by the European intellectual trends of their day, including socialism and secularism, as well as nationalism. While individuals with a wide range of beliefs and backgrounds shared the aim of the creation of a Jewish state, the leading role in developing the ideologies and actually advancing the cause of political Zionism was taken by young Eastern European Jews who shared a belief in secular and democratic socialism. Within Palestine from about 1910 a succession of socialist parties developed that led directly to the Israeli Labor Party, the dominant force in *yishuv* and Israeli life from the 1920s through the 1960s. This was the party of David Ben-Gurion, Yitshak Ben-Zvi, Golda Meir, Moshe Sharett, Levi Eshkol, and many other prominent Israeli leaders and thinkers.

However else they may have differed, this group of men and women had turned their back on the old ways of Jewish life and looked forward to a new day featuring a rational, educated, secular, democratic, productive, healthy and athletic, progressive Jewish society in the homeland of the Jews. As they understood it, the life of the Jews as a despised and alien minority had forced them into unproductive occupations (as moneylenders, peddlers, rabbinical students, and intellectuals), had kept them superstitious and under the control of rabbis and elders, had kept them afraid and segregated and subject to the whims and questionable mercies of the gentiles.

They saw themselves as pioneers *(khalutsim)* and workers. (Ha-Poel Ha-Tsair, "the young workers," was the name of one of the early parties.) They built a series of powerful institutions: trade unions, parties, a network of collective agricultural settlements *(kibbutsim),* paramilitary groups (at first to fight off raids from hostile Arabs; later to fight for independence against the British mandatory power), the General Federation of Trade Unions (Histadrut), sports federations and cultural organizations, a university and an institute of technology. They were brash, full of ideologies and ideals, self-assured, intense, and determined. And they were self-consciously turning their backs on the ways of their parents and their ethnic group, which they thought was antiquated, unprogressive, and unhealthy.

The leaders of the emerging Israeli society and state saw themselves as building a new society, a new land, a new people—and, indeed, they were. Their songs, their publications, their youth groups, their propaganda all stressed the building of modern new institutions: schools, farms and collectives, towns and cities, sports clubs, a cultural life of the theater and music—both classical and newly created "folk" dance and music. They argued that Jewish society in Europe had been "unnatural" because they were forced into a few occupations, forbidden to own and work the land, isolated from the normal range of productive activities. These pioneers would rebuild themselves as they rebuilt the deforested and barren land. ("We are coming to the land—to build and be built in it," said the words of a popular song.) In this old-new land, the Jews would be farmers and police, fishermen and sailors and firemen, artisans and skilled workers. They would do all the work of a normal economy and society. (And for a long time those on the *kibbutsim* claimed that women would be liberated from the drudgery of housework and child care and would do the same work as the men — and vice versa.) They would be modern, and make great use of science, medicine, and technology. They would be a model for the rest of the Middle East. The prosperity and modernity which they were bringing would be infectious, and would affect their Arab neighbors for the better, they said.

Although they had spurned many of the ways of their parents and other Jews, and were very antitraditional and secular, they believed in the unity of the Jewish people. *Am Yisrael am ehad* ("the Jewish people is one people") and *Kol Yisrael haverim* ("All Israel — comrades") were and are common slogans. Their modern nationalism drew upon ancient ideas of connections among and the essential oneness of the Jewish people.

Despite their antitraditionalism, they thought it their duty to build a *Jewish* state. Artists, musicians, writers, and thinkers concerned themselves with the problem of creating a new-old culture, looking backward past the traditions of European Jews to some presumed authentic Middle Eastern past, with greater connection to supposed Biblical roots. In this quest, "Oriental" Jews living in preindependence Palestine, and even Arabs, sometimes served as models for those seeking "authenticity" (Lewis 1984).

The Mass Immigration (aliya)

The State of Israel was formally established on 14 May 1948 and the 650,000 Jews of Israel were plunged into a war for survival against the six Arab nations on their borders. It was a country with severe shortages, unable to produce most of its food, with few arms, greatly outnumbered and in need of reinforcement. At the same time, several hundred thousand European Jews were living in displaced persons camps in Europe or interned on Cyprus by the British. Other countries wouldn't accept them, and they needed settlement, homes, new lives. And in the Middle East and North Africa there was a similar number of Jews desirous of immigration to the new Jewish state. Many, like the Jews of Yemen, were motivated by their own Zionism, a long-held desire to return to The Holy Land, the Land of Israel (Erets Yisreal), the Land of Zion.

(The Jews of Yemen always believed that they were only in temporary exile — for about 1,500 years.) Others were forced out of their homes by riots and danger in their countries, especially in Libya, Iraq, and, later, Egypt. And so there was no lack of needy immigrants for a land needing people to settle it, work it, and fight for it.

To many it really seemed like prayers and prophecy coming true. *Every day* for almost two millenia religious Jews had prayed regularly for the "ingathering of the exiles", the return of the Jewish people "from the four corners of the earth." (These formulae are in every Jewish prayerbook everywhere in the world.) And here it was actually happening. Jews were coming "home" from all over the world; not merely from Poland and Russia, Germany and Romania, but from Morocco and Yemen, Kurdistan and Tripolitania, Bombay and Broadway. And it is at this point that Israel's problems with Jewish ethnicity really begin.

The Absorption of Immigrants: Theory and Practice

The leaders of the new state, in all fields, were presented with tremendous challenges. They led a newly formed government and a country with a relatively poor and undeveloped economy, at war with and under siege from the six surrounding Arab nations. At the same time they had to make provision for the feeding, settlement, housing, employment, education, health, and welfare of immigrants that doubled the total population in three years, tripled it in a little over a decade.

To add to their problems, none of the newcomers could speak the language of their new country (Hebrew) — but they spoke more than fifty other languages among themselves. Most of the people who came from Europe had been homeless or living in concentration camps, death camps, and displaced person camps for almost a decade. They arrived penniless, destitute, some with severe psychological problems. Many of those who had come from North African and Asian countries had no modern schooling, little or no training for work in an industrial society, and major health problems due to conditions in their countries of origin. These were the realities of life in the Jewish state after 1948 when the mass immigration was in full flood. These were the challenges to the governmental and military leaders, the teachers, health workers, and planners in settlement, housing, industry, agriculture, and every other field of endeavor.

Attitudes to Jewish Ethnicity

As far as Jewish ethnicity was concerned, it would appear that the Israeli elite had few doubts at first. They saw the Jewish people as one, and in July 1950 passed The Law of Return guaranteeing to all Jews the right to settle in Israel, the Jewish state, with full rights and responsibilities as citizens. They envisioned full integration and unity, politically, culturally, and socially, among all Jews.

The government of Israel and the various institutions within the state and society aimed to settle, educate, employ, and integrate the newcomers without distinction — at least in theory. They were in the process of building a new society and a new culture, and they expected the new immigrants to participate in it and help build it. But they also expected them to discard many of their old ways, their "*galut* (Diaspora) mentality"—as they thought they, themselves, had done. One new Jewish nation would be formed out of the mass of humanity that had suddenly arrived on their shores. As David Ben-Gurion, the first prime minister and leading political figure and thinker, expressed it in 1953,

> Within the state the differences between various kinds of Jews will be obliter-
> ated in the course of time, the communities and tribes will sooner or later fuse
> into one national and cultural unity. Common education, the Hebrew lan-
> guage, universal service in the Israel Defence Forces, the establishment of a
> common minimum standard of living, the entry of workers from various
> countries and communities into a single labour federation, mixed marriages
> between various tribes, common political action in noncommunal parties, and
> so on, will produce a new type of Jew with the favourable qualities and charac-
> teristics of all the tribes of Israel. (Quoted in Isaac 1959)

There could hardly be a clearer statement of the basic premises of the Israeli elite in the early 1950s.

Problems of Absorption

During the 1950s, along with the imperatives of settlement and housing, the development of industry, agriculture, the armed forces, the educational, and health systems was the need to "absorb" the immigrants. Social workers, psychologists, educators, sociologists, specialists of all kinds turned to the problems of absorption *(klita)*. The "ingathering of the exiles" *(kibbuts galuyot)* was being accomplished; now for the "fusion of the exiles" *(mizug galuyot)* (See Schechtman 1961).

Housing and work had to be found for the Jews from Europe as well as for those from North Africa and Asia, and the former, as survivors of the Holocaust, often had special health and psychological problems as well. But the major problems seemed to be posed by the "Oriental Jews" *(eydot ha-mizrah,* "Eastern communities") as the North African and Asian Jews came to be called (for the literature of this period see Eisenstadt 1954; Frankenstein 1953; Patai 1953, 1961).

The immigrants from Europe had come from the same cultures and societies as the Israeli elite. There were differences of class, education, and outlook among European Jews, but these were minor compared to the cultural chasm between the European Jews and many of those from Asia and Africa. Or at least the planners and decision-makers thought there were.

In fact, the "Oriental" Jews differed among themselves as much as they did from European Jews. Among the Jews of Morocco there were urban-dwelling French speakers, with education, wealth from local and international trade, even cabinet ministers. There were also artisans and peddlers, with little or no education outside of the synagogue, who came from remote villages in the Atlas Mountains. And there were urban poor from the slums of Casablanca. From Alexandria and Baghdad came successful middle class bankers, teachers, and merchants, but there were also villagers from the mountains of Kurdistan who were very close in culture to their Kurdish farmer and herder neighbors. The Jews of Yemen had lived in one of the most isolated countries of the world, remote from the influences of the developing "modern world," as artisans in an agrarian society something like that of Europe in the tenth century.

At first there were no facilities for the newcomers and most of them had to be housed in "transit camps," in tents or tiny prefabricated cabins. Those officials and specialists who worked with the new immigrants were impressed and troubled by many of the cultural differences that they perceived. First there were the obvious differences in material culture, hygiene, and domestic practices. Some of the immigrants from the Middle East were not familiar with electricity, with indoor plumbing, with Western-style utensils, appliances, and furniture, with traffic and urban bustle.

A sympathetic French observer wrote about Yemenite immigrants,

> The principal task was . . . to teach the Yemenites the use of the fork, that many threw away after wounding themselves; to demonstrate that a bed is a comfortable accessory—if you sleep on it and not under it; that sheets aren't intended for the manufacture of shawls or dresses. To teach them the use of a chair, or a table, of a washbasin; of a garbage can; to prove that the use of a latrine is, from all points of view, preferable to the "open air"; and that stones have a disastrous effect on the drainage of latrines. . . . Running water amused them; the shower amazed them. (Berreby 1956, 105)

Needless to say, the veteran Israelis whose job it was to help "absorb" these newcomers were not enlightened relativist anthropologists who could look upon these cultural differences with equanimity. Geertz (1973, 53) tells us that the Javanese say, "other fields, other grasshoppers," but these functionaries were charged with the serious business of creating new Israelis out of this "raw material." Nor were all the differences as "benign" as we might judge those mentioned above to be.

Among the Yemenites, for instance, there were serious health problems. Malaria, skin diseases, parasites, tuberculosis, trachoma, venereal diseases, and bilharzia were quite common among the new immigrants. Many children suffered from chronic malnutrition but Yemenite parents at first would not entrust their children to the nurseries and clinics. Women refused to be examined unclothed by male doctors nor were they, at first, willing to give birth in hospitals. Seriously ill patients would sneak out of hospitals under their own steam or with the aid of their kin (See Lewis 1989, 59ff.).

And there were apparent social problems as well. The Israeli elite, as "modern" secular socialists, were not about to sanction polygyny, child marriage, and/or patriarchalism. Giora Yosephthal, a prominent leader in the Labor Party and the head of the

Absorption Department was quite explicit about the problems he saw:

> We have given a high priority to expanding our social services, primarily for the benefit of those who were most neglected in the social structure of their lands of origin: the children and the women. We fought—and not unsuccessfully—against the patriarchal structure of the backward countries, in which the father was the unchallenged potentate in the family in whom all rights and privileges repose, and we tried to create a Western type of social climate, one which is centered around the education of the child.
>
> The transformation from an authoritarian to a modern society, to a critical, democratic society, in which a person's status is determined by his ability, character, and achievements, and not by family connections, cannot be achieved in a few years. The struggle between the patriarchal society and the child-centered society was waged in order to allow the child to pass childhood in conditions conducive to normal maturation. *We tried as best we could to change the living patterns the immigrants brought with them.* (G. Yosephthal 1966, 268. Emphasis mine)

Here we have another revealing statement of the perceptions, values, and intentions of the leaders of the new state. They had a clear mandate: make the immigrants over into the kinds of modern Jews and Israelis that their ideology had envisioned.

Ideology, Social Science, and Ethnocentrism?

It is not really surprising that the veteran Israeli elite wanted to transform the *eydot ha-mizrah*. Aside from their normal and expectable ethnocentrism (which should not be ignored), they believed that they had a mission to build a new kind of state, a new society, and a new culture. They thought that they, themselves, represented all of these modern things, while the newcomers represented the opposing forces: traditionalism, patriarchalism, fatalism, obscurantism. They were no more tolerant of the extreme orthodox Jews who came from Europe. On the contrary, the European Jewish tradition is precisely what they were rebelling against. The "traditional" Oriental Jews reminded them of their own backward past. If they did not find their own heritage worth saving they were not likely to go out of their way to preserve that of these others. The ways of the Jews of North Africa and Asia also seemed to resemble those of the Arabs of Palestine and the neighboring countries, whose "unprogressive" culture and society were certainly not positively valued (cf. Lissak 1983, 33–34; E. Cohen 1983, 115–17).

But the leaders of the Jewish State had more to draw upon for their attitudes than their own ideology. In 1948 there was a very strong bias in liberal and radical Western thought in favor of unitary states and nations, undivided by disruptive "primordial" sentiments, "tribalism," and "nationalism." The term "ethnicity" had not yet gained currency, and the prevailing idea in the West was certainly that progress lay in setting aside old, outmoded loyalties. And at that time the United States, with its "melting pot" seemed to be the ideal for many. (Both Ben-Gurion and Golda Meir are credited with saying of Israel, "We have no time to be a melting pot; Israel must be a pressure cooker." The pressure cooker metaphor is still widely used in Israel.)

They also had the backing of the social science of their time. In 1948 acculturation and assimilation appeared to be the law of the future. Social science was still under the spell of a straight line, progressive acculturation model. Again the experience of the United States seemed to point the way. It seemed clear that the power of the mass media, of a national education system, common citizenship and civil rights in a modern democracy, common and universal participation in the military forces (for virtually all men and a great many women), collegial relations in the work force — all would have the power to acculturate the citizens of the modern state to one another. This would lead to assimilation, especially through intermarriage (See Kivisto 1990).

Modernization theory, which developed in the 1950s, must have clinched the case for acculturation. It seemed as though the laws of development were known and the future was obvious. Once upon a time all the world had been "traditional," only to be supplanted in the West (in the first instance) by "modernity." (See George Theodorson 1953, for example.) So it would be in the rest of the world. Tradition, marked by particularism and ascription, by religion and the irrational, fatalism and tribalism, patriarchal control over women and youth — all would be driven out by the power of industrialization and urbanization, consumerism and mass communications, bureaucracy, and democracy. Modernity would conquer tradition in the rest of the world just as it had in Europe. Primordial sentiments would melt before the needs of industrial society and the pressures of urban life (cf. Smith 1981). Although a product of "bourgeois" functionalist social science, the same basic view, in other terms, was shared by Marxists as well (cf. Bendix 1967).

In that era planners for change all over the world saw "tradition" as antithetical to "development." This was equally true in Israel, where the European Jewish elite saw their own history and their future in these terms.

Israeli social scientists, led by S. N. Eisenstadt (1953, 1954), wrote about the absorption of immigrants, their resocialization, their remaking into modern Israelis (see also Bar-Yosef 1968). The traditional ways of immigrants might impede progress for a while, but in time these would be surmounted. One sociologist, Y. Ben-David claimed that the problem was not one of cultural differences but of progressive cultural change: "The important point is that even groups hailing from the same country do not see, in their common origin or in the cultural tradition therein involved, any important or vital social value" (1953, 33). And so the planners and workers set about to build this unitary society.

In those days there didn't seem to be many voices urging cultural pluralism and an understanding of the culture of these immigrants from North Africa and Asia. One anthropologist, Raphael Patai (1953) made such a plea, but it does not seem to have been widely noticed. A few scholars, notably S. D. Goitein, undertook to study some aspects of their culture, while Gurit Kadmon, a leading figure in the folk dance movement, captured the dances of many groups on film, and later encouraged the organization and presentation of this aspect of their culture. The second president of Israel, Yitshak Ben-Zvi, wrote a book about the history and ways of some of the more isolated groups, and an institute was founded in his name, devoted to the study of the various Diaspora communities.

But these were not the leading perspectives of that period. The primary efforts of Israelis in positions of authority, charged with the absorption of immigrants and the development of the country and its people were directed toward the construction of one Jewish population, undivided by divisive and retrogressive loyalties and traditions brought from the *galut* (Diaspora).

To summarize, the leaders of Israel were supported in their views by their sense of their own past; by their ideology; by their belief that the Jewish people is, and must be, one people; by then-current liberal and Marxist ideology; by the social science of the period. It was not merely the result of "Ashkenazi ethnocentrism," though there certainly was plenty of that as well.

Results of the Policies of Acculturation and Assimilation

As the quotation at the beginning of the paper suggests, at one time there was great optimism, officially at least, about the success of the policies of *mizug galuyot,* the fusion of the exiles. Official statements, enthusiastic foreign supporters of Israel, many Israelis and even some social scientists were confident that the policies and the institutions that were created were having the effect of producing one people, intermarrying, beginning to forget the old country origins and the differences between these groups. Over and over in the 1970s one heard middle-aged parents say things like, "My daughter just asked me "What is Sephardi and Ashkenazi?" She and her friends don't even know! " Or they would talk about their friends at work and their buddies in the army who come from different ethnic groups, and how it no longer makes any difference.

From time to time, however, there would be sudden eruptions of ethnic conflict and competition and public awareness of the problems. One of these took place in 1970 when a group of young men, most of Moroccan origin, calling themselves "The Black Panthers" (after the American Black model) declared that they were fed up with the Ashkenazi establishment, neglect, poverty, and the stigma attached to their ethnic origin (see Smooha 1972). This has been followed by a series of flare-ups, often around election time, pitting "Oriental" against "European."

Simultaneously, in the political and intellectual climate that developed in the late 1960s in Israel, as in the U.S. and elsewhere, the problem of the ethnic divide in Israel, "the two Israels," the dominant Euro-American Jews and the subordinate Afro-Asian Jews, became a topic for the newspapers and journals. It was pointed out that the Euro-Americans (Ashkenazi) enjoyed greater prosperity, higher status, more education, and had more access to power than the Afro-Asians (Sephardim, *eydot ha-mizrah*). And it was claimed that the result of the policy of *mizug galuyot* has been the "deculturation, marginalization, educational and cultural deprivation" of these people. (See Toledano 1973; Iris and Shama 1977; Smooha 1978; A. Lewis 1979; Rubenberg 1986; D. Bernstein and Swirski 1982; for examples of this view.)

It is not easy to generalize about the outcome of these policies; they were very far-reaching and there is no single or simple answer. Rather, there have been, as we should expect, variable and complex results. And the situation is still in a state of flux.

Socioeconomic Status

Despite very rapid gains and upward mobility in absolute terms, on the average Jews of European and American origin have been more "successful" in socioeconomic and political terms than the Jews of Asian and African origin. (See J. Bernstein and Antonovsky 1981; Matras 1985.) There is still considerable room for debate over the extent to which this "gap" is due to the policies for absorption rather than to the original inequalities among these groups that derive from their preimmigration homelands. There is no denying the reality of Ashkenazi discrimination or the negative impact of some policies, such as those that sent the Moroccans, in particular, to settle in ethnically homogeneous new towns in marginal areas in the country. (See Iris and Shama 1977.) But one may also expect that people who came with middle-class aspirations, a degree of modern education and technical expertise, veteran status or access via family connections to those in power, will get ahead faster than those who arrived without these advantages. (Bernstein and Swirski [1982, 66–67] argue that Ashkenazi immigrants did not in fact have all these advantages because they came from the periphery of the capitalist world, but the case they make seems most unconvincing.)

Compare, for example, the recent remarkable success of middle-class Cuban, Chinese, Vietnamese, and Korean immigrants to the United States, to the much slower movement of earlier generations of European immigrants from peasant backgrounds. Unfortunately there do not seem to be any studies that compare the "success" of Jewish immigrants from Baghdad, Algiers, Alexandria, Rabat, or Beirut, who came already "middle class," to that of European Jews, as well as to Asian and Africans from more rural backgrounds, less "middle class."

One might wonder, however, what would have happened if the Israeli elite had *not* adopted policies aimed at assimilation and acculturation! What would the results of such policies have been, if Jews from Yemen and Morocco, Iran and Kurdistan, Cochin and Bombay, Georgia and Turkey had been encouraged to study in and develop the fifty or so languages they brought with them; if they had been encouraged to continue with polygyny and child betrothal and not urged to put their faith in schools and clinics?

It is certainly true that the policies were sometimes implemented poorly and unfairly. Immigrants from Asia and North Africa may have been given the less favorable conditions and poorer treatment than those from Europe and North America. But in terms of the overall policies, what alternative models were available for them to consider in the early 1950s? What attitude toward ethnic traditions would have been more successful in fostering rapid educational, economic, and political advancement?

The Substance of Ethnic Differences

Despite the ideology of Jewish unity and the assumption that the major institutions of the state should and would work for the acculturation and assimilation of all immigrants, Jewish ethnicity was always a reality of life in Israel. There are ethnically homogeneous villages *(moshavim)* and neighborhoods that are heavily Yemenite or Iraqi or Moroccan, and so on. Synagogues are overwhelmingly based on ethnicity. While there is a tendency for Ashkenazi Jews of whatever origin to pray together, the synagogues of Yemenites, Moroccans, Egyptians, Tunisians, Indians, Georgians, "Sephardim" (Greek, Turkish, Bulgarians) and others are usually distinct and separate. (To some extent this is necessary because, although the prayerbooks are virtually identical for all Jewish groups, the pronunciation of the Hebrew, the melodies and cantillation, and the style of worship may be quite different. It may be quite confusing, and therefore disturbing, for an observant Jew of one tradition to join congregants following a different one.)

There are ethnically based dance groups, cultural associations, mutual aid and burial societies, and even political parties (see Herzog 1985). On and off since 1948 there has been a Yemenite political party running in the national elections (without much success), and more recently North African, especially Moroccan, Jews have fielded their own parties. (They do not label them as explicitly Moroccan/North African.) Some ethnic organizations were initiated by members of those groups; others were fostered by the major political parties or the Histadrut (General Federation of Labor) in an attempt to win more followers from those groups. Ethnic leaders were recruited and ethnic interests played upon for political purposes. Ethnic politics were decried, scorned, and employed.

It is popular for Afro-Asian Jews to complain that in school they were forced to read the Hebrew poetry and stories of such writers as Bialik, Chernikovsky, and Berdichevsky, who were born in Europe. This is true, but these were the writers who helped create the new Hebrew literature for the developing new culture of the Jewish homeland. And the Jews from Asia and Africa were not forbidden to develop their own literature or traditions, even if these were not taught in the schools for the first twenty years. The maintenance and development of their artistic traditions were, in fact, often encouraged. This is particularly true of the Yemenites, whose rich heritage of poetry, music, dance, and the decorative arts was supported by outside agencies from as early as the 1920s. And the Yemenites, with or without external encouragement, continually nourished and elaborated this heritage, until today (cf. Lewis 1984).

The Yemenites began arriving in Palestine as early as the 1880s, at exactly the same time as the first Zionist settlers from Europe. They were a visible minority of the Jewish population during the development of the culture of the Jewish community, and their traditions caught the imagination of the new community's artists. They saw in them authentic Middle Eastern traditions, and ones that were distinctly Jewish as well. Yemenite artists, craftsmen, musicians, and dancers, on their own and in collaboration with Ashkenazi artists, contributed greatly to the new Jewish society, especially to its designs and decorative arts, music, and dance: folk, "classical" and "modern." The first well-known singers and recording artists were Yemenite women; the first Israeli dance group to tour the world was the Yemenite Inbal company. While these particular manifestations of Yemenite culture were heavily influenced by European traditions of music, dance, and performance, many other Yemenite musicians and dancers continued to perform and develop their heritage within the community. And today many young Yemenites have the education and the motivation and the opportunity to seek the "authentic" in their traditions (see H. S. Lewis 1984, 1989).

In recent years the musical traditions of North African and Asian Jews have become more and more popular in Israeli society. Musicians have found a new, enthusiastic audience; the modern technology of music recording and playback permits rapid diffusion of their music throughout the society. This musical genre appeals more to the "oriental" part of the population, just as the Western "classical" tradition appeals to Jews of Western origin. The point is that both traditions exist, are widely disseminated, and flourish.

Despite fears and talk of "deculturation" other groups as well as the Yemenites continue to draw upon and develop their own religious, cultural, and social traditions. There have been an increasing number of studies of cultural life among other Israeli groups in the last decade as there has been more and more to investigate. (Among the pioneering works see Deshen 1974; Deshen and Shokeid 1974.)

In recent years there has been a remarkable development (almost "explosive" in its extent and suddenness) of religious pilgrimages *(hilula)* by Moroccan Jews. These pilgrimages, which existed all along, began to be organized on a very large scale in the 1970s. Since 1985 a major shrine has developed around the tomb of a rabbi who gained fame for his abilities to heal. On the anniversary of his death hundreds of thousands of Jews, mostly from Morocco and elsewhere in North Africa, gather at his tomb in a small city in the Negev. But numerous other centers are also on the pilgrimage circuit. New "saints" and new shrines are developing all the time. (Cf. Weingrod 1990. For a series of papers suggesting some of the richness and complexity of Jewish ethnicity in Israel see Weingrod 1985.)

Ethnically specific social and cultural patterns are still being maintained and developed in Israel, despite the original ideology, the policies, and the alarms of critics of the government and establishment. Today there is greater legitimacy for this and the ideology itself has been modified.

The Re-thinking

By the early 1970s, after the Black Panthers captured the spotlight in Israel, about twenty years after the formulation of the original policies of *mizug galuyot,* the Israel political and educational elite recognized that they had a problem. The pressure cooker had not worked as it was supposed to. Many of the teachers and social workers and government officials became aware of and sensitive to the complaints of the *eydot ha-mizrah,* and a growing number of political, academic, and journalistic critiques. They responded with policies and programs meant to correct the original disdain for, or ignoring of, the history, culture, and traditions of the "oriental" Jews.

The Ministries of Education and of Religion became involved with these issues, as did some political parties and the Histadrut. Teachers and community workers and others were invited to workshops and conferences on the subject. Papers and books were written, and guidelines and suggestions distributed to schools and community centers.

Money was appropriated for the purpose of "enriching" school curricula, after school programs, and the cultural programs of the community centers. All manner of events were supported and organized, celebrating the "traditions" of all the ethnic groups — but with special emphasis, of course, on those from Asia and Africa. And so there were Yemenite evenings, and Moroccan culture exhibitions, and Georgian Jewish dance groups, lectures, publications, and conferences and workshops devoted to the attempt to rectify the original mistakes, by taking into account the traditions, the rich heritages, of the "oriental" Jews.[2]

Persian and Yemenite organizations sponsor "weekends," subsidized gatherings of thirty to forty young couples at a hotel or resort (see Goldstein 1985). There they can enjoy each other's company, religious services in their tradition, lectures, music and dance, and other ethnically specific activities.

Perhaps the most spectacular result of the encouragement of "traditions" was the development of the great annual celebration of the Moroccan Jews, the *mimouna*. The *mimouna,* a development of a practice of Jews in Morocco, takes place at the end of the Passover festival. On the evening that it ends, and during the next day, Jews of Moroccan origin (increasingly joined by others) prepare special foods, invite friends to their homes to partake, and may go the next day to public parks to picnic, enjoy the spring weather, sing and dance, meet with others, perhaps watch entertainment. They may even be honored and bored by the speeches of politicians who come to pay their respects—and hope for political credit (cf. Goldberg 1978; Weingrod 1990).

The much smaller Kurdish community has a similar celebration of its own, *saharanei* (Halper and Abromovitz 1984), while the most recent immigrants from Africa, the Ethiopians, have been encouraged to maintain and develop their *sigd* festival (Ben-Dor 1987).

It seems most significant that there has never been any serious resistance to this revision of the thinking of the elite. There was never a countermovement against the idea of advancing the interests or honoring and developing the traditions of groups from different countries. Whatever individual prejudices there are, these are rarely voiced publically and have no standing in the Jewish community.

Jewish Ethnic Diversity and National Integration

The critical and revisionist writings of the 1970s and 1980s, as well as much popular pessimism, give the impression of a deeply divided Jewish society, in contrast to the rosy predictions and propaganda of the two previous decades. But is it so divided? Despite the persistence of ethnicity among Jews derived from different countries, it seems clear that, in fact, the original policies have produced a high degree of consensus of the sort originally foreseen and desired by the leaders in the 1940s and 1950s.

There is no doubt that there are conflicts and resentments in Israel between Jews who have come from different countries. Above all, there is a general sense on the part of Jews from Asia and Africa that European Jews have been guilty of discrimination and prejudice against them and have given preference and precedence to their fellow ethnics. On the other hand, some Jews of European origin may feel that Jews from Asian and African countries do not have the same "standards" or capabilities ("yet") that members of their own group do. These days many Ashkenazi intellectuals, with "left-wing" or "dovish" beliefs deplore the increasing religiosity, the lack of support for socialism, the "hawkishness" and ultranationalism that they believe characterizes the "Oriental" Jews.

But these conflicts are overbalanced by general agreement about the nature of the state, and by the realities of everyday life.

1. There is remarkable consensus among Israel's Jews, of whatever origin about the oneness of the Jewish people and the legitimacy and significance of Israel.[3] There is no "Oriental"— European split on this score. As far as Jews of all backgrounds are concerned, Israel is the national homeland of the Jews. All Jews. There is nothing remotely like the conflicts in Canada, Belgium, or even the United Kingdom among the Welsh and the Scots. There is agreement on the basic Jewish nature of the state and on its legitimacy.

There is little doubt that almost all Israeli Jews approve of the idea that "the Jewish people is one," and that Israeli Jews should be united. It is also clear that the Afro-Asian Jews support the aims of the state, and its claims to be the homeland of the Jews. Very few would have any sympathy with those small groups of Ashkenazi Jews who deny the validity of Israel and dispute its right to exist. They are proud of being Jewish and Israeli. Their dispute, insofar as they have one, is with the Ashkenazim who are seen as discriminating against them, not giving them their due. But they accept the centrality of their Jewishness and their citizenship in the Jewish state.

2. Israel's leaders have succeeded in making Hebrew the national language of the Jews, the only one used in regular public

discourse. (Arabic is an official language, too, but spoken by primarily Arabs.) As in the United States, where it has been understood that all newcomers who want to participate in the society and culture would learn English, so in Israel all newcomers learn Hebrew. Other languages are not forbidden, and the elderly may continue to speak Arabic, or English, or German, or Yiddish, but the children all learn Hebrew, and it is the language of all the (Jewish) institutions in the land. Bilingual education for Jews, or the development of languages from the Diaspora, has not been an issue since the establishment of the state.[4]

3. In general, intermarriage among Jews of different national origins has been looked upon as the ultimate mechanism for and measure of integration. Social scientists, politicians, and anyone interested in the success of Israel looked on with approval as the rates of intermarriage between Asian and African Jews, on the one hand, and European and American Jews, on the other, rapidly rose (see Matras 1985, 14–15). Beyond the actual rising rates of intermarriage, however, it seems clear that people generally express the ideal of intermarriage among all Jewish groups. I found this attitude very strongly marked among Yemenite Israelis in 1987.

While carrying out research with a community of about 1300 Yemenites in a small city in 1977, I found that they actually were marrying out of their ethnic group only 15 percent of the time — a low figure for that era. When I did a follow-up study in 1987 I discovered that, in the preceeding decade, the rate of out-marriage had risen to 50 percent for men and 62 percent for women! Although the extent of actual intermarriage in this case is extraordinary, the ideology behind it is not. In conversations with dozens of young people, married and soon to marry, I was assured, over and over again, that they felt it possible — and *right* — to marry Jews of *any* background. Some agreed that it would be *easier* to marry other Yemenites, but only two or three said "only another Yemenite for me." But almost all expressed the ideal that intermarriage among Jews of different backgrounds was desirable for the future of Israel. And virtually all said that they could marry a Jew from any other background. They might express attitudes for or against a particular group (Ashkenazim are too cold; Moroccans are too hot-blooded, for example) but all agreed that who one married was a matter of luck and love, and "it could be anybody"—that is, any Jew. (The norm for marrying a Jew seems stronger than that for marrying another Israeli, incidentally.)

So, forty years after the founding of this state, its very heterogeneous Jewish population accepts its legitimacy as the Jewish state, accepts the central significance of the Hebrew language for all, and seems to accept the importance as well as the legitimacy of marriage among Jews from the different ethnic groups. This is no small accomplishment.

4. There is far too much to be said on the subject of "integration" to do anything more than allude to it. It might be summarized this way: On the one hand, Jewish Israel is a unitary society. People learn to behave like Israelis in the major public arenas such as the workplace, school, the army, and the marketplace. A degree of conformity to public norms in these settings is expected, and obtained. (See Ben-Rafael 1982 and Ben-Rafael and Sharot 1991 for a view that stresses integration even more strongly.)

On the other hand, there is still considerable scope for ethnically specific activities, attitudes, norms, and relations. The realm of family, synagogue, and, sometimes, the local community, may be heavily influenced by aspects of culture, behavior and social relations adapted from among those brought from countries of origin. And, as Harvey Goldberg points out (1987, 47–48), "the side of ethnicity based upon individual choice not only can help maximize a person's social position, but can be an *expression of individuality*. . . . Ethnic related symbols are becoming common signs of the individual in 'post-industrial' society."

Conclusions

In 1976 Yancey, Ericksen, and Juliani published an influential paper that argued that American ethnic groups were not products of their supposed "foreign heritages" but were actually the result of "the exigencies of survival and the structure of opportunity" in the United States. This perspective proved rather popular in ethnic studies, and at least two writers, Swirski and Katzir (1978; Swirski 1981) applied it to the Israeli context. They argued that a new ethnic group, "Oriental Jews", was being produced as the result of the emerging unequal division of labor in Israel.

In contrast to their reading of the evidence, it would appear that Diaspora-based identities are flourishing despite active government intervention and a powerful ideology (a moral imperative, really) meant to deemphasize and discourage them. Manifestations of ethnic "culture" are increasingly evident despite the very real force of acculturation to Israeli economy, society, and culture. The state neither destroyed nor created these groups, which depend for their existence upon the loyalties, attitudes, and heritages that they brought with them from the Diaspora. They may be based on ties, not only to Yemen, Morocco, and Tunisia, but to such places as Habban, San'a, Meknes, and Jerba, centers of Jewish culture that the leaders of the state barely knew existed.

The founders of the State of Israel grew up and began their leadership in a world in which even the term "ethnicity" did not exist and in which the things for which we now use the word were deemed backward, destructive, and doomed to disappear. By the 1970s the ideological climate in much of the world had begun to change. It was more legitimate to speak of tradition and ethnicity in Israel as it was in the United States and in many other parts of the world. "Multiculturalism," a term for the 1990s, was not yet in use, but some such idea was developing in Israel among those who dealt with problems of education and integration. The world had changed since 1948, and many said, in effect, "we made mistakes; we didn't understand the importance of these traditions." Some intellectuals of Eastern European origin are even reaching the stage where they can take a new and more appreciative look at their own ancestral traditions and at the language that their parents or grandparents spoke, Yiddish.

Throughout this paper I have stressed "the leaders," "the elite" rather than "the state" in order to avoid reification and imputing directions, needs, imperatives, to "the system." Implicitly, at least, I have also had in mind the millions of Israelis who have made choices and behaved in accordance with *their* values and perceptions of their situations and thus forced a change of view upon the leadership. It was not "the state" that planned the absorption of immigrants in Israel, nor is it "the state" that decided it had made a mistake. It was human beings, "actors" or "agents," facing a particular set of circumstances and forced to make choices that explains the policies that were followed. These could only be handled in the light of their perceptions, their desired ends, and in terms of their current understandings of the nature of ethnicity, "tradition and modernity," and Jewishness. The changes in their policies and in their perceptions are the result of feedback from the realities in Israel and changes in the perception of ethnicity in the world more generally.

Notes

1. In the 1970s African and Asian Jews were seriously underrepresented in positions of influence in the Knesset, in the cabinet, and so on. Since that time there has been a great expansion of their power, in part due to the response to the demand for changes, in part due to the passage of time and the rise of these leaders through the ranks of the parties, the military, and local government. By the early 1980s the deputy prime minister, the chief of the defense forces, and the head of the powerful Histadrut were from Morocco, Iraq, and Yemen, respectively. In the Likud-led government formed in June 1990, at least seven of the nineteen cabinet ministers, including the current foreign minister are of Afro-Asian origin. There has been an even more marked advance in their role in regional and municipal government.
2. It is important to note that, despite the widespread use of the category "oriental Jews" in Israel, no such ethnic group has developed. Although many Jews from Asian and African countries may be united in their resentment of perceived discrimination and inequality, this has not served as the basis for the creation of any sort of entity, either social, cultural, or political (cf. Ben-Rafael 1982). They generally see themselves as Jews, Israelis, and as members of specific country-of-origin groups, such as Yemenite, Tunisian, Kurdish, Moroccan.
3. The only disagreements on this score are found among two very different groups of Ashkenazim. On the one extreme, there are small sects of ultraorthodox who deny the validity of a Jewish state before the coming of the messiah. As the messiah has clearly not yet come, they reject the Jewish state. At the other end of the spectrum, there is a tiny group of individuals who favor a binational secular Palestinian Jewish-Arab state, who consider themselves to be "Canaanites" rather than "Jews."
4. There are newspapers published in Ladino (Judeo-Spanish), Hungarian, Romanian, and other languages, but these have a limited future since they are read primarily by the older generation. But it is worth noting that there has been no attempt to prevent publication in languages other than Hebrew.
5. Indeed, even today there is great hostility on the part of many liberals and radicals to ethnic phenomena. Many can see only bad things to come from an

emphasis on ethnic solidarity. Writers such as Patterson (1977), Stein and Hill (1977), and Steinberg (1981) write of the evils of these retrograde sentiments, while fears grow about the spread of ethnopolitical/nationalist claims in the 1990s.

References

Bar-Yosef, Rivka. 1968. "Desocialization and Resocialization." *International Migration Review* 2:27–43.

Ben-David, Joseph. 1953. "Ethnic Differences or Social Change?" In C. Frankenstein (ed.), *Between Past and Future*, pp. 33–52. Jerusalem: Henrietta Szold Foundation.

Ben-Dor, Shoshana. 1987. The Sigd of Beta Israel: Testimony to a Community in Transition. In M. Ashkenazi and A. Weingrod (eds.), *Ethiopian Jews and Israel,* pp. 140–59. New Brunswick, N.J.: Transaction Books.

Ben-Rafael, Eliezer. 1982. *The Emergence of Ethnicity.* Westport, Conn.: Greenwood Press.

Ben-Rafael, Eliezer and Stephen Sharot. 1991. *Ethnicity, Religion, and Class in Israeli Society.* Cambridge: Cambridge University Press.

Ben-Zvi, Itzhak. 1957. *The Exiled and the Redeemed.* Philadelphia: Jewish Publication Society of America.

Bendix, Reinhard. 1967. "Tradition and Modernity Reconsidered." *Comparative Studies in Society and History* 9:292–346.

Bernstein, Deborah and Shlomo Swirski. 1982. "The Rapid Economic Development of Israel and the Emergence of the Ethnic Division of Labor." *British Journal of Sociology* 33:65–85.

Bernstein, Judith and Aaron Antonovsky. 1981. "The Integration of Ethnic Groups in Israel." *Jewish Journal of Sociology* 23:5–23.

Berreby, Jean-Jacques. 1956. "De l'Intégration des Juifs Yéménites en Israel." *L'Annee Sociologique,* 3rd series:69–163.

Cohen, Erik. 1983. "Ethnicity and Legitimation in Contemporary Israel." *The Jerusalem Quarterly* 28.

Deshen, Shlomo. 1974. "Political Ethnicity and Cultural Ethnicity in Israel During the 1960s" In Abner Cohen (ed.), *Urban Ethnicity,* pp. 281–310. London: Tavistock Publications.

Deshen, Shlomo and Moshe Shokeid. 1974. *The Predicament of Homecoming: Cultural and Social Life of North African Immigrants in Israel.* Ithaca: Cornell University Press.

Eisenstadt, Shmuel N. 1953. "The Process of Absorption of Immigrants." In C. Frankenstein (ed.), *Between Past and Future*, pp. 53–81. Jerusalem: Henrietta Szold Foundation.

———. 1954. *The Absorption of Immigrants.* London: Routledge and Kegan Paul.

Frankenstein, Carl. 1953. *Between Past and Future.* Jerusalem: Henrietta Szold Foundation.

Geertz, Clifford. 1973. *The Interpretation of Cultures.* New York: Basic Books.

Goldberg, Harvey. 1978. "The Mimouna and the Minority Status of Moroccan Jews." *Ethnology* 17:75–85.

————. 1985. "Historical and Cultural Dimensions of Ethnic Phenomena in Israel." In A. Weingrod (ed.), *Studies in Israeli Ethnicity: After the Ingathering,* pp. 179–200. New York: Gordon and Breach.

————. 1987. "The Changing Meaning of Ethnic Affiliation." *The Jerusalem Quarterly* 44:39–50.

Goldstein, Judith. 1985. "Iranian Ethnicity in Israel: The Performance of Identity." In A. Weingrod (ed.), *Studies in Israeli Ethnicity: After the Ingathering,* pp. 237–57. New York: Gordon and Breach.

Halper, Jeff and H. Abromovitz. 1984. The Saharanei Celebration in Kurdistan and Israel. In S. Deshen and M. Shokeid (eds.), *Jews of the Middle East* [Hebrew]. Tel Aviv: Schocken.

Halpern, Ben. 1969. *The Idea of the Jewish State.* Cambridge, Mass.: Harvard University Press.

Hertzberg, Arthur, ed. 1960. *The Zionist Idea.* New York: Meridian.

Herzog, Hanna. 1985. "Ethnicity as a Negotiated Issue in the Delegates' Assembly and the Knesset (1920–1977)." In A. Weingrod (ed.) *Studies in Israeli Ethnicity,* pp. 159–78. New York: Gordon and Breach.

————. 1973. *Immigration and Settlement.* Jerusalem: Keter Books.

Iris, Mark and Avraham Shama. 1977. *Immigration Without Integration: Third World Jews in Israel.* Cambridge, Mass.: Schenkman.

Isaac, J. 1959. Israel: A New Melting Pot? In W. D. Borrie (ed.), *Cultural Integration of Immigrants,* pp. 234–65. Paris: UNESCO.

Kivisto, Peter. 1990. "The Transplanted Then and Now: The School to the New Social History." *Ethnic and Racial Studies* 13.

Laqueur, Walter. 1972. *A History of Zionism.* New York: Holt, Rinehart and Winston.

Lewis, Arnold. 1979. *Power, Poverty and Education.* Ramat Gan: Turtledove.

Lewis, Herbert. 1984. Yemenite Ethnicity in Israel. *Jewish Journal of Sociology* 26:5–24.

————. 1989. *After the Eagles Landed: The Yemenites of Israel.* Boulder, Col.: Westview.

Lissak, Moshe. 1983. "Ideological and Social Conflicts in Israel." *The Jerusalem Quarterly* 29.

Matras, Judah. 1985. Intergenerational Social Mobility and Ethnic Organization in the Jewish Population of Israel. In A. Weingrod (ed.), *Studies in Israeli Ethnicity,* pp. 1–23. New York: Gordon and Breach.

Patai, Raphael. 1953. *Israel Between East and West: A Study in Human Relations.* Philadelphia: Jewish Publication Society of America.

————. 1961. *Cultures in Conflict.* New York: Herzl Press. Patterson, Orlando. 1977. *Ethnic Chauvinism.* Briarcliff Manor, N.Y.: Stein and Day.

Rubenberg, Cheryl A. 1986. "Ethnicity, Elitism, and the State of Israel." In J. F. Stack (ed.), *The Primordial Challenge: Ethnicity in the Contemporary World,* pp. 161–184. Westport, Conn.: Greenwood.

Schechtman, Joseph B. 1961. *On Wings of Eagles: The Plight, Exodus, and Homecoming of Oriental Jewry.* New York: Thomas Yoseloff.

Smith, Anthony D. 1981. *The Ethnic Revival in the Modern World.* Cambridge: Cambridge University Press.

Smooha, Sammy. 1972. "Black Panthers: The Ethnic Dilemma." *Trans-Action,* 9.

———. 1978. *Israel: Pluralism and Conflict.* Berkeley: University of California Press.

Stein, Howard F. and Robert F. Hill. 1977. *The Ethnic Imperative: Examining the New White Ethnic Movement.* University Park: Pennsylvania State University Press.

Steinberg, Stephen. 1981. *The Ethnic Myth: Race, Ethnicity, and Class in America.* New York: Atheneum.

Swirski, Shlomo. 1981. *Not Disadvantaged, But Disenfranchised: Oriental and Ashkenazim in Israel.* Haifa: Research and Critique Series [Hebrew].

Swirski, Shlomo and Sara Katzir. 1978. *Orientals and Ashkenazim in Israel: An Emerging Dependency Relationship.* Haifa: Research and Critique Series.

Theodorson, George. 1953. "Acceptance of Industrialization and Its Attendant Consequences for the Social Patterns of Non-Western Societies." *American Sociological Review* 18:477–84.

Toledano, Henry. 1973. Time to Stir the Melting Pot. In M. Curtis and M. Chertoff (eds.), *Israel: Social Structure and Change.* pp. 333–347. New Brunswick, N.J.: Transaction Books.

Weingrod, Alex, ed. 1985. *Studies in Israeli Ethnicity: After the Ingathering.* N.Y.: Gordon and Breach.

———. 1990. *The Saint of Beersheba.* Albany: State University of New York Press.

Yancey, W. L., E. P. Ericksen, and R. N. Juliani. 1976. "Emergent Ethnicity: A Review and Reformulation." *American Sociological Review* 41:391–403.

Yosephthal, Giora. 1966. *The Life and Opinions of Giora Yosephthal.* Edited by Ben Halpern and Shalom Wurm. New York: Schocken.

9

Conclusion: Ethnicity, the State, and Moral Order

Ronald Cohen

"Jewish settlers attacked and beat Israelis trying to deliver food and medicines to Palestinian children following a raid on Palestinians in which a thirteen year old girl was shot dead" (*The Globe and Mail* 3 June 1989:A2). "About the same time an Israeli Rabbi used biblical references to justify the conclusion that spilling non-Jewish blood is a lesser offense than the spilling of Jewish blood. Responding, the Chief Rabbi of Israel proclaimed that all human beings are made in God's image (*New York Times,* 6 June 1989:5).

These West Bank incidents can be repeated for innumerable occasions, times, places, and peoples. Although not discussed directly they point to the fundamental issue underlying all of the chapters of the book. One with more ramifying implications affecting many other problems. Can there be a universal moral order based on claims to a common humanity—what Marx called species being. Or is morality at least to a very important extent an integral product of tradition, tribe, society, and ultimately the nation state applicable first and most accurately to ethnic units? Is Kantian universalism questioned by cultural relativism and its assumption that genuineness comes out of the particularism of

231

specific streams of human adaptation by real people in real world places?

It's an old question. But these chapters throw it into a new context. For the state once it emerges throws such problems into relief, even though it has yet to solve them. Scholarship is ambivalent. At one time or another writings on the state and ethnicity have taken each side of the argument claiming that particularism is both superior and an advance on universalism, and vice versa that universalism is the way forward to human progress and the march of history towards human betterment. Each viewpoint then sees or acts as if the other is regressive, reactionary, or backward. In what follows I wish to examine this issue, using the papers in the volume as a stimulus and the question itself as an heuristic enabling me to come to grips with the emergent relations between ethnicity, the state, and the moral order. It is apparent in the papers and even more dramatically in current events that these relations are not stable. State sovereignty is weakening under global and regional pressures from above, while simultaneously recognizing the legitimate rights of ethnic units from within.

The issue is dramatic and intense with passion, violence, suffering, even horror, for those caught up in its rushing currents. Some see glory in it. A melding of the self into the shaping and flow of historic forces that speak of victory over enemies and/or promise justice and advancement for themselves and "their people." Others see the conflict as irrational, a cruel illogic in which they must suffer for stigmata whose meanings foretell lives long on vulnerability, short on power. Using the Israeli example again, recent accounts of the tensions in the area show how ethnic conflict produces only losers (Shipler 1985; Emerson 1991). In state-supported ethnic oppression and counterrebellion these authors argue that no one, no group, no individual wins or can win. And yet the forces involved, and the stakes at risk are so deeply felt, so much a major feature of life that the interethnic conflict becomes part of the culture, almost of normalcy for the groups involved. In many instances, in the Middle East, in the Punjab, for the Kurds, the Tibetans, the Eritreans, the Irish, the Quebecois, the Tamils, the southern Sudanese, many in Corsica, Basques in Spain, to name only a few, the price is often high in human suffering and sacrifice but for those involved, often the vast majority, the goals are worth it. So the struggle goes on.

Ethnicity and State Origins

In anthropological terms, using comparative and long-term perspectives, multiethnicity and statehood are two sides of the same coin. The evolution of centralized political systems starts with chieftaincy in which centralized institutions are weak, dealing for the most part with relations to outsiders along with some mediation of internal disputes. Alien individuals and groups are rapidly incorporated, often in one to two generations, through cultural assimilation. At the same time, chiefly power is contained within its Malthusian nemesis. Factional disputes over leadership or delicts involving collective responsibilities or access to natural resources increase in frequency as group size enlarges making fission normal and frequent. However, the state evolves compensatory mechanisms to contain this enervating feature enabling it thereby to become the most powerful organization in species history (Cohen 1976, 1978, 1980). Once the centralized state emerges with authority to mediate disputes, and its capacity to demand tributes and other revenues as well as militia from its subject groups, pluralism or increased multiethnicity becomes one of its most common features. Conversely, fission, the ubiquitous hallmark of prestate political processes decreases very significantly whilst multiethnicity becomes a way of adding power through numbers of supporters that overrides sole dependence upon births.

But there are multiple pathways to statehood and ethnicity plays varied roles. In many, probably the majority, of instances the emergent state is composed of numerous ethnic groups variably related to one another but invariably ranked. This generally means a plethora of culturally distinct local groups under dominant royals and nobles — more and less culturally different — in control of the central government from a citadel capital town. In others, states emerge from hostilities between ethnic groups and surrounding polities. In such instances claims of common ethnicity are used to mobilize previously autonomous groups under a unified leadership. As with all states this step creates expansionist potential under the newly emergent centralized government. In effect state centralization and its attendant political order occur through the dominance of one ethnic group among a competing set of them creating a plural polity from the beginning, or by a single ethnic group choosing to unify and defy its enemies rather than running away or being absorbed by one or several of them (Cohen 1980 etc.).

In the first instance, statehood is triggered most often by conquest. Notably, cultural assimilation to the great tradition of the dominant group and their capital citadel happens very slowly, although it does occur authoritatively in at least one instance (Inca) in which conquest involves dispersing the new group in order to speed up assimilation (Toland 1988). In most instances, however, localized and rank differences help sustain ethnic distinctions for long periods, especially those based on differentiated ecological and occupational adaptations such as farmers and graziers, or traders, and so on.

In varying degree all of these early state systems share the power granted to them by their new political order. By far the most important feature of this emergent increase in power lies in the selection and retention of new criteria for membership in the polity. Unlike all previous formations the state differentiates the role of citizen and/or subject, making for a quantum leap in mobilizing capacity, revenues, and territorial control. Hammurabi used the promise of a common rule of just laws to legitimate conquest and incorporation of adjacent polities under his own (Yoffee 1988). The ancient Egyptians used conquered ethnic groups and multiethnic slave groups to build their monuments, and early states used multiethnic subordination to create and maintain massive and frequent military campaigns (Smaldone 1977; Ferguson 1984; Cohen 1986). The capacity to deal with both pluralism and to institutionalize ways and means of minimizing fission through authoritative dispute settlement enhanced the adaptive capacity of centralization increasing its power many times over. In effect, with the emergence of the state, cultural pluralism may vary independently of political membership. The members may be either citizens or servile noncitizens in their relation to central and local authority, and they may be of the same or different ethnic categories to others especially to the rulers. Historically then, the state is the first organizational form in human evolutionary history to incorporate the capacity for the everyday management and mobilization of plural societies. The payoff in potentially enhanced power is infinitely greater than any previous form of political system.

People are strength. They produce more goods, more revenues, more soldiers, and thus more power. The emergence of the state allows for ethnic group enclaves to reproduce their heritable culture within the polity while assimilating more slowly. They also make available their own traditions, technology, and socio-political alliances as variants for selection and retention by the more polyglot whole creating a polity and society characterized by hybrid vigor, albeit potentially more conflictful. In the prestate era people from elsewhere were most often added as individuals or at most as families. In contrast the state enables the incorporation of quite large even culturally distinct populations — an enormous leap forward in the capacity of political systems to increase control over territories, resources, and trade routes, with bigger, better, and more organized armies that carried out campaigns on an almost annual basis (Cohen 1986). This in turn meant an emphasis on access to militia and the rapid development of military strategy and technology. The early state was strongly oriented to war. People, whatever their culture, were its military fodder and its source of revenue for an entire class of managers and rulers whose differentiated sumptuary life-style made them dependent on their ability to demand a share in resources of land, labor, production, and trade. The main point, however, is clear. In evolutionary terms the state benefitted in terms of reproductive success from its emergent capacity to organize a plural society by differentiating political obligations from cultural heritage. It was a major step forward in social evolution but one that is often overlooked. But it important to be clear about it. Statehood is correlated with multiculturalism. In comparative and historical perspective uniethnic states are the exception not the rule.

Universalism and the State

Given the stimulus of multiculturalism and its organizational capacity for an immense leap in power, the state soon became the dominant political form in the world. Within three to four millenia after its earliest appearance, the state in one form or another claimed hegemony over the entire population of the world. Non-states became parts of larger state systems with more and less degrees of absorption into the ethnizing processes of the state as it struggled towards a more unified culture under the leadership of its dominant ethnic or clan grouping. On the other hand, this process is never complete. Migrations, varying degrees of assimilability, and the emergence of new ethnic units (as in Sumatra, or with the Palestinians) ensure that pluralism and statehood remain correlated. And almost from the beginning successful states—Egypt, Alexandrian Greece, the Mongols, China, Inca, Maya, Aztec, Borno, Ghana, the Islamic caliphates and that of Rome, became seriously expansionist. Imperial expansion introduced complex administrative authority over local peoples at state peripheries and beyond to areas of vital concern. The search was for power; control over access to trade routes and resources, especially those quite far off. So whilst the state stimulated the growth of an emergent common ethicity, its expansion reintroduced or stimulated new ethnic groups under its leadership, constantly rejuvenating its pluralism.

Possibly the most fascinating cultural correlate of the state has been its stimulation, selection, and retention of universalist ideologies, philosophies, theology, and constitutionalism. Out of the Mediterranean world especially, but present in the Far East as well, state and empire, especially the latter have promulgated the emergence of ethnic-based, indeed species-wide, do's and dont's. From Hammurabi's code to Roman law to modern constitutions and the rule of law, once a panethnic nation state is set into being, there are correlated developments. Universal moral principles applicable beyond the moral boundaries set by ethnicity expand the moral universe. These may not fit all comers, but clearly they signal a feature of political culture fostered by this new structure. In effect this is the state-associated attempt to create a set of supraethnic universal values and rules. Given the organizational format of a multiethnic polity it was necessary to develop moral rules that applied to everyone regardless of their ethnicity. The multiethnic state thus provides the social soil out of which emerged concepts of a legitimizing panethnic God and his universally applicable moral rules. Although we now know that Hammurabi did not live by his code (Yoffee 1988), it is also clear his concept of universally applicable laws was a means of seeking and legitimizing multisite (and multiethnic) support for his state's expansionism.

In the Western tradition notions of cultural superiority by the Romans in relation to Northern Europeans, and the need for administrative comparability throughout the empire, stimulated a universally applicable set of laws, governmental structures, roads, and even language. Ultimately, after the fall of the Empire and the concomitant rise of Christianity from its ashes, there arose a new and strongly universalist religion whose tenets and dieties were/are concerned with the individual and collective responsibilities of humanity as a whole. Other world religions such as Islam and Buddhism associated with expansionist statehood made the same universalist claims.

Importantly for human development, notions of cause effect relationship concerned with both the supernatural and the natural world were also deeply affected as they moved from ethnic based traditions to the realm of a universalist conception of common, empirically understandable processes whose discovery/conception contributed to technology in all major sectors of civil life. Ethnic-based science remained within ethnic boundedness. But the state and its universalist, multiethnic character created the basis for the panethnic accumulation of knowledge. Together with writing and the accumulation of knowledge in libraries associated with religious, that is, moral experts and practioners the door opened on our modern scientific conceptualization of the world as seen and imagined in terms of cause-effect explanations. This in turn led the way to immense power as the state and religion developed the notion of a research tradition. This involved investment in intellectual advance through the search and dissemination of new knowledge. In the West, within Islam, and in the Far East those in control recognized that this form of exploration could enrich and empower the state.

Universalist thought persisted throughout the early history of the European states with notions of virtue, theology, of government, and science. Scholarship itself was panethnic with Church Latin as a lingua franca and the great monasteries as repositories of research and universalist teachings. Almost all of the great medieval thinkers, Augustine, Bodin, Vico, Confucius, Ibn Khaldun, and many in the Renaissance (e.g., Descartes, Spinoza) sought out universalist logics and understandings. Their epistemology and schemes of morality and government were meant to be species wide, or at the very least relevent to their own civilization, to Christendom, Islam, or Buddhism.

Possibly the zenith of universalist writings and approaches occurs in the eighteenth century. Whether they were defending an older monarchical order or pointing the way to a new one, the Enlightenment writers argued that there were rational reasons for inequality and state power. The state, and the underlying causes of human history and progress stem from humankind's common humanity in the same physical world. Thus it seemed evident that a universally applicable set of moral rules could be derived for society, government, commerce, the family, and so on. These reflect universal principles of rights and duties that can be "discovered." And they should be applicable equally to all humankind. Humbolt (Meineke 1976, 43) writing about this time (end of eighteenth century) called for a comparative anthropology of various ways of life to discover the general laws governing history, culture, and morality. This would then allow us to extract the highest and most valuable among human values and cultures and apply them to the advancement of humanity as a whole. In England, Thomas Carlyle (1837, 1987) wrote a novel suggesting that ethnic and rank differences were superficial outward appearances covering up universals that should be the true guiding principles of humankind's behavior. This was followed ultimately by the nineteenth century founders of social science Comte, Morgan, Spencer, Tylor, Durkheim, and Maine to mention only a few.

On this point, Marx went much further. In reaction to the particularism of his day, especially in Germany, he joined universalist thought with ideology and a political program. For Marx and many of his followers, ethnicity was a superficial property. A mystified category that obscures the inequality and the universal causal processes of history — the class struggles between rulers and ruled representing owners and workers for control of the means and fruits of production. Programmatically, working people of the world must be made to understand their common predicament. From that point on, ethnicity will fade or take its "true" place. Each local "nationality" can then be appreciated by everyone, ethnic member and nonmember alike, for its specific artistic and historic value. Within this utopian vision, citizenship and ethnic-national loyalties will wither as humanity achieves classless nirvana ending the egregious greed and individualism of capitalism and its instrument of exploitative control, the state. Instead individual humans must be educated to seek the collective good (not just for their own group but for humankind as a whole) as the means to their personal satisfactions (Pearson 1990).

This, then is the basis for the logic of universalism. Humanity and God are one. The moral universe does not end at the ethnic boundaries. Under apparent cultural and national differences lies a single, common trajectory of human progress. Rules governing its development and guiding its moral order apply equally across cultures under a universal diety concerned with the world as a whole. From the Enlightenment forward the notion of a common condition for all humankind and their particular historic pathways permeated social thought. And these common conditions were seen to be objective and scientifically knowable. Underlying the entire human experience are "natural," that is, measurable trends and outcomes along with their discoverable causes and effects. In Liebnizian fashion, particular settings, peoples, states, ethnic groups, or classes and organizations, and so on, are examples of these universal processes. Ethnic peculiarities are merely superficial distinctions that hide the common features of panethnic human experience, rights, duties, and mechanistic processes of cause and effect that generate both multiculturalism and the state. It is our responsibility to discover these natural phenomena and then to use this knowledge to change things. In effect human progress was seen as dependent upon discoverable laws governing economics, politics, society, and culture.

Under such a paradigm, which is exceptionally strong in the Western tradition, ethnicity, even the state, are stepping stones on the way to an orderly and controllable panhuman world order. One species, one set of needs, and an evolving means of recognizing the universal causes and rules that must be discovered and then manipulated to achieve a common human welfare. And that welfare reflects a universal moral order under the final authority of a unified and universal God. Both ethnicity and modern states are thus staging points on the way to emancipation for all peoples which depends upon the emergence and acceptance of cross-culturally applicable morality, and hence to progress.

Particularism and the Ethnic State

Fortunately or unfortunately, depending on your viewpoint, scientific materialism, universalism, one worldism, humanism, cosmopolitanism, or any other well-meaning attempt to set ethnicity aside or weaken its effect seems to have faltered. Whatever else happens in cultural and political history, ethnicity seems to have survived. It may reappear as if it had only been dormant, or it emerges under new labels often as not incorporating different populations. In effect ethnicity seems to fulfill needs not easily provided for by other categories of identity, and to survive despite the trouble it creates, often resulting in violence and loss of life (Horowitz 1985). Events seem to be saying that ethnicity cannot be dismissed as some kind of retrograde obstruction or the reflection of a "deeper" reality such as inequality and class struggles. Rather, it seems to be a phenomenon, like many others, that is inherent in and that characterizes the human experience. Marx was wrong. We don't progress beyond it, we can't move forward without it.

Elsewhere (Cohen 1978a) I have analyzed ethnicity and its determinants into a set of we/they distinctions having both subjective and objectively derived referents. Whether self-defined, attributed by others, or both, these usually descent-based markers constitute a process of ethnic identifications dependent upon real world causes. The most widespread of these triggers is the we/they situation in which the we is defined by the presence of an outsider—the Other(s). Thus, X is an American in Paris, an Italian in Houston, and a Texan in New York. Other triggers or markers include a real or putative common historical experience that provides a sense of shared fate, leaders who seek constituencies and use ethnic loyalties and fears to mobilize supporters, a common language, religion, territory, a restricted set of occupations, physical appearance, and greater or lesser than chance access to scarce resources. The determinative effects of each marker varies over time. The greater the correlation among them, the greater is the boundedness or dividing lines and the distance between those ethnic groups involved. The descent basis reflects the fact that ethnicity is generally acquired by birth into an ethnically homogeneous household. Marriages are governed by ethnic boundaries making interethnic unions far rarer than could occur by chance.

I also noted (ibid.) that over time the plural state is an ethnic creating unit. Given time and a stable government, the state has the capacity to induce a common we-feeling, a common language or a lingua franca, possibly a common religion and educational system, but certainly a common set of laws reflecting an emergent statewide morality, and patriotism including life-threatening committment to the state as a corporate entity. Indicators include intermarriages among citizens, a common set of loyalties to a leader, in earlier times generally a monarch, and recognition by outsiders as an ethnic group identifiably associated with a state. In this sense the state levels out cultural differences over time. England was plural to begin with, say in the eleventh century, as was Christian Europe with its local ethnic groups beginning to coalesce into contemporary states under monarchs who ultimately succeeded in unifying centrifugal feudal administrations. In England by Elizabethan times internal differences between Anglo-Saxons, and Normans, less so with peripheral Celts, were considered minor in the face of the centralized monarchy and its growing power to unify administration. Religion had been nationalized (for Protestant Europe) under the state and even in Catholic Europe there was national competition for control of the Church (leading to a Pope in Avignon rather than Rome). The Bible was translated and printed in local languages supporting the emergent states as autonomous political actors rather than as a segment of Christendom under weak feudal monarchs. Trade and commerce were developing on a national basis especially with the inception of the royally chartered trading companies (precursor to the modern business corporation) working in India and Canada.

And the process is a continuing one even in contemporary times. Although the United States began as a plural society, and still is, there is an identifiable American ethnicity based on the emergent populist culture of the Republic (Lipset 1990). The leveling process varies with the degree of protection and political expression given to ethnicity. The French of Canada differ from their relatives in the U.S. In the USSR governments followed the Marxist-Leninist theory of state and ethnicity that predicted the end of ethnic rivalries and conflict in a socialist environment in which the state protects the collective equality among ethnic groups. Meanwhile, local republics were set up to reflect and nourish cultural differences under local political authority. Ethnicity could be expressed politically as long as it did not challenge revolutionary (i.e., central government) authority, or represent "class" differences. In this way ancient roots, territoriality, and the cultural adaptation correlated with it could be continued, indeed protected under the guidance of the Soviet state, that is, union of republics. Unfortunately, in the USSR, Yugoslavia, Ceylon, Iraq, to mention only a few, events so far have not supported the theory. Ethnic loyalty and its accompanying patriotism is not solely dependent upon "class" differences among ethnic groups. And as we have seen, it is not necessarily antiprogressive for local polities to challenge the central government.

The European perception of concomitance between ethnicity and the state has been one of history's more serious mistakes. As we have noted statehood is inherently multiethnic. Ethnic homogeneity within autonomous states is a rarity. In general and throughout social evolution, ethnic conflict and competition helps make states, and therefore most states are and always have been plural. And it increases through time. As the world's state system evolved, the total number of states has decreased logarithmically while unit size has increased (Carneiro 1978). This means that multiethnicity per state has increased in probability terms over the period from early states to the present. Statistical data certainly support this generalization for contemporary times.[1] What makes this point important, however, is the deep-rooted European belief that states are or somehow ought to be correlated with uniethnicity. While there may be some states that have a single ethnic group predominating as in Japan, the generalization reflects a cultural orientation rather than any valid statement about the real world.

Possibly, the most well-articulated analysis of this position is that of Meineke (1907:1976). He summarizes the history of the idea of an ethnic state in Germany first theoretically, then historically from the late eighteenth to the end of the nineteenth century. In so doing he contrasts "cosmopolitanism" or universalism on the one hand with its theoretically progressive successor, the nation state. For Meineke the state evolves and is established to protect and express the particularism of an ethnic group whose common language and culture requires the political strength of statehood. Once achieved such a state contributes to humanity's progress by a politically protected attempt to preserve and expand its ethnicity. In this sense the historic and evolutionary function of the state is to sustain uniethnicity, not promulgate or utilize multiethnicity or "cosmopolitanism." This latter quality—synonomous with universalism—was theorized to corrode the source of the state's unique strength. Distilling this thesis from a series of German thinkers from the 1790s to the late nineteenth century, Meineke claims that social evolution moves forward only when an ethnically homogeneous people develop their own state. The reverse idea, fostered by the Enlightenment, that humans operate in accordance with a set of basic natural rights and precepts leading to a social contract and a set of universal rules governing all states and their *human* not ethnic identity, he found reactionary and unacceptable. For him and a long list of others that he discusses, universal principles of morality and order are too generalized. They may serve as overall guidelines, but they lack sufficient detail to cope with real world problems to be found in everyday life within a specific society, and in the unruly cutthroat world of interstate competition. These details are, however, always present in the moral and cultural adaptations to be found in the long term rootedness of particular ethnic traditions. In more general evolutionary terms, it is this feature, ethnic statehood, he believes, that provides the variety upon which natural selection operates. For the particularists humanity is made up of species of cultures each of which is competing for survival in an unforgiving jungle in which the best adaptions will survive and provide a model culture for ever more numbers of their conspecifics whose own cultures will be lost in the struggle. Evolution in this sense is a form of cultural darwinism. And in order for this natural process to work at its most accelerated and purist form, ethnicity must be given corporate political expression in a Hobbesian world of internation state competition. This gives nature and history the chance to choose the best in humanity's sociocultural varied (ethnic) experience for survival, thereby ensuring progress for the species as a whole.

Thus generalized rules governing all human activity, universalism, hides the real meaning of human history and progress epitomized by eighteenth-century rationalism, by the cross-culturally valid claims of the church of Rome, by Jews who wished to be both full citizens of national states yet remain culturally and even morally distinct, and by social science, especially Marxist evolutionism to name only the most obvious. In the end, however, these ideas are impediments to human advance. Progress is not achieved through the development of an increasingly higher culture evolved from a "cosmopolitan fusion," that is, a multiethnic citizenry. On the contrary its conditions of emergence depend upon the state being the political expression of a single ethnic tradition (Meineke 1976, 43). In the view, therefore, the main direction of evolution is not towards a set of universal principles about human social, political, and economic organization. On their own this kind of theorizing is insufficient because it leaves out the richness and variety of human adaptation in particular and "mightily rooted" (ibid., 70) ethnicities. Each of these is similar to an individual with its own personality, its essential strengths and weaknesses, competing for it place in the world and its reproductive success. The ethnic state is the means by which culture and ethnicity become competing actors on the world's stage. To muddy this process through ethnic pluralism, cosmopolitanism, intermarriage, or the fostering of multicultural rights within the state is to work against history and progress which for Fichte (in Meineke 1976) are the primary sources of inspiration and principles for any particular state. In this view the state is not a rational contract and a negotiated constitution based on a set of universal rights and duties. It is the penultimate expression of a single culture. Universal ideas about human rights, about property, or the rule of law, are its rational beginnings. But its character, its prospects, and its competitiveness lie in its ethnic character and its capacity to control the purity of these roots through political action and the maintenance of a uniethnic state. As Fichte (ibid., 42) noted, "[E]very state is deeply ailing in which political organization does not coincide with the national spirit." (i.e., with its uniethnic roots and their preservation and protection through the use of state power.)

In sum, the state is and should be the expression of uniethnic progress. Law and morality are rooted in both universalism—Christendom for Europe, Shintoism for Japan, Judaiism for Israel, or Shiite Islam for Iran, and in the morality of ethnic roots as these evolved within the ethnic group's own "national" culture. In sharp contrast there is life and death competition in the international environment; no law, no morality, only decline or expansion, conversion of other ethnicities to one's own through conquest, imitation, and diffusion. Military strength is a sine qua non in such a world as is export trade and expanding spheres of political, economic, and cultural interests beyond the uniethnic state borders. Within the state multiethnicity weakens the virility and creative energy of assumed uniethnic roots. In response the local culture must become sovereign and protect itself against a cosmopolitanism that ennervates its "national spirit."

Hitler did not invent Nazism, he merely cut the cord that joined cultural nationalism to its universalist antecedents in order to explain Germany's defeat and the only way forward to its destiny as a great nation. Earlier writers had accepted much of the universalist moral principles expressed in the French revolutionary doctrines of 1793. However, they added the romantic notion that ethnic group peculiarities were humankind's way of experimenting with ways of making these universal but abstract and overgeneralized principals work into the hurly burly of real world conditions among specific peoples. Nazism downgraded universal moral principles and "natural rights" by blasting ethnicity into position as the highest value and single most important determinant of national success or failure. Ethnicity and its continuity with the past in purified (Aryan) form trumped all other values and rights. When indigenous ethnicity is endangered from without by other nations, or by non-Germans within, all universalist moral rules must be set aside. Instead people must "think with their blood," that is, ethnicity and its welfare should dictate moral and political rationality.

By the end of the century, economic forces, and the general

expansion of Europe into the Third World was interpreted and justified by this same argument. The "civilizing" mission became the validation of European ethnic competition and superiority. In this same language of justification it also explained to the actors themselves the necessity for a "scramble" for colonies. In the theory of ethnic statehood adoption of metropole culture by the "inferior races" would validate the historic success and superiority of the metropole. Lord Lugard and his wife campaigned in England for rapid colonization of Africa under English rather than French, Belgian, German, or Portuguese tutelage on three counts, first it was their moral duty to do so. Just as Rome brought civilization to Britain centuries ago, now Britain must do the same for the uncivilized peoples of Africa. Second, if Africa was to be controlled by Europe, why not by the best that Europe had to offer, the British, and their field-tested understanding and practice of constitutional government. And third, if England did not join the competition, it and its own ethnic project would lose the economic benefits and even more importantly the international test of fitness provided for by colonialism.

Results

The results of Europe's development of cultural nationalism are well-known. In the nineteenth century it was the argument used to unify Germany and Italy, to expand colonialism, and to create inter-European competition and conflict. That wasn't new. European states were seen as political actors with essentially uniethnic populations, French, British, German, Italian, and so on. Never mind that France had several indigenous languages, that Britain had a rebellious Celtic fringe, that Germany had deep internal divisions between Prussia and the rest of the new nation, that Belgium, Holland, Austria, and Switzerland were acknowledgedly multiethnic. European nationalism had a strong sense of uniethnicity per nation state defying the empirical facts, and fostering cultural darwinism—an ideology that used as guiding principal the notion that the interstate-interethnic world was a jungle in which the best and strongest ethnicity-become-statehood would survive and flourish proving their worthiness and pride in a mythically originated superiority. Under such misguided assumptions, European racism leading to variably oppressive overseas regimes, and to Nazism although tragic and morally reprehensible was in fact quite logical. The latter case proved the penultimate development of cultural nationalism spawning the horror of the Holocaust within a superheated ethnocentricism that was intoxicating, passionate, and in the end draconian in its capacity to see ethnicity as the root of progress and the Other or the non-German as beyond the borders of the moral universe, that is, outside the realm of moral consideration. Paradoxically, yet understandably given the widespread romanticism of a uniethnic basis for statehood and dependence of ethnic survival on the founding and flourishing of an ethnic state, the same historical misinterpretation also helped foster Zionism or cultural nationalism for Jews, leading to the steady growth of Jews in the Near Eastern population and the eventual founding of the state of Israel.[2]

Given the lack of realism in the ideology of cultural nationalism it is not surprising that multiethnicity expanded in the twentieth century. Where colonial expansion would plant a mother ethnicity among the "less civilized" its brief intrusion led simply to a large array of new multiethnic states on the world's stage. At the same time the older European states and their outlying seedlings in the commonwealth, the U.S., Latin America and Asia have in turn produced even larger more multiethnic ethnic states plus migrations from older colonies to the more prosperous nation states. Sweden has its Turkish workers; Germany has Yugoslavians and Africans, France Algerians, and Africans; Britain has immigrant populations from all over the poorer corners of its former empire. Hispanics and Asians are the fastest growing populations in North America.

Granted the state still ethnizes, and contrarily ethnicity within plural states contains continuities independent of statehood. Blacks from the Caribbean in Canada and U.K. seem quite different after twenty years compared to their counterparts who went to the U.S. But as Bromley (1984) noted for Ukranians in the USSR and in Canada there are also commonalities. Thus the brogue accent obtained from the early numerical dominance of the Irish in the English-speaking Caribbean, single parent families, and other peculiarities are common despite their migrant destinations. Many ethnic characteristics carry on as heritable traits in spite of new environments.[3]

The main point is worth repeating. Over and over again, the previous chapters demonstrate that the state as a uniethnic unit is a myth. Diamond's discussion of China is most apposite here in showing how the "Chinese" are in fact ethnically plural. In almost all cases, states are rooted in, and foster or maintain, pluralism. And where homogeneity is claimed or idealized (Japan, Germany, Israel, Quebec, Armenia, Slovenia, or Swaziland) cultural differentiation is either present already, or inexorably interwoven into the social fabric. Despite its implied claim to being a "distinct" ethnic society, Quebec is significantly multiethnic. Besides the English minority, the Africans, and the Haitians, there are native peoples, and even a subgroup of Quebecois French in the Saguenay who claim that as far as the rest of the province is concerned they are a separate "country" with a separate history and a special culture. In moral terms, and after a century and half of romantic, often belli-cose, and sometimes horrifying cultural nationalism, it is only natural that the liberal interpretation of history has swung towards the obligations of democratic states to pluralism. At least this has been the case up to now. But strangely something new is happen-ing. Something enabling the old myth to play an important part in humanity's next step forward.

The Weakening of the State

Just as statehood and its imperialist expansionism were reaching their zenith in the twentieth century, the very opposite process was beginning and would gather strength throughout the century. The dangers of interstate competition and conflict signaled by two world wars, the Cold War and "mutual assured destruction" all pointed to the need for some form of emergent international orga-nization and law, limitations on how wars could be fought, trade agreements, regional cooperation, and organization along with the largest number of internationally recognized rights covenants of any period in recorded history. From 1926 to 1981 thirty-six international codes of human rights were signed by regional and world-wide groups of sovereign state governments (Cohen 1992). Each of these declarations (theoretically) committed sovereign state signators to a contract in the international arena that decreased their autonomy. In effect an interstate community is being formed in which each participant must recognize authority outside the state across the entire species. Though not fully recognized as yet, international tribunals that adjudicate such covenants have obviously increased their authority enormously in the latter twentieth century. In the economic sphere, national borders are becoming less significant as transnational corporations, stock markets, currencies, and increasing amounts of economic planning move outside single states to an interstate environment. Most pressing, the issue of environmental hazards and disease control require international cooperation and compliance with agreed upon remedies. Finally, recent events that are bound to accelerate have found both single nation states and the U.N. demanding that human rights violations within a particular country be corrected and that the international community has a "right" to override state sovereignty in the cause of human rights. The Kurdish predicament in the Gulf War set a precedent. There is now an activated claim by the U.N. to aid and protect refugees, that is, human rights *within* a state. If upheld over time by further precedents this means as some have already claimed (Hansen 1992) that bona fide refugees possess rights that trump nation state sovereignty. It is not insignificant that this case, like other similar ones, for example, the Armenians in the USSR involve ethnic rather than other types of social conflict.

The upshot is that in the real world of the twentieth century the state is becoming progressively weakened by the necessities of a shrinking world. The Hobbesian relations among states assumed by cultural nationalism has had to be curtailed by international agreements and an emergent form of suprastate authority. More will come. Instead of a misguided cultural darwinism practiced by putatively pure ethnic states, real world developments have shifted unit boundaries. Given the outcomes of cultural nationalism, the suicidal destructiveness of modern warfare and the interdependence of global life forms, it has been necessary to shift the unit to that of humankind as a whole for a start, with the possible addition, perhaps, of all living matter. In other words to a surviving unit whose primary characteristic is its pluralism.

And as if this wasn't enough, the state is also being weakened from within. Statism, the belief that progress and socioeconomic stability requires rational planning and detailed guidance from a centralized managerial bureacracy is on the decline. Doubtless an important residue of needed regulatory authority will remain. But Hayek's (1944, 1971) lifelong critique of the inefficiencies and dangers of overcentralized governmental control of society and economy has proven prophetic. Information loss between real world work places and centralized hierarchical government control centers in statist economies supports maladaptive policies, sycophantic blockage of feedback correctives, injustice, tyranny, and ultimate economic and political failure (ibid.). Events in Eastern-bloc socialist countries and the statist Third World have proven him right. Only enormous numbers of ordinary and experienced individuals processing information about their needs and their participation in the economy, polity, and society can support a prosperous and adaptive state. The contempary rush to more market-driven economies among previously centralized statist regimes bears out these earlier insights. It also privatizes and disperses central authority.

Democratization and increased local power in the political domain is a correlated feature. The worldwide democratization movement reflects a desire to have local peoples use information and requirements closer to home to regulate their everyday lives. In Africa, country after country is seeing the demand for multiparty competition at all levels. In effect this worldwide movement is shifting political control away from single regime central government, empowering and enhancing local decision-making, and moving to protect the rights of minority ethnic and other interest groups to mobilize or bargain for increased power. The process has been occurring in the more developed nations as well. The statism of the 1930s has now slowed down by a counter trend to increase local government responsibilities. This is correlated with growing central government deficits, and poor performance by many central bureaucracies. Interest in local government is also increasing. In the U.S. in 1940 only one third of all households were owner occupied. By 1980 this had changed to two thirds. Thus a majority of the population have their major capital investment affected by decisions of local governments. Meanwhile central governments have been sloughing off social programs to the state and local level. Governments in the capitalist, socialist, and Third World states are moving to sell off public corporations to the private sector. In the Scandinavian countries social research and criticism is now concerned with findings that statism is responsible for producing personal demoralization. Although people revere and will not give up their advanced social welfare programs, researchers find that there are costs. Under conditions in which the state does the lion's share of caring about human welfare and suffering individuals paradoxically become increasingly (with each generation) demoralized and self-serving. Morality is the job of the state. There is measurably less need in civil society to acquire and foster empathy, sympathy, or personal concern for the public good (Wolfe 1989). Divorce, suicide, juvenile indiscipline and immorality, and mental health problems are all on a significant upward climb. As Wolfe (1989) points out, the antidote may be for local communities, local neighborhoods, to take over more control and responsibility, teaching each person and family the importance of participation in, and the ongoing construction of, the moral life of the community. Localism, plural centers of control and decision-making which accept local differences-making responsibility both plural and more immediate is now being advocated. In sum, it is as if modern industrial society and its peripheral cadets in the Third World had reached a zenith of state power and control in the mid-twentieth century. In so doing the negative outcomes have started to outweigh the positive achievements. But the internal reaction, that of increased localism and the active dismantling of centralized governmental control along with a worldwide movement for increased democratization, means that pluralism is on the rise. Local control requires less standardization and more support for local differentiation. Can the state survive this erosion from without and within? The answers will fill the headlines in the next several decades.

Ethnicity and State: the Emergent Synthesis

Above all else the various contributions indicate that ethnicity is alive and well at the end of the twentieth century. Although states can and do ethnize their citizenry over time, pressure cooker tactics such as those described for Israel, or the USSR in its newly admitted abortive attempt to create "Soviet Man," continue to crash on the unforgiving rocks of entrenched ethnic heritability.[4] Whether states ethnize or not, they do form the primary political arena within which ethnicity operates. And statehood is changing. As we have noted, forces outside and inside the older state are working to weaken its autonomous control over policies and praxis. Such forces represent the contemporary version of Enlightenment universalism and the particularism of cultural nationalism. What has become clear in recent times is the fact that both universalism and particularism are necessary in a world of increasing complexity, specialization, and the dangers of nuclear and other forms of self-imposed mass destruction.

Universalism with its threads going back to Rome, to early Christianity, along with many other world religious movements, and the eighteenth-century Enlightenment are the natural soils out of which human rights declarations and actions have developed in our own day.[5] Similarly with international efforts devoted to environmentalism, and with the worldwide demands for increased democratization. Each of these developments assumes universal qualities of human existence from which can be derived a logic in favor of particular rights, actions, procedures and goals that are applicable to the species as a whole. Some, like international disease monitoring and control are immediately understandable, others like the international protection of internal refugees and minority rights within a state, are less clear. In effect this means that important qualities of morality have as their referent the human community as a whole, given that the problems dealt with morally are becoming increasingly universal in their causes and effects. Traditionally, the moral order has been, an ethnic concern or at most a religious "community." Despite teachings and lip service to notions of universalism the full practice of a moral order has been correlated with ethnic boundaries. Trade always fosters some interethnic moral order and the state demands it for obligations owed to the state and its laws. For many peoples, obligations of community, of trust, of sharing and a sense of shared fate are only fully practiced within a moral universe defined ethnically. A limited set of common moral obligations must exist for economic relations to function, so too with common membership in a polity. But for many peoples around the world, as these chapters attest, the full gamut of moral relation are restricted to family and to one's own ethnic group. Where the state develops an ethnicity of its own then patriotism and ethnicity and moral life begin to coalesce.

Universalist theory sees little if any place for ethnicity in matters of rights, duties, indeed the entire panoply of moral principles. Marx (1987) writing about the "Jewish Problem" saw this clearly. Progress requires a universalizing of morality that he felt was impossible without the worldwide victory of communism and the death of the capitalist state. Today, although communism as theory and practice has failed, it is apparent that emergent universal moral rules are growing apace. The world has shrunk and our survival requires that we live by a widening set of species-wide agreements about morality and correlated rules of conduct for individuals and collectivities. Logically and empirically this involves legitimizing suprastate, even enforceable, authority, especially when not to do so endangers the global population and its sustaining environment.

On the other hand, and in a more complex fashion, particularism is also finding acceptance. Clearly the weakening of the state has provided an opportunity for cultural nationalism or ethnic statehood, to revive all over the world. Universalist principles and their institutionalization increase with the scale and differentiation of human interactions. And a sense of wider membership in the entire species expanding to include all life forms develops as well. Under such circumstances ethnicity gives way to common humanity and its emergent demands. But paradoxically as the chapters point out, there is a correlated increase in particularism as well. As we differentiate into ever more discrete particles of roles, *personhood,* which unifies and energizes social life, has less not more room for recognition and some form of legitimized expression.[6] Generalizations, rules, discoverable causes and effects can be directed at institutions, roles, statuses, and aggregates of these organizational units. As the world shrinks, airports, clothing, music, education, even economic theory and political ideology are beginning to universalize. But personhood involves vast amounts of sensitivity, of judgments, and more or less integrating features for social participation, along with continuous spontaneity of reaction to self and others that slips through the grossly overgeneralized universal rules and principles applicable across all ethnic boundaries. The essential core of human activity is a particularistic actor, not a scientifically generalizable and programmable set of predictable role behaviors that model and reflect the human condition but leave enormous amounts of details and relationships out of the depiction and the way the rules of the game are interpreted and enacted. Outside the unique biological and psychological qualities of the person lie the features they hold in common with others as a matter of birth and rearing. Common roots, language, accent, expectations, and vast numbers of common understandings and familiar ways of reacting and acting are reproduced within networks of intermarrying families defined by ethnicity. This suggests that ethnicity is the naturally occurring tangible social orbit within which personhood is most meaningfully expressed and experienced. And I repeat, innumerable commonalities within ethnic groupings from physical appearance, to a way of moving one's body, to facial expressions, to life-styles, child training, and attitudes to life, death and achievement may link coethnics but have not, for the most part been given role specific jobs to do in a specialized work force or home place. This does not mean that people are not linked to their wider groupings of religion, citizenship, even their common humanity. But the limited degree of expectations that go with roles and statuses and the universal rules of decency and justice that may apply to them are extraordinarily limited in comparison to the complexities of personhood for which there are no specific roles (i.e., named and/or bundles of activities directed to specifiable goals). Persons as whole entities do not relate to complex modern organizations nor necessarily to other persons. Hence alienation, the programmed tension between person and role. But ethnicity provides the widest sense of descent group solidarity and of the myriads of meanings and patterns of behavior that go with it. In a world of growing impersonality, ethnicity provides an immediate and often unconscious fellow-

ship of identity and community that is increasingly missed as scale
of action and universalized intensification of specialization creates
fewer opportunities for an holistic expression of personhood. It is in
this sense that it is an antidote to alienation.

And ethnic nationalism, giving political expression to ethnic
identity means that the we of me has authority and power to foster
and sustain the growing significance and importance of this source
of comfort in an increasingly differentiated and alienating social,
economic, political, and cultural environment. To be engaged by
cultural nationalism in Quebec, or Slovenia, or Latvia means that
people are passionate in their support of this identity. This is especially true if they help define common life chances in a social
environment of inequality which is far from uncommon. If an
identity group membership is at all correlated with access to scarce
resources especially to low access then it is not surprising that the
next step is towards political action and hence to cultural nationalism. Similarly if it defines selfhood, provides a sense of continuity
with past generations so that the self shares in this historic experience then enhancing its political autonomy and power ensures
continuity of the most pertinent we of me beyond the net of kinship. Contrarily, if the state is successfully ethnizing its constituent
ethnic and other interest groups, that is, creating a new state based
identity then older ethnicity can be predicted to decline in relation
to a fellow feeling with the state as a whole. Nevertheless, there is
some validity to the older cultural nationalism. Older adaptations
are a storehouse of possible ways of dealing with the problems of
modern life. They therefore serve as a reservoir of possible solutions
to older, newer, and emergent problems.

Particularism and universalism are two sides of the same coin
that of humankind's capacity to invent the means for its own
survival. And our own puny attempts to understand this process
must reflect the same kind of bifocal view. There are universal and
widely applicable generalizations that can be made about this and
other process. These can in turn be seen mechanistically as the
results of ongoing features that influence their stability and change.
But that positivistic project may be hopelessly quixotic in seeking
ultimate understanding through incremental refinements of
models and theories that are easily and quickly overturned by

events. In even more general terms, then, scientific, generalization-seeking solutions must exist along side the rich depiction of complexity signalled by artistic expression and ethnography and area studies. One seeks a body of valid universals applicable to all human experience, the other seeks to understand the peculiarities of a specific cultural experience or even a small part of it. Although this is another subject, its eclecticism is implied in both this volume and this particular chapter. We don't advance by changing myopically from universalism to particularism or vice versa either in cultural policy, morality, or scholarship, we grow by using both.

Notes

1. Although figures vary over time and surveys are a modern product a recent one is instructive. Of 132 states studied only 9 percent were ethnically homogeneous (Walker Connor, cited in Weiner 1991, 7). Another 19 percent had one ethnic group making up over 90 percent of the population while the same proportion (19 percent) had one ethnic group making up over 75 percent of the people. This left 53 percent of the sample with no one group making up more than 75 percent of the country, and of this group a significant portion (30 percent) had no single named ethnic group containing more than 50 percent of the entire state. Possibly this was less so in the past when states were smaller, transportation and migration less easily available. However, to my knowledge there were no major urban centers in early states without migrants, foreign traders, craftsmen, and even foreign consulates and embassies. Throughout Europe's history. The Church, long-distance trade, roads, a universalist past, empires of the past, and alliances among states made multiethnicity part and parcel of European society from the early trading cities onwards. In Eastern Europe Jews were spread across even the small towns and villages in small or larger quarters (or shtetls) giving even the most remote towns an awareness of multiethnicity as part of normal social life even if the Other (Jew, Tinker, Basque, Tamil, Native American) was outside the moral and social, but not political, order of state society.
2. Whatever else it is, and it is many stranded, Zionism is a form of cultural nationalism rooted in the same intellectural culture that held Europe in thrall in the nineteenth century. But cultural national legitimacy required a state or at least a territory or homeland validating ethnic survival. Whether on the right or the left, or among Jewish leaders themselves, Lenin's position was accepted. Jewish nationality lacked the necessary ingredients for recognition because they lacked a common language and a traditional and sovereign political territory of their own. More generally throughout Europe they lacked the ingredients for inclusion in the cultural nation unless they were willing to give up their own ethnicity completely and join the universalist moral community of Christendom, and the particular local version of it in a local state. Some did. Others did not. And the recalcitrants accepted cultural nationalist theory and

founded a social movement devoted to the establishment of a Jewish national state in the biblical homeland. And this led in turn to today's unresolved conflict between Palestinians and Israelis over claims to indigenousness.

3. This is meant to be ambiguous. Whether such traits are biologically and/or culturally transmitted or both is a matter for research not opinion. Although I lean strongly in favor of culture I am aware of the complexities involved that commingle these two sources given the fact that ethnic groups are also breeding populations (See Boyd and Richardson 1985: Cohen 1991). The notorious aggressiveness and drive for localized political autonomy of celtic fringe groups in the British Isles commented upon by observers from Roman times to the present and also claimed to be part of southern "cracker" culture in the U.S. may be a form of learning passed from one generation to the next. It may also be a genetic proclivity based on favoured breeding for these traits. Or both of these may be explained by the worldwide correlation of such traits with pastoralism and segmentary lineage systems also found in celtic groups at the peripheries of Roman Britain.

4. As late as 1985 and 1986 at least one leading Soviet anthropologist reported that even in the Baltic states a levelling process was taking place that involved significant "Russification" of all local cultures. Challenged by his colleagues, V. Tischkov who espoused this view (at joint meetings by U.S. and Soviet anthropologists on ethnicity) held on to it throughout the conference. Although the topic of "Soviet Man" was carefully skirted by the conference, a number of papers referred to notions of the ethnizing of the state and the levelling of cultural differences under the authority of the state.

5. This purposely omits the relativist position put forward by a number of writers (e.g., Vincent 1984) who accept the African Peoples Charter of Human Rights as evidence that human rights can be more particularistic and relative to non-Western cultural traditions. This position is in my view untenable and mischevious in its enablement of governance activities that abrogate individual human rights (Cohen, Hyden, and Nagan 1992).

6. Personhood is the whole living human actor accorded the rights given to any individual in a community. Controversy surrounds its limits—somewhere between conception and the second-term fetus in Western culture to begin with, and between brain-dead vegetative states and heart failure on the other. Exact definitions for any particular case are variably determined by social debate, technology and its availability, medical ethics, and the force of religious values (Jones 1990). In many cultures tests of survival beyond a certain time period are made to new borns before they are accorded personhood in the community. Death before that time generally implies no proper burial ceremony.

References

Bromley, Yu. V. 1984. *Theoretical Ethnography* (Translated by V. Epstein and E. Khazanov). Moscow: Nauka.

Carlyle, T. 1987 (1837). *Sartor Resartus*. Oxford, New York, Toronto: Oxford University Press.

Cohen, R. 1977. "Rex and Regina: The Queen Mother in Africa." *Africa* 47:14–30.

Cohen, R. and R. Service, eds. 1978. *Origins of the State.* Philadelphia: ISHI.

Cohen, R. 1978a. "Ethnicity: Problem and Focus in Anthropology." *Annual Review of Anthropology 1978,* 379–403.

Cohen, R. 1986. "Warfare in Pre-Capitalist and Post-Capitalist States." In R. Rubinstein and E. Foster (eds.), *Anthroplogical Approaches to War.* New York: Academic Press.

Cohen, R. 1992. "Endless Tears." In R. Cohen, G. Hyden, and W. Nagan (eds.), *Human Rights in Africa.* Gainesville: University of Florida Press.

Cohen, R. G. Hyden, and W. Nagan eds. 1992. *Human Rights and Governance in Africa.* Gainesville: University of Florida Press.

Carneiro, R. 1978. "Political Expansion as an Expression of the Principle of Competitive Exclusion." In R. Cohen and R. Service (eds.), *Origins of the State,* 205–23. Philadelphia: ISHI.

Emerson, G. 1991. *Gaza.* New York: Atlantic Monthly Press.

Ferguson, R. B., ed. 1984. *Warfare, Culture, and Environment.* New York: Academic Press.

Hayek, F. 1944. *The Road to Serfdom.* Chicago: University of Chicago Press.

Hayek, F. 1971. *Law, Legislation, and Liberty.* Chicago: University of Chicago Press.

Horowitz, D. L. *Ethnic Groups in Conflict.* Berkeley: University of California Press.

Lipset, S. M. 1990. *Continental Divide: The Values and Institutions of the United States and Canada.* New York: Routledge.

Manganaro, M., ed. 1990. *Modernist Anthropology.* Princeton, N.J.: Princeton University Press.

Marx, K. 1987. *On the Jewish Question.* In J. Waldron (ed.), *Nonsense Upon Stilts.* London and New York: Methuen.

Meineke, F. 1970. *Cosmopolitanism and the National State,* translated by R. B. Kimber, with an introduction by Felix Gilbert. Princeton, N.J.: Princeton University Press. (Published first in German in 1907.)

Pearson, L. 1990. *Children of Glasnost: Growing Up Soviet.* Toronto: Lester and Orpen Dennys.

Shipler, D. 1986. *Arab and Jew.* New York: Times Books.

Smaldone, J. P. 1977. *Warfare in the Sokoto Caliphate.* Cambridge: Cambridge University Press.

Toland, J. 1988. "Inca Legitimation as a Communication Process." In R. Cohen and J. Toland (eds.), *State Formation and Political Legitimacy.* New Brunswick N.J.: Transaction Books.

Weiner, M. 1991. "The Impact of Nationalism, Ethicity, and Religion on International Conflict." Paper delivered to Peoples and States Seminar, MIT Center for International Studies, 2 May 1991.

Wolfe, A. 1989. *Whose Keeper?.* Berkeley: University of California Press.

Yoffee, N. 1988. "Context and Authority in Early Mesopotamian Law." In R. Cohen and J. Toland (eds.), *State Formation and Political Legitimacy.* New Brunswick N.J.: Transaction Books.

About the Contributors

ANGELA S. BURGER is professor of political science at the University of Wisconsin, Marathon Campus, in Wausau. She earned her Ph.D. at the University of Wisconsin-Madison, and has authored Opposition in a Dominant Party System: A Study of the Jan Sangh, Praja Socialist and Socialist Parties in Utter Pradesh, India (1969), as well as articles on the police, paramilitary and disaster management in South Asia.

RONALD COHEN is professor of anthropology at the University of Florida. He has held positions in Anthropology at University of Toronto, McGill University, Northwestern, and Ahmadu Bello Universities. In 1985 and 1986 he worked with a group of American and Soviet scholars on problems of ethnicity and national unity. Major publications include *The Kanuri of Borno* (1967, 1987), *From Tribe to Nation*, edited with John Middleton (1971), *Dominance and Defiance* (1971), *Origins of the State* edited with E.R. Service (1978), *Legitimacy and State Formation*, edited with J. Toland (1988), *Human Rights in Africa*, edited with G. Hayden and W. Nagan (1992).

NORMA DIAMOND is professor of anthropology at the University of Michigan, and an associate of the Center for Chinese Studies. She has done field research in Taiwan and the Peoples Republic of China. She has published several articles based on her research in a peasant village in Shandong province in 1979-80. A paper titled "The Miao and Poison: Interactions on China's Southwest Frontier" appeared in the January 1988 issue of *Ethnology*. She is working on a social history monograph on the Hua Miao.

BLANCA MURATORIO is associate professor at the department of anthropology and Sociology, University of British Columbia and Research Associate at the Latin American School of Social Sciences (FLACSO, Ecuador). She is the author of *Etnicidad, Evangelización y Protesta en el Ecuador: Una Perspectiva Antropológica* and *Rucuyaya Alonso y la Historia Social y Económica del Alto Napo 1850-1950* (English edition forthcoming). She is currently conducting research on Napo Quichua women's work and symbolic universe.

SUSAN RODGERS is associate professor of anthropology at the College of the Holy Cross in Massachusetts. Her recent research has focused on issues of symbolic change in the southern Batak Angkola culture of North Sumatra, Indonesia, as Angkola has moved more and more firmly into the national orbit. She has additional fieldwork interests in the area of *adat* rituals as these have changed as Sumatran ethnic groups have become more fully integrated in the Indonesian nation.

ANYA PETERSON ROYCE is professor of anthropology at Indiana University. Her books include *Prestigio y Afiliacion en una comunidad urbana: Juchitan, Oaxaca* (1975), *The Anthropology of Dance* (1977), *Ethnic Identity: Strategies of Diversity* (1982), *Movement and Meaning: Creativity and Interpretation in Ballet and Mime* (1984), *The Silver Age of the Commedia dell'Arte* (in press), and *Splendid Muse* (an historical novel, in press). She is currently working on a book on politics and identity in the Zapotec city of Juchitan, Oaxaca.

EMILE SAHLIYEH is associate professor of international relations and Middle East politics at the University of North Texas. In addition to numerous articles and chapters on the Arab-Israeli conflict, he is the author of *In Search of Leadership: West Bank Politics since 1967* (1988) and *The PLO After the Lebanon War* (1986). He is editor of and contributor to *Religious Resurgence and Politics in the Contemporary World* (1990).

JUDITH D. TOLAND is a senior lecturer in the University of Wisconsin Center's Post Secondary Reentry Education Program. As a political anthropologist, her research has included the study of political legitimation in the early Inca state, the emerging ethnic identity of the Hmong in Wisconsin, and violence and the social control of women. She is currently working on a study of incarceration and the maintenance of dependency within the Correctional System. This is her second edited volume for Transaction.

JOAN VINCENT is professor of anthropology at Barnard College, Columbia University. She has been carrying out fieldwork in Northern Ireland periodically since 1973. As a visiting fellow at the Institute of Development Studies, the University of Sussex, she is currently completing *Seeds of Revolution: The Culture and Politics of the Irish Famine: Fermanagh 1836-1856.*

Index

Abromovitz, A., 221
Absorpion Department, 212
Acehnese, 159
Adamson, W., 10
Adat, 14, 149, 155, 157, 160, 161, 165–167, 171, 172
Afghanistan, 196
African Americans, 18
Agama, 151
Al Sai'qa, 191
Al Nadi Al Arabi, 184
Al-Muntada Al Adabi, 184
Alexander the Great, 90
Alexandria, 210, 217
ALF, 190
Algeria, 188, 217
Aliya, 207, 208
All Pak, 91
Anakboru, 155, 157–159, 161–166, 169, 170
Anderson, B., 23, 127, 138
Angkola Batak, 13, 14, 147–176
Anglo Irish Agreement, 141
Anglo Irish, 133, 142
Anglo Saxon, 13, 17, 142, 241
Animism, 7
ANM, 186
Antonovsky, A., 216
APG, 186, 187
Arab League, 186, 192
Arab Israeli War, 182
Arabs, 15, 143, 177–223
Arafat, 190
Argolla, La, 47
Arnold, Matthew, 5
Aronson, D., 14
Arteta, Leonidas Pallares, 21, 24, 25, 27, 28
Ashkenazi, 215–218, 222, 223
Assam Rifles, 95, 99
Atahuallpa, 26, 28

Atkinson, J., 51
Augustine, 238
Australia, 128, 204
Ayala, Enrique, 46–48
Azerbaijan, 127
Aztecs, 28, 236
Aztlan, 18

Ba'ath party, 186
Baghdad, 193, 210, 217
Baluchistan, 90, 92
Bar Yosef, R., 214
Barth, F., 4
Bayley, D., 94, 100
Beijing, 58
Beirut, 217
Ben Dor, S., 221
Ben Raphel, E., 224
Ben David, Y., 214
Ben Zvi, Yitshak, 205, 214
Bendix, R., 214
Bere lele, 106, 115
Berkhofer, R., 32
Bernstein, D., 216
Berreby, J.J., 211
Bhinneka Tunggal Ika, 154
Bhutto, Benazir, 92
Bhutto, Prime Minister, 92
BIA, 17
Bingley, Capt. A.H., 83
Black Panthers, 215, 220
Bodin, 238
Bombay, 208, 217
Border Polls, 141
Bornu, 236
Boru, 167
Bourgeoisie, 23, 46, 49
Bowden, T., 81
Brass, P., 103
Brazil, 128
Breckenbridge, C., 30

Broadway, 208
Bromley, Yu. V., 247
BSF, 95, 96, 99
Buddhism, 75, 84, 86, 238
Bulpitt, J., 124, 136, 138
Bupati, 158
Burger, A., 87, 100
Burghers, 85, 86
Bush, G., 18

Cacique Charupe, 26
Cacoa, 23, 27, 46
Camano, Jose Maria Placido, 46, 47
Camat, 159
Camp David, 193
Canada, 241, 247
Caras, 6, 25, 27, 30
Caribbean, 247
Carlisle Indian School, 36
Carlyle, Thomas, 238
Carneiro, R., 242
Carrasco, Cesar Agusto, 104
Casa de la Cultura, 106, 107, 117, 118
Casablanca, 210
Castro, Gen. Heliodoro Charis, 118
Castro y Velazquez, J., 31, 40
Catholicism, 12, 13, 127
Celts, 13, 142, 241
Ceylon, 242
Charton, Ernesto, 38, 40
Chicano, 18
China, Peoples Republic of, 5, 6,
    55–78, 84
Chinas, Lopez, 113, 114
Chiriboga, M., 46, 47
COCEI, 12, 104, 107, 116, 118
Cochin, 217
Coercion, 8, 9
Cold War, 248
Communism, 253
Comte, 238
Confucius, 238
Corkery, D., 133
Cortez, Col. Francisco, 109
Costumbrismo, 40, 41
Cousin, F., 40
CRP, 95, 96, 99
Cuenca, 48
Cultural Revolution, 56, 69, 70

Culture
    combative, 4,
    dominant, 3, 4, 23
    hegemonic, 4, 5, 7, 9, 10, 24, 46,
        142
    subordinate, 3, 4
    symbols, 4, 124
Culture Guides, 160

Dalihan na tolu, 155
Darwin, Charles, 32
De Vos, G., 4
Decalo, S., 82
Democracy, 17, 250
Descartes, 238
Deshen, S., 219
Despres, L., 18
Deutsch, K., 70
DFLP, 190, 192
Diapora, 202, 203, 209, 214, 223, 225
Diaz, Porfirio, 105, 110, 111
Diaz, Felix, 110
Direct rule, 126, 139
Dissanayake, T.D.S.A., 87
Doniz, Rafael, 104
Dual Polity, 138, 139, 141
Durkheim, Emile, 238

Ecuador, 5, 6, 21–54
Edelman, M., 79
Eqypt, 16, 186, 188, 193, 204, 208,
    217
Eisenstadt, S., 210, 214
Ellingwood, D., 83
Eloy Alfaro, 47
Emerson, R., 120
Emerson, G., 232
Engels, F., 56
Enloe, C., 17, 81, 82
Erickson, E.P., 224
ERPLF, 89
Eshkol, Levi, 204
Espada, Marcos Jimenez de la, 41
Ethiopia, 221
Evans of Meath, Bishop, 131
Eydot ha mizrah, 210, 212, 216, 220

Fabian, J., 43
Faisal, Prince, 183, 184

Falklands War, 143
Fatah, 188, 190, 191
Ferguson, R.B., 234
Fichte, 244
First, R., 82
Fisk, R., 138
Fitzpatrick, R., 12, 13, 134–136,
    142, 143
Flores, Dr. Antonio, 26, 27, 46–48
Forth, 157
Foster, R., 130, 132, 133
Foucault, M., 5
Fox, 157
France, 184, 247
French Revolution, 48, 245
Funeral rituals, 151

Gailey, C., 8
Gallegos, Plutarco, 111
Gallegos de Donoso, 41
Garcia, Don Joaquin, 108
Gaza Strip, 180–182, 185–187,
    193, 194, 196, 198
Geertz, C., 21, 23, 49, 211
Germany, 208, 243, 245, 247
Ghana, 236
Ghandi, Indira, 94
Ghandi, Sanjay, 100
Ghandi, Mahatma, 85
Goitein, S.D., 214
Goldberg, H., 221, 224
Goldie, T., 34, 49
Goldstein, J., 221
Government of Ireland Act, 124
Gramsci, A., 9, 10, 18
Great Britain, 123, 184, 247
Greece, 236
Green Line, 189
Guayaquil, 27
Guchachi'reza, 106, 115
Guendabianni, 11, 107, 118
Guendalisaa, 11, 105
GUPS, 189
GUPT, 189
GUPW, 189
GUPWM, 189
Gurit Kadmon, 214
Gurkas, 84
Gurrion, Adolfo, 111–113

Ha Poel Ha Tsair, 206
Habban, 225
Haj Amin al-Husaini, 185
Hallo, W., 41
Halper, J., 221
Halpern, B., 205
Hammurabi, 234, 236
Han Chinese, 6, 56–78
Hansen, 249
Harahaon, 157, 158
Hashemite Regime, 186
Hassaurek, F., 28, 40, 41
Hatoban, 163
Hawaii, 150
Hayek, F., 250
Headhunting, 152
Hebrew, 208, 217, 223, 224
Hechter, M., 129
Heeger, G., 92
Hertzberg, A., 205
Hewitt, J., 129
Hicks, 157
Hill, J., 49
Hilula, 219
Hinduism, 84, 93
Hispanic, 17
Histadrut, 206, 218, 220
Hitler, Adolph, 245
Hmong, 18
Hobsbawm, E., 28, 43, 49
Holocaust, 247
Hong Kong, 56
Horowitz, D., 81, 86, 240
Horton, Willie, 18
Hoskins, 152
Hrebenar, R., 79
Hua Miao, 7, 55–78
Huayna Capac, 26
Hugo of St. Victor, 2
Hula, hula, 167
Hull, R., 126
Huntington, S., 82
Hussein, Sadat, 195
Hussein, King, 183, 196
Huta, 159

Ibn Khaldun, 238
Imagined community, 6, 23, 127
Incas, 25–28, 236

India, 8, 16, 83, 84, 93–100, 204, 241
Indonesian Unity, 14
Indonesian Chinese, 150
INS, 17
Intifada, 15, 194, 196, 197
IPS, 94
IRA, 139, 141, 142
Iran, 6, 204, 217
Iraq Iran War, 195
Iraq, 15, 184, 204, 208, 242
Ireland Act, 126
Iris, M., 216
Irish Free State Act, 126
Islam, 149, 179, 181, 238, 245
Israel, 15, 185, 193, 195, 197, 201–
    229, 231, 232, 252
Israeli Arabs, 181, 182
Isthmus Zapotec, 11, 103–122

Jakarta, 150
James VI of Scotland, King, 135
Japan, 56
Javanese, 150
Jerba, 225
Jews, 16, 143, 180, 182, 185, 201–
    229, 231, 247
Jews, Oriental, 16, 207, 210, 212,
    222, 225
Jews, European, 16, 207, 210
Jimenez, Sotero Constantino, 117
Jivaro, 6, 25, 34
Johnson, J., 81
Jordan, 180, 186, 187, 188, 193, 195
Juchitan, 104–106, 109, 114, 117,
    119, 120
Juliani, R.N., 224
JVP, 88, 89

Kabupaten, 158
Kachin, 148, 153, 157
Kahanggi, 155, 161
Kahn, J.S., 129
Karen, 147
Karo, 150, 157, 167
Katzir, S., 224
Kearney, R., 86
Kecamatan, 159
Keyes, C., 12
Khalutsin, 206

Khurdistan, 208, 210, 217
Kibbuts galuyot, 210
Kibbutsim, 206, 207
Kipling, R., 90
Kivisto, P., 213
Kodi, 152
Kuper, L., 137

La Raza, 18
Lake Toba, 150
Laqueur, W., 205
Larrea, C., 47
Law of Return, 202, 209
Leach, E. 147, 148, 153, 157
Lears, T.S.J., 49
Lebanon, 127, 184, 195
Lena, Cenobio Lopez, 115, 116, 119
Lewis, A., 216
Lewis, H., 207, 211, 219
Leys, C., 82
Li Zhaolun, 65
Libya, 16, 204, 208
Linnekin, J., 150
Lipset, S.M., 242
Lisboa, Miguel Maria, 40
Lissak, M., 213, 218
Lofchie, M., 82
Lord Lugard, 246
Louis XIV, 28
LTTE, 89

Madero, Francisco, 111, 112
Madrid, 6, 21, 22, 24
Maine, 238
Mair, L., 127
Maju, 14, 152
Malay, 148, 156
Malmsheimer, L., 34
Mandailing, 156, 157, 169
Mandarin dialect, 58–62, 69, 70
Marakub, Baginda, 165, 166, 168
Marancar, 161
Marga, 157
Marpaung, Bgd., 164
Marx(ism), 9, 77, 138, 214, 215,
    231, 238, 240, 242, 253
Master fictions, 6, 23, 24
Matras, J., 216, 223
Matus, Macario, 114

Mayas, 236
MCA, 183
McCormack, 133
Medan, 150
Meineke, F., 238, 243, 244
Meir, Golda, 205, 213
Meknes, 225
Mera, Juan Leon, 41
Mestizaje, 5, 23, 49
Methodist faith, 68, 70
Mexico, 103–122
Middle Kingdom, 41
Millais, John Everell, 28
Mimouna, 221
Minangkabau, 150, 156, 159
Minorities, 6, 56, 60, 77, 93
Missionaries, 67, 68
Mizugguluyot, 16, 210, 215, 216, 220
Modernization, 4, 68, 71
Mohammed Ali Jinnah, 92
Molina, Arcadio G., 108, 109
Molina, Jose Ramon Caraveo, 119
Mongols, 236
Monsivais, Carlos, 104
Montalvo, Juan, 28
Montesquieu, 108
Mora, 155, 157–161, 163–166,
    169, 170
Morgan, 238
Morgan Lewis Henry, 56
Morocco, 16, 204, 205, 208, 210,
    216–218, 220, 223, 225
Moshavim, 217
Moslem Brotherhood, 186
Multiculturalism, 225, 235, 239
Munsterberg, M., 37
Muratorio, B., 28
Murra, J., 26
Myth of Rights, 17

Nairn, T., 129, 137, 138
Namibia, 196
Nassar, Gamal Abdel, 186, 193
National Party of Scotland, 125
Native Americans, 17, 18
Nazism, 245, 247
Neza Cubi, 11, 106, 114, 115
Neza, 11, 106, 112–114
NGC, 193

Nias, 168
Nicholas, Capt. A. 83
Normans, 241
Northern Ireland, 12, 123–146

Oaxaca City, 106, 116, 117
Operation Holdfast, 86
Opium, 64
Orangeism, 13, 136
Orangkaya, 161–163
Orozco, Damaciano, 106
Ortiz, Crespo, G., 46–48
Osculati, Gaetano, 40
Otavalo, 6, 25, 28, 30
Other, 1, 5–7, 12, 18, 23, 34, 46,
    49, 240, 247
Ottoman Empire, 182
Oudh, 83, 84
Outer Island Indonesia, 150, 151

Paccha, 26
Pakistan, 8, 83, 84, 90–93
Palembang, 150
Palestine Red Crescent Society, 191
Palestine Congress, 184
Palestine, 202
Palestinians, 15, 177–200, 231, 236
Pan Arabism, 186
Pancasila, 167
Pandian, J., 4
PANE, 157
Parsiis, 93
Particularism, 240, 252, 253, 255,
    256
Pastoralism, 7, 13, 56, 63, 66
Patai, R., 210, 214
Pearson, L., 239
Peoplehood, 3, 4, 13, 18
Perez, Victor de la Cruz, 114
Persian Gulf crisis, 15
Personhood, 253, 254
PFLP, 190, 191
Pimental, Emilio, 111
Pineda, Rosendo, 110, 111, 113, 118
Pinto, Joaquin, 37, 39–42
Plaid Cymru, 125
Plantation of Ulster, 128, 129
PLO, 15, 181, 182, 189–197, 249

Pluralism, 2, 203, 233, 234, 248, 250, 251
PNC, 191, 194
PNF, 193
Poland, 204, 208
Pravel, Maj. Gen., 94, 99
PRCS, 189
Presbyterianism, 136
Prescott, 28
PRI, 104, 119
Prigogene, I., 1
Progresismo, 46, 49
Protestantism, 67, 127
PRRI Rebellion, 152
Punjabi Muslims, 83, 84, 90

Qing Dynasty, 57, 60
Querrero, Agustin, 37, 41, 44, 45
Quito, 30
Qureshi, S.A., 91

Rabat, 217
Rabushka, A., 12
Ramsey, S.R., 58
Richter, W., 92
Rivera, Diego, 117
Roberts, M., 86
Robinson, P., 130
Rodgers, S., 160
Romania, 208
Royce, A., 103, 105
Rubenberg, C., 216
Ryan, M., 32, 34

Sa'an Toraja, 151
Saharanei, 221
Said, E., 4
Salas, Rafael, 37, 40
Salomon, F., 26, 30
Samaniego, Salazar, F., 40
Samuels, D., 18
San'a, 225
Sanchez, Luis, 109
Scheingold, S., 17
Sephardim, 202, 215–217
Seventh Day Adventists, 70
Shama, A., 216
Sharett, Moshe, 205
Sharot, S., 224

Shepsle, K., 12
Shintoism, 245
Shipler, D., 232
Shokeid, M., 219
Shtetl, 205
Siala plant, 170
Sider, G., 23, 46
Sigd, 221
Sikhs, 93, 94
Simpson, 32
Singapore, 56
Sinhalize, 9, 84–90
Sipirok, 157
Siquieros, David, 117
Siregar, Baumi, 160, 162–164
Slash and burn agriculture, 7, 56, 63
SLFP, 85, 86
Smaldone, J.P., 234
Smith, A., 214
Smooha, S., 215, 216
Son, 106
South Tapanuli, 149, 152, 153, 155, 160, 161, 169, 170
South Africa, 137, 204
Southhall, A., 14
Spain, 21, 105
Spencer, 238
Spinoz, 238
Sri Lanka, 8, 84–90, 127
State Legitimation, 3, 8, 10, 23, 80
Stenger, I., 1
Stutzman, R., 30
Suku, 161
Sulawesi, 151
Sumatra, 14, 147–176, 236
Sutan Tinggi, 161
Swirski, S., 216, 224
Syria, 180, 183, 184, 186, 195

Taiwan, 56
Talleyrand, 81
Tamaguari, 26
Tamils, 9, 84–90
Tang Dynasty, 58
Taoism, 75
Taru, Manuel Musalem Santiago, 119
Taussig, M., 32
Taylor, A., 36

Thatcher, Mrs., 139, 140, 143
Theodorson, G., 213
Thomas, Raju, 93
Thompson, W., 82
Three Support Stones on the
    Hearth, 161
Three Self Church, 71
Tibet, 77
Toba, 156, 157, 161
Toland, J., 3, 8, 234
Toledano, H., 215
Toledo, Francisco, 106, 117
Toledo, Ramigio, 109
Toqueville, de, 108
Totora, 25
Tripolitania, 208
Tsantsa, 34, 36
Tunisia, 16, 204, 217, 224
Turkey, 16, 204, 217
Tylor, 238

UDI, 134
Uganda, 137
Ulster Scot, 12, 13, 127, 133, 135,
    136, 139, 142
Ulster Unionism, 13
Uniethnicity, 243, 244
United Nations Resolution, 242, 88
United States, 9, 17, 28, 128, 179,
    204, 223, 225, 242, 251
United Arab Republic, 187
United Nations, 4, 249
Universalism, 231, 235, 237, 239,
    240, 252, 253, 255, 256,
USSR, 1, 123, 196, 204, 208, 242,
    247, 249, 252

Van Wouden, 157
Vanguard Party, 134, 138
Vargas, J., 37, 40, 43
Velasco, Juan de, 26
Veliz, C., 82

Vico, 238
Vincent, J., 124, 125, 128, 137
Volkman, T., 151
Von der Mehden, F., 81

Wake, Archbishop, 131
Wana, 151
Weiner, Charles, 47
Weingrod, A., 219, 221
Wenhua, 6, 74
Wenming, 6, 75
West Bank, 15, 180–182, 185–187,
    193, 195–198, 231
West Sumba, 151
Whitten, N., 49
Wilenz, S., 6, 24
William of Orange, 132, 135
Wolf, Teodor, 46
Wolfe, A., 251
Wona Kaka, 152
World War I, 182, 183

Yancy, W.L., 224
Yangtze River, 57
Yellow River, 57
Yemen, 16, 204, 207, 208, 210, 217,
    225
Yemenite Inban Company, 219
Yemenite Jews, 203, 210, 217, 218,
    220, 223
Yi, 64, 65
Yiddish, 223
Yishuv, 202
Yoffee, N., 234, 237
Yosephthal, Giora, 211
Young, C., 7, 13
Yugoslavia, 2, 242

Zaparo, 25, 30, 34
Zapotec Style, 11
Zionism, 181–185, 205, 207, 218,
    247